# JUSTICE AND PROFIT IN HEALTH CARE LAW

The issue of justice in the field of health care is becoming more central with concerns over access, cost and provision. Obamacare in the United States and the Health and Social Care Act 2012 in the United Kingdom are key examples illustrating the increasing pressure put on governments to find just and equitable solutions to the problem of health care provision. *Justice and Profit in Health Care Law* explores the influence of justice principles on the elaboration of laws reforming health care systems. By examining the role played by key for-profit stakeholders (doctors, employers and insurers), it tracks the evolution of distributive norms for the allocation of health care resources in western welfare states. Essentially, this book sheds light on the place given to justice in the health care law-making process in order to understand the place we wish to give these principles in future health care reforms.

# Justice and Profit in Health Care Law

*A Comparative Analysis of the United States and the United Kingdom*

Sabrina Germain

·H A R T·

OXFORD · LONDON · NEW YORK · NEW DELHI · SYDNEY

HART PUBLISHING

Bloomsbury Publishing Plc

Kemp House, Chawley Park, Cumnor Hill, Oxford, OX2 9PH, UK

HART PUBLISHING, the Hart/Stag logo, BLOOMSBURY and the Diana logo are
trademarks of Bloomsbury Publishing Plc

First published in Great Britain 2019

First published in hardback, 2019
Paperback edition, 2020

A catalogue record for this book is available from the British Library.

**Library of Congress Cataloging-in-Publication Data**

Names: Germain, Sabrina, author.

Title: Justice and profit in health care law : a comparative analysis of the United States
and the United Kingdom / Sabrina Germain.

Description: Chawley Park, Cumnor Hill, Oxford : Hart Publishing, 2019. |
Includes bibliographical references and index.

Identifiers: LCCN 2018049648 (print) | LCCN 2018055846 (ebook) |
ISBN 9781509902729 (Epub) | ISBN 9781509902705 (hardback) |
ISBN 9781509902712 (ePDF)

Subjects: LCSH: Medical policy—United States. | Medical economics—United States. |
Medical policy—United Kingdom. | Medical economics—United Kingdom. |
BISAC: LAW / Health. | LAW / Comparative. | LAW / Medical Law & Legislation.

Classification: LCC RA395.A3 (ebook) | LCC RA395.A3 G392 2019 (print) |
DDC 338.4/73621—dc23

LC record available at https://lccn.loc.gov/2018049648

ISBN: HB:  978-1-50990-270-5
PB:  978-1-50994-542-9
ePDF:  978-1-50990-271-2
ePub:  978-1-50990-272-9

Typeset by Compuscript Ltd, Shannon

To find out more about our authors and books visit www.hartpublishing.co.uk. Here you will find
extracts, author information, details of forthcoming events and the option to sign up for our newsletters.

*Pour Joséphine et Sasha,*
*mon âme et ma lumière*

# FOREWORD

This is an ambitious book. It has a specific aim to present the philosophical problems in the state's involvement in healthcare provision. If justice is an ambition of society, then how does this influence the legislator's choice of frameworks within which health care is provided? Is the state to be a provider of health care, funded through taxation, or is its role to ensure that the private sector is capable of providing appropriate care, leaving the state as a provider of last resort? Chapter two tries to set out the philosophically defensible positions which exist within contemporary liberal political discourse. The remainder of the book then tries to examine how the legislatures of the USA and of the UK have struggled with these questions in implement successive waves of healthcare reform since the Second World War.

The focal issue is the place of private healthcare providers. Of course, the public sector cannot afford to provide everything, so there will always be a place for supplementary services provided by voluntary groups or purchased from commercial providers. But the issue becomes more urgent when private providers are conceived as central to core healthcare provision. For many, the idea that you can only get necessary healthcare if you can afford it goes against fundamental values of social justice and social solidarity. On the other hand, the administrative bureaucracy that universal, state-run provision involves may be thought to cramp innovation and lack incentives to efficiency in deciding what should be provided and at what cost.

The attention paid to the UK and the USA in this book shows how countries which are similar in many ways can make significantly different policy choices and embrace different philosophies. The chapters in this book unpack this background to the legislative debates. They document carefully the arguments used in preparatory materials and in the legislative process. The active role of different private actors (insurers, doctors and employers) is documented and the way they not only articulated their own perspective but were able to shape the debate. But, at the same time, the broader character of the debate in each country is also presented, showing that lobby groups pursuing their own interests are not the only influences on legislative debates. The debates have to be justified within a broader framework of arguments of justice, solidarity and subsidiarity.

Sabrina Germain does not simply make a contribution to the analysis of healthcare law. She offers an attempt to understand lawmaking as a rational exercise. It is common to attribute base motives to politicians – that they are only trying to get themselves re-elected or that they are supporting their political friends. Germain's book starts with a different perspective. Legislators are seen as engaging in a rational exercise of making choices and justifying them. We live in an imperfect world and politicians, like all of us, are imperfect people. But this book demonstrates how politicians have tried to decide what justice requires in choices which affect large numbers of people and where the consequences are very unpredictable. Based on imperfect information, they have tried to produce systems of healthcare which protect the vulnerable, fit with broader economic models and are fiscally affordable. The medical professions and the wider public are not of one mind on the right answer to such questions, and the same is true of legislators. I hope this work will lead us as readers to be more appreciative of the difficulties of being a legislator and of the seriousness with which the activity is undertaken by most in politics.

In both her specific focus on healthcare law and policy and in her general contribution to an understanding of the legislative process, Sabrina Germain offers insights that can be taken forward not just by scholars of the USA and the UK, but also in relation to other countries. I was privileged to have a number of conversations with her as she developed the early stages of this work. I am glad to see it come to fruition in such an impressive way and trust that it will stimulate further studies by other scholars.

John Bell,
*Cambridge*
*5 October 2018*

# ACKNOWLEDGEMENTS

Writing a book was a childhood fantasy, writing a monograph has been an extraordinary challenge in adulthood. With a few modest words, I wish to thank all of those who have helped me fulfil this dream.

I should start by highlighting the financial support of Cornell Law School, and the Berger International Legal Studies Program and thank Dean Charles Cramton for his assistance throughout my doctoral degree as my thesis forms the basis of this book. I am also thankful for the institutional support of the University of Cambridge and the Centre for European Legal Studies during the last years of my doctoral studies.

I am most indebted to the members of my doctoral committee at Cornell Law School: Professor Muna Ndulo for his patience, encouragement and great empathy and Professor Robert C Hockett and Professor Chantal Thomas for their many insightful comments on the draft of my thesis. I am also deeply grateful for the relentless support of Professor John Bell at the University of Cambridge. Discussions with Professor Bell have been illuminating and this project would never have been possible without his critical input.

I also owe many debts to other individuals for their comments on the early drafts of the book. In particular, Professor Michael Frakes, Professor Adam Kolber, Professor Aziz Rana, Dr Michael K Gusmano and Luke Mason. I believe that their feedback has made a significant contribution towards the originality and timeliness of this book. I am also tremendously thankful for the excellent research assistance of my dedicated students, Jamie Delaney and Paula Poniatowska.

My gratitude of course also goes to Hart Publishing for making this book possible. I am most thankful for the excellent work of Sinead Moloney, commissioning editor, and the production and marketing team.

Over the past five years, I was also happy to have the friendship of Paulina Szczepan, Ankit Chhabra, Dr Sabrina Gilani, Dr Anastasia Chamberlen, Dr Henrique Carvalho-Raudau during the moments of doubt and the short but intense episodes of laughter. I am also very grateful for the camaraderie of my colleagues Dr Tawhida Ahmed, Dr Nora Honkala, Dr Noreen O'Meara, Jeffrey Thompson and Dr Adrienne Yong as I wrote up the last portion of this book.

Last but not least, I want to acknowledge the profound influence of my family on my writing. I was fortunate to have had the encouragement of my sister Alexandra and the outstanding support of my parents, Dr Lesly Germain and Me Ghislaine Hardy. I cannot thank my parents enough for teaching me the importance of an education and instilling in me the foundations of intellectual independence.

Their love for medicine and a strong sense of justice were a tremendous source of inspiration for this book.

Even though acknowledgements cannot be equal to the measure of their sacrifice, I also wish to thank my husband Sasha and our beautiful daughter Joséphine. Their infallible support has helped me more than I can say and their resilience has made me realise how much growth can arise from challenging oneself. They have celebrated my moments of enlightenment and, as life continued outside this project, helped me cope with overwhelming losses, and this I will never forget. The words of this book are filled with the love and compassion they have selflessly given me, and it is to them that I wish to dedicate every single one of them.

Sabrina Germain
*London*
*July 2018*

# CONTENTS

# ABBREVIATIONS

| | |
|---|---|
| ACA | Affordable Care Act |
| AFL–CIO | American Federation of Labor and Congress of Industrial Organization |
| AHA | American Hospital Association |
| AIDS | Acquired Immune Deficiency Syndrome |
| AMA | American Medical Association |
| BMA | British Medical Association |
| CCG | Clinical Commissioning Group |
| CESCR | UN Committee on Economic, Social and Cultural Rights |
| CHI | Commission for Health Improvement |
| CHIP | Children Health Insurance Program |
| ERISA | Employee Retirement Income Security Act |
| FDR | Franklin D Roosevelt |
| GP | General Practitioner |
| HSA | Health Savings Account |
| HIPAA | Health Insurance Portability and Accountability Act |
| HMO | Health Maintenance Organization |
| ICESCR | International Covenant on Economic, Social and Cultural Rights |
| LIFT | Local Improvement Finance Trust |
| MAA | Medical Assistance to the Aged Program |
| MP | Member of the British Parliament |
| NHS | National Health Service |
| NICE | National Institute for Health and Care Excellence |
| OAA | Older American Act |
| OECD | Organisation for Economic Co-operation and Development |
| PBR | Payment by Result |
| PCG | Primary Care Group |
| PCT | Primary Care Trust |
| PFI | Private Finance Initiative |

| PMI | Private Medical Insurance |
| POS | Point of Services |
| PPO | Preferred Provider Organizations |
| QALY | Quality-Adjusted Life Year |
| UDHR | Universal Declaration of Human Rights |
| WHO | World Health Organization |

# TABLE OF CASES

# TABLE OF LEGISLATION

**International Legislation**

# 1

# Introduction

> The ideas of economists and political philosophers, both when they are right and when they are wrong, are more powerful than is commonly understood. Indeed, the world is ruled by little else ... I am sure that the power of vested interests is vastly exaggerated compared with the gradual encroachment of ideas.[1]
>
> John Maynard Keynes

Vegetables have recently taken over discussions around issues affecting health care systems. A line of argument suggests that public powers should no longer be addressing health care, and like peas or broccoli, the allocation of these resources, to finance or provide health care services, should be left to the market. Proponents of this approach believe that health care is no more special than vegetables in the achievement of good health,[2] therefore why should it not be bought off the shelf? For instance, Jonathan Haidt, advocate of the 'vegetable rhetoric', explains that central to making peas available to the general public is the chain of manufacturers and suppliers involved in their production and marketing. Farmers, truckers, supermarket employees, and even miners and metalworkers contribute to making the peas available at an extremely low price. He attributes the affordability of the produce to the presence of competition among the suppliers at every stage of production and to the innovative techniques that helped reduce the aggregate price of the can. In a similar manner he claims that the allocation of health care resources would be most optimal and the price lowest if it were treated like a can of peas, i.e. left in the hands of the market and subject to competition.[3]

---

[1] John Maynard Keynes, *The General Theory of Employment, Interest and Money* (New Delhi, Atlantic Publishers and Distributors, 1936) 383–84.

[2] R Hanson, 'Why Health is not Special: Errors in Evolved Bioethics Intuitions' (2002) 19(2) *Social Philosophy and Policy* 153 doi.org/10.1017/S0265052502192077.

[3] J Haidt, *The Righteous Mind: Why Good People are Divided by Politics and Religion* (New York, Vintage Books, 2012) 303–04, Haidt imagines, to help consumers with the purchase of their groceries, a food insurance scheme with a substantial premium of $2000 and a co-payment fee of $10 payable at every shopping session. According to him, a certain point will be reached where food insurance prices will inevitably rise because supermarkets will only be willing to stock the produce that rewards them with the highest insurance payments and not the ones that provide the greatest value to the insured. An uncontrollable spiral of price increases will then be unleashed, and the price of a 'subsidized' can of peas will reach $30. A contribution to a tax-based subsidised scheme to cover all consumers' inflated grocery bills will then be imposed.

Similarly, vegetables have also made their way to the American Supreme Court during discussions pertaining to the validity of President Obama's Affordable Care Act (ACA).[4] The purchase of health care insurance was then compared with the consumption of broccoli. Justice Scalia argued that although imposing the purchase of vegetables on American citizens may produce good health outcomes, it would be unimaginable and ludicrous to do so. Nevertheless, as pointed out by Justice Ginsburg, health care presents attributes that have no parallel in modern life, since 'the inevitable yet unpredictable need for medical care and the guarantee that emergency care will be provided when required are conditions non-existent in other markets. That is so … of the market for broccoli as well'.[5]

Granted it may be argued that health care is no more special or unique than other determinants of health, such as nutrition, environment or safety, but it is greatly reductionist to equate it to a consumer good. For after all, health care is not just a vegetable. The importance it has in our lives and communities makes it a worthy subject of justice. Indeed, according to Norman Daniels, even in those societies, which tolerate or support significant inequalities in the distribution of social goods, most of their members feel that an equal distribution of health care resources is still justified.[6] The moral significance of health care derives directly from the importance of health in our lives. Its importance does not stem from the opportunity or advantages it creates but from its potential to alleviate suffering and absolute harm.

The indisputability and seriousness of health care needs therefore make the distribution of health care resources stand out from the distribution of any other good. It is the fundamental and critical nature of these resources that requires that their distribution follow principles of justice.[7] This is precisely why political philosophers have become interested in theorising the just allocation of health care resources. More specifically, the feeling that available resources are now seriously out of synch with our needs mandates that principles of justice be used for a better allocation.[8] Unfortunately, however, political philosophy seems to be at a distance from the reality of law and policy.[9] The waves of health care reforms experienced in Western welfare states partly reflect the law's inability to embody justice principles that could provide methods for tackling pressing issues.[10] Indeed, even though political philosophers have thought of multiple models to justly allocate resources, problems of availability and access to care remain major challenges.[11]

---

[4] *National Federation of Independent Business v Sebelius* 567 US 519 (2012).

[5] ibid, II D 1a.

[6] See generally, N Daniels, 'Health-Care Needs and Distributive Justice' (1981) 10 *Philosophy & Public Affairs* 146.

[7] N Daniels, *Just Health Care* (Cambridge, Cambridge University Press, 1985) 4.

[8] D Weinstock, 'Health Care in Political Philosophy: What Kind of a Good is it?' (Centre de recherche en éthique de l'Université de Montréal, 2010) 1.

[9] MJ Sandel, 'The Procedural Republic and the Unencumbered Self' (1984) 12 *Political Theory* 81, 81.

[10] See generally, RB Saltman and J Figueras, *European Health Care Reform* (Copenhagen, World Health Organization, 1997).

[11] DJ Hunter, *The Health Debate* (Bristol, Policy Press, 2016) 2.

The relationship between justice and health care, then, raises several questions that are central to this book. Considering the above debates in political philosophy, we may wonder whether it is the mismatch between the theory and the practice of law-making that is to blame for failing health care systems; or is it simply that theories of distributive justice do not inform the decisions of actors involved in the crafting of health care policies? The book suggests that the link between these two worlds needs to be examined more concretely to improve the organisation and the distribution of care. The very existence of a connection between moral philosophy and health care law has thus far been underestimated and unappreciated by law and policy scholars and as this book will show, understanding whether theories of political philosophy have made their way into law is an essential first step in solving health care issues. Rationing is, and will remain, at the top of governments' priority lists since only a finite amount of resources will ever be available to satisfy the infinite health care needs of populations.[12] Therefore, we should be able to explain how ideas of justice can be used to craft more adequate laws to ration, finance and provide health care services.

This book engages with literature in political philosophy and historical sources relating to the evolution of health care reforms in two Western welfare states, namely the United States and the United Kingdom, to understand the influence of theories of justice on health care policy over time. The legislative committees' debates that are presented in this book illustrate the deeper ethical and moral trends that were brought forward during the discussions leading to health care reforms. Attention is given to actors belonging to the for-profit sector: doctors, employers and insurers because of the different, but equally influential, roles they have played in the edification of both systems. Remarkably, these actors are also thought to be less sensitive to the social justice rhetoric.

Essentially, this book sheds light on the place given to theories of justice in the health care law-making process and on the place that we wish to give these theories in the crafting of future reforms. It is also a reflection on health care reforms as expressions of their broader social context. Health care law and policy are the products of path dependency evolving differently in the United States and the United Kingdom. These findings potentially have significant implications for health care law and policy in Western welfare states, especially regarding the need for change in these areas.

## I.  Justice, Profit and the Law

In theory, no health care system could ever be sustained without adjusting the distribution of resources according to certain rules,[13] and so, political philosophers continue to propose solving rationing issues with distributive justice principles.[14]

---

[12] D Wilsford, 'The Logic of Policy Change: Structure and Agency in Political Life' (2010) 35 *Journal of Health Politics, Policy and Law* 663, 664.

[13] E Elhauge, 'Allocating Health Care Morally' (1994) 82 *California Law Review* 1449, 1493–95.

[14] See works of Norman Daniels, Amaryta Sen and Carie Fourie on the subject.

At a clinical level, bioethics philosophers generally believe that the health care decision-making process should revolve around four principles: *autonomy*, encompassing the principles of self-governance, liberty, privacy, and freedom of choice; *non-maleficence*, encompassing the moral duties of doctors not to execute acts of torture or to behave harmfully towards their patients; *beneficence*, encompassing the moral duties of doctors to act for the benefit of others; and *justice*, the duty to treat like cases alike when allocating resources to patients.[15] In line with these principles, doctors select treatments based on an assessment of the disease and then run a cost–benefit analysis for each treatment option. At both stages, questions of justice and solidarity are weighed.

At a systemic level, it is less clear whether normative arguments, based on philosophical or moral standards, are the basis of policy goals or whether they are even used as normative tools to achieve certain outcomes. Evidently, because of the multi-layered and complex nature of health care policy-making, goals and outcomes rarely overlap. Although these normative theories have often been criticised for providing only broad guidelines with no concrete application, they may help situate health care in an ethical framework that can achieve fair distributive decisions.[16]

Ideas of justice are no more essential than institutional input, but they may have a different place in the decision-making process and it is important to determine what that place has been so far in order to determine what we want it to be in the future. Policies may reflect powerful economic interests, and ideas about the good society. Interests and ideas both shape policy choices and it is usually a matter of understanding how they come together to do so to be able to improve the access, delivery and financing of health care services.

## A.  Profit and Health Care

Arrangements for the delivery and financing of health care services vary across countries. However, most Western democracies have aligned themselves with an 'international standard' for health care.[17] One of the main features still distinguishing the organisation of health care systems in Western welfare states is the share of publicly financed services in the total health care expenditure.[18] At one end of

---

[15] TL Beauchamp and JF Childress, *Principles of Biomedical Ethics* (Oxford, Oxford University Press, 2001) 12.

[16] C Fourie, 'What Do Theories of Social Justice Have to Say About Health Care Rationing? Well-being, Sufficiency and Explicit Age-rationing' in A den Exter and M Buijsen (eds), *Rationing Health Care: Hard Choices and Unavoidable Trade-Offs* (Antwerp, Maklu, 2012) 73–74.

[17] J White, 'The 2010 US Health Care Reform: Approaching and Avoiding How Other Countries Finance Health Care' (2013) 8 *Health Economics, Policy and Law* 1, 14–15.

[18] D Brady et al, 'Path Dependency and the Politics of Socialized Health Care' (2016) 41 *Journal of Health Politics, Policy and Law* 355, 356.

the spectrum lies the United States with less than half of its total spending coming from public funds, and at the other, is the United Kingdom[19] that finances over 80 per cent of health care services through taxes.[20] The amount of private sector activities related to health care is inversely proportional to the state's involvement in both of these countries. All of this inevitably impacts the organisation of these systems.[21] Indeed, the share of publicly financed services translates the degree of 'socialisation' of medicine. Some political scientists have attributed this variation to the different role played by the for-profit sector in each of these countries, while others believe that culturalist explanations can justify the difference in health care and social policy.[22]

Political elites and the public, as cultural agents, may perceive the importance of health care and relay their perspectives to law-making institutions differently, but looking at culturally similarly situated welfare states the culturalist argument becomes difficult to defend. The United States and the United Kingdom are countries that share a common cultural background and are both common law jurisdictions. They have achieved a similar level of development and political freedom. However, the American health care system has always been singled out as the exception in comparison to its European counterparts given the extremely prominent role played by the private sector in health care.[23] The medical profession, employers and insurers have had a critical impact on the edification of the system and neither culture nor political allegiance can properly explain their dominance.[24] This book explores how the for-profit actors are in great part responsible for the lack of universal care in the United States.[25] Having long resisted and contested the idea of compulsory insurance they have shaped health care policy and have had a significant impact on the law-making process.[26]

Comparing and contrasting the American health care system with the National Health Service (NHS), it is obvious that the share of activity of general practitioners acting as independent contractors, of medical consultants engaging in the private practice of medicine, and of other medical professionals providing health care services privately in the United Kingdom, does not compare with the American for-profit sector's stake in its health care system. The role of the private

---

[19] In this book, references to the United Kingdom after the devolution of power in 2002 relate only to NHS England.

[20] Brady et al, above (n 18) 356.

[21] H Maarse, 'The Privatization of Health Care in Europe: An Eight-Country Analysis' (2006) 31 *Journal of Health Politics, Policy and Law* 981.

[22] See generally, C Geertz, *The Interpretation of Cultures: Selected Essays* (New York, Basic Books, 1977).

[23] White, above (n 17) 1.

[24] EM Immergut, *Health Politics: Interests and Institutions in Western Europe*, 6th edn (Cambridge, Cambridge University Press Archive, 1992) 1–67.

[25] P Starr, *The Social Transformation of American Medicine* (New York, Basic Books, 1982) 6.

[26] ibid, 256. Further details on the history of the American health care system and the role of the for-profit system will be given in ch 3.

sector is different in the United Kingdom as the for-profit stakeholders have not been equally hostile to a government-led health care system.[27] From the inception of the NHS and throughout its modern history the for-profit sector in the United Kingdom has helped preserve universality of care. In some respect, the medical profession has presented itself as the shield protecting the NHS's core values as further demonstrated in this book.

Actors from the for-profit sector in America and the United Kingdom are at the heart of the organisation of their systems and greatly impact governmental decisions regarding the allocation of health care resources, be it directly or indirectly. That is not to say that political institutions do not play a major role in the drafting of health care laws, but it is important to understand how these institutions are permeable to the for-profit sector's input to fully grasp the nature of health care policy in both countries. Therefore, the influence of political philosophy on the crafting of health care laws should also highlight the role of the state in the allocation process.[28]

## B. Discourses of Justice

Political philosophy mandates the analysis of public discourses to understand the law's deep-lying objectives, even if those are not necessarily being reflected in the legislative outcome. Jürgen Habermas in his book *Between Facts and Norms* points to the argument made by some philosophers about the absence of absolutes and grounds for morality in modern, liberal and pluralistic societies, such as Western welfare states, but explains that a moral foundation nonetheless exists within discourses.[29]

For Habermas morality is not metaphysical but pragmatic and present in the use of language. A statement about the morality of a matter made to establish what is right for society participates in the edification of the moral foundation. Habermas' conception of morality sees discourse as a mechanism for conflict resolution and language as instituting social order. Of course, laws and political institutions also participate in the coordination of the social order. Thus, law is a medium for social integration and politics is a support to morality. The realm of politics is itself divided into two spheres: the informal sphere constituted by civil society where actors exchange informal and spontaneous discourses; and the formal sphere of political institutions such as Parliament or Congress, Cabinets

---

[27] JS Hacker, *The Divided Welfare State: The Battle over Public and Private Social Benefits in the United States* (Cambridge, Cambridge University Press, 2002) 221–69.

[28] Brady et al, above (n 18) 361.

[29] See generally, J Habermas, *Between Facts and Norms: Contributions to a Discourse Theory of Law and Democracy* (Chichester, John Wiley & Sons, 2015).

or elected assemblies where members of the political community engage in the decision-making process and formulate laws and policies.[30]

Habermas argues that for politics to elaborate a valid legal rule, a normative and a factual aspect must come together.[31] Thus, a legitimate rule cannot be 'self-validated' since it requires that members engage in a dialectic process and reach an agreement as to the rightness of the law.[32] Norms must go through a democratic process to be enacted and this requires the use of a specific form of communication. Policies and laws are the reflection of civil society's discourses transferred and formalised in the discourse of the political community.[33] In this respect, positive law is the mechanism that complements and stabilises key stakeholders' communicative actions. Discourses and their moral foundation also infuse ethical values in a legitimate law.[34] Thus, this theoretical underpinning establishes that discourses conveying ideas or theories of justice, formulated during the elaboration of health care laws, are proof of a connection between moral philosophy and the reality of law and policy. The formal sphere of legislative institutions also provides tangible evidence of moral discourses recorded in various reports and legislative drafts. More particularly, as this book will show, the discourse of for-profit actors during the negotiations and drafting stages explains how and why ideas of justice have made their way into health care policy.

The impact of the for-profit sector on the enactment of health care reforms in the United States and the United Kingdom results from its ability to participate in the legislative framework. The presence of language employed by doctors, employers or insurers in these contexts may reflect a justice theory and demonstrates its social recognition. Indeed, language and communication styles also reflect visions of the world, identities and the roles individuals play in social relations. Discourses are socially embedded and, to a larger extent, reflect social movements and our perception of a society at a particular time and place. Analysed in different contexts, social domains, or different institutions they reveal factors that contribute to social change.[35] Thus, in order to unpack the social context of health care reforms, this book pays close attention to the language of legal and policy discourse.

For-profit actors' speeches are interlocutory acts that have raised a set of criticisable claims and, when they have made their way in the final version of a legislative act, have received universal validity.[36] Positive law therefore represents

---

[30] J Gordon Finlayson, *Habermas: A Very Short Introduction*, Vol 125 (Oxford, Oxford University Press, 2005) 108.

[31] ibid, 93–115.

[32] ibid, 108.

[33] Habermas, above (n 29) 110.

[34] ibid, 99.

[35] MW Jørgensen and LJ Phillips, *Discourse Analysis as Theory and Method* (London, Sage Publications, 2002) 61.

[36] Habermas, above (n 29) 4.

a mechanism that structures different stakeholders' communicative actions.[37] Essentially, flowing from Habermas' theory, this book suggests that discourses of justice formulated by for-profit actors have led to the enactment of legitimate health care reforms as the product of a larger social consensus in the United States and the United Kingdom.

## C. Legislative Intent

The United States and the United Kingdom are unique case studies in the realm of health care policy. The United States remains the only Western democracy without a universal health care system, and the United Kingdom is the first country to offer free comprehensive health care services to its entire population.[38] The differences in the organisation and objectives of these systems make the comparison even more interesting and relevant. Looking at these contexts together also provides evidence that normative thinking in health care policy is not just the reflection of national preferences. Despite fundamental differences, both Western welfare states have developed mature health care systems and, as demonstrated in chapters four, five and six, have seen the drafting of health care reforms impacted by for-profit actors and ideas of justice. For the sake of clarity, it should be specified that the analysis presented in this book focuses only on American federal health care laws and the laws pertaining to the NHS of England (even though health care laws enacted prior to 1999, some of which discussed hereafter, were also applicable to NHS Wales, NHS Scotland and NHS Northern Ireland).

The American Congress through formal and specialised committees collects testimonies from its members, officials of the executive branch, policy experts and interest groups (including the for-profit sector) to evaluate the necessity to create new law in certain domains. The reports of these hearings constitute influential information used to draft legislative proposals. These documents also provide key elements to make sense of the controversies arising at the early stages of the policy-making process.[39] Committee hearing reports have the most probative value in determining Congress' legislative intent, more so than the reports of the discussions taking place in the House of Representatives or on the floor of the Senate, which only offer technical information on the negotiations of the wording of the law. As further discussed in the book, abstracts from these reports relate language of justice used by for-profit actors to comment on potential laws pertaining to the financing and provision of health care services. These documents are a primary source of information for the analysis of key policy moments in the United States.

---

[37] ibid, 37.

[38] N Vetter, *The Public Health and the NHS: Your Questions Answered* (Oxon, Radcliffe Medical Press, 1998) 33.

[39] 'Congressional Hearings' (US Government Publishing Office), available at: www.gpo.gov/fdsys/browse/collection.action?collectionCode=CHRG.

In the United Kingdom, the government's request for an inquiry can ignite the legislative process. The review leads to the drafting of a White Paper: an authoritative report presenting the issues, potential solutions and tentative timeline to implement new legislation. The document presents the reasons for a reform, usually voicing the reactions of different groups and mentioning potential controversies surrounding the project. The White Paper contains many elements that are later incorporated in the Bill.[40] Following the publication of the White Paper and before the law receives royal assent, the draft Bill is read three times before Parliament. The Second Reading of the Bill provides the most information about the intent behind the future law. Depending on the activity of each House the draft law is presented either before the House of Commons or the House of Lords. During this process House Members discuss the principles that motivate the enactment of the new law. Second Reading reports also shed light on the role of certain Members in the legislative process and on the role (although indirect) played by pressure groups in the elaboration of health care reforms.[41] Interest groups such as the for-profit sector do not enter the walls of Parliament to discuss future legislation, but often relay their opinions to their representatives, who may carry the group's support or grievance inside the institution. Similarly, to Congressional Hearing reports, abstracts from transcripts of the Second Reading of a draft Bill may reveal discourses of justice. They are therefore analysed in chapter six to shed light on key health care reforms.

## D.  History and Health Care Reforms

The book focuses on a 70-year period starting with the birth of modern medicine and the discovery of antibiotics and penicillin[42] going all the way to President Obama's health care reform in 2010 and the UK Coalition government's health care reform in 2012.[43] This period marks years of great economic, social and political change in both countries with watershed policy moments and major turning points. The presence of discourses of justice in the policy and law-making process during this era testifies to the fact that these occurrences are not isolated events but enduring trends in both welfare states.

Indeed, health care policy must be understood as part of a political, economic and social context. National health care programmes are the product of a constellation of factors taking place at particular points in time. The history surrounding

---

[40] Select Committee on the Constitution, *The Legislative Process: Preparing Legislation for Parliament*, 4th Report (2017–19, HL 27) 14.

[41] ibid.

[42] 'Antibiotics changed the focus of medical care from prevention of disease through inoculation and hygiene to cure of illnesses'. See K Patel and ME Rushefsky, *Healthcare Politics and Policy in America*, 4th edn (Armonk, NY, ME Sharpe, 2014) 54; see generally, MC Bernstein and JB Bernstein, *Social Security: The System That Works* (New York, Basic Books, 1988).

[43] Health and Social Care Act 2012 c 7.

the enactment of major health care reforms in the United States and the United Kingdom recounted in subsequent chapters brings about a different perspective on the connection between political philosophy and institutional outcomes.

Obviously, historical events and their sequencing matter as they provide a specific conjecture favouring certain interest groups and their ideas.[44] A bird's-eye view of American and British health care policies helps us determine whether ideas and theories of justice have been ingrained and preserved in the systems as part of a set policy, or whether they have made their way into the legislative process as an accident of history.[45] Ideas of justice are certainly part of a larger social narrative, but they have also been instrumental in helping actors set trends for the distribution of health care resources. The book thereby explores path dependency theory as a tool to unpack the complex nature of political philosophy's relationship with the practice of law and policy making.

Path dependency theory suggests that similar outcomes in public policy are the result of a political trajectory born out of historical events.[46] More than a mere description of historical phenomena, the theory emphasises the significance of social variables to explain how policy 'got to where it is'. Essentially, it demonstrates how and why past events lead to repetitive policy outcomes and offers a systemic understanding of history.[47] Policy moments often consolidate the path, but sometimes their importance is such that they deviate the trajectory.[48]

Institutional arrangements attempt to prevent divergence because of the high cost associated with reversal of a policy.[49] Public policy tends to create large constituencies that have a great interest in maintaining social programmes and benefits, and some actors and organisations participating in these programmes become stakeholders with vested interests and therefore are reluctant to encourage any change in policy. The state must continue to meet set standards and normative expectations.[50]

Findings later presented in the book confirm that the medical profession and other for-profit actors in the United States and the United Kingdom have helped

[44] JS Hacker, 'The Historical Logic of National Health Insurance: Structure and Sequence in the Development of British, Canadian, and US Medical Policy' (1998) 12 *Studies in American Political Development* 57, 59.

[45] Throughout the book the adjective 'British' is used to talk about reforms in England, Northern Ireland and Wales, except for acts and events post-devolution (2002) for which 'British' is used to qualify acts pertaining to NHS England only.

[46] See generally, AL Stinchcombe, *Constructing Social Theories* (Chicago, IL, University of Chicago Press, 1987).

[47] Brady et al, above (n 18) 355.

[48] D Wilsford and LD Brown, 'Path Dependency: A Dialogue' (2010) 35 *Journal of Health Politics, Policy and Law* 681, 687–88.

[49] M Levi, 'A Model, a Method, and a Map: Rational Choice in Comparative and Historical Analysis' in M Irving Lichback and AS Zuckerman (eds), *Comparative Politics: Rationality, Culture, and Structure* (Cambridge, Cambridge University Press, 1997).

[50] Brady et al, above (n 18) 360–61.

set policy paths that were, at times, diverted with the enactment of a health care reform. The for-profit sector in both countries seems to be responsible for setting trends for the allocation of health care resources and for upholding certain elements of justice to reinforce their respective positions. Thus, path dependency theory provides an important perspective in the assessment we make of the legislative systems' sensitivity to conceptions of justice.

Not all political scientists support the path dependency theory or the findings derived from it. Famously, Lawrence Brown has been particularly critical of the theory as he considers that there are no good reasons to justify using it as a prism for the analysis of public policy.[51] He argues that the theory has no major added value since policies are merely the outcome of an institutional push and pull, and therefore the theory becomes an invitation to describe the political phenomenon rather than to make sense of it.[52] Brown makes a valid point about the extensive negotiations involved in the law-making process; however, the theory still offers a valid account for the design and organisation of health care systems. As this book will argue, path dependency theory is key in explaining successive waves of reforms and the recurrent issues relating to access, cost and sustainability of health care services in the United States and the United Kingdom. This is further explored in chapters three to six.

## II.  Essential Elements of the Book

Medical professionals, employers and insurers, in the United States, and the general practitioners, medical consultants and independent sector in the United Kingdom, have all had a great impact on policy making and health care reforms. Their ability to participate in the legislative framework highlighted throughout the book demonstrates how their actions in and outside the legislative sphere have shaped decisions relating to the financing and provision of health care services. Their 'institutional' influence also sheds light on path dependency constraining health care policy in both countries. From the beginning of the twentieth century to the present day, for-profit actors have certainly been instrumental in maintaining some of the attributes of both health care systems. In this respect, the United States and the United Kingdom provide exemplary case studies. Their cultural similarities and their unique approach to health care financing and delivery allows us to put into perspective the level of engagement the for-profit sector has had with ideas of justice. This systematic comparison puts forward the different roles these actors have had in the only mostly privately run system and the first

---

[51] See generally, LD Brown, 'Pedestrian Paths: Why Path-Dependence Theory Leaves Health Policy Analysis Lost in Space' (2010) 35 *Journal of Health Politics, Policy and Law* 643.
[52] ibid, 643.

universal health care system in the world. The analysis is concentrated on watershed moments in the history of the American and British health care systems to better highlight specific aspects of health care policy in both countries. This also allows a parallel examination of what were the factors in both systems that led to these hinging points.

Universality of care is a major underlying theme of this book as it has helped develop the necessary theoretical framework to lead a coherent and consistent historical and comparative analysis of legislative work. Essentially, *Justice and Profit in Health Care Law* is the first book to examine whether the lack of an overlap between theories for the just allocation of resources and the process leading to the enactment of a law, has led to reforms unsuccessfully tackling problems affecting mature health care systems in Western welfare states. An analysis of the role played by American and British for-profit actors, deemed least sensitive to ideas of justice, provides pertinent insights into health care law and policy making, and the comparative dimension of this study offers an unprecedented outlook on both the legal and policy aspects of health care provision.

## A. Methodological Considerations

Discussions, arguments and negotiations between powerful stakeholders have led to legislative proposals that are sometimes turned into laws. The strategic and rhetorical use of language is most crucial to this process. Stakeholders often directly relay their interests to the sphere of law and policy making through discourses uttered in political and legislative institutions. Setting and framing issues with language establishes precise conceptual boundaries, which have a significant impact on legislative outcomes.[53] The book therefore adopts a discourse analysis methodology to determine whether for-profit actors have used ideas of justice to relay their interest in health care law, and whether their discourses have influenced the health care allocation process in the United States and the United Kingdom. The enquiry examines the concrete linguistic occurrences made by these for-profit stakeholders during the negotiation of important health care reforms.

The appendix to the book encloses key words associated with the five allocation models used to theorise the just allocation of health care resources. These words constitute a reading grid used to analyse reports of legislative preparatory work. Contextualised, these occurrences provide evidence that discourses relating to these distributive models were used to convey ideas of justice in health care law.[54] This methodological approach also mandates that historical elements be taken into consideration, as on many levels they have made an impression

---

[53] See generally, J Russell et al, 'Recognizing Rhetoric in Health Care Policy Analysis' (2008) 13 *Journal of Health Services Research & Policy* 40 doi.org/10.1258/jhsrp.2007.006029.

[54] See appendix for the detail of textual occurrences analysed in the primary sources.

on the production of the actors' discourses. Thus, the textual analysis of pattern in and across occurrences is supported by the historical analysis presented in chapter three and in chapter five. Throughout the enquiry, historical and socio-logical sources also clarify the influence elements of a broader context have had on interlocutors.

The purpose of this project however is not to enter into socio-psychological study that attributes meaning to the leading actors' discourses and behaviours. The book makes no claim of inside information on the motivations and private views of for-profit actors. The enquiry only presents how and when theories of politi-cal philosophy and organising principles have made their way into the legislative process as exemplified by the discourses of these key policy actors. Essentially, the book proposes a theory of legal development and advances methodological elements for the study of legal change.[55]

## B. Outline of the Book

The chapter following these introductory remarks ('Understanding Health Care as a Question of Justice') presents theories of political philosophy that outline methods for the just allocation of health care resources while addressing the fundamental philosophical, political and legal debate on universality of care as a requirement for the attainment of justice. Some of these conceptions of justice (egalitarian, utilitarian and communitarian) confer a special status to health care and argue in favour of a universal system. Others (libertarian and neo-liberal) value individual freedom or a certain laissez-faire, which should not be infringed to promote free access to health care. All five theories are fleshed out in order to understand their potential influence on health care policy-making. This chapter intends to set the table for subsequent discussions on whether these normative schemes have been instrumental in setting goals or organising the financing and provision of health care services in the United States and the United Kingdom over the past 70 years. The purpose of this chapter is not, however, to critically assess each theory but to offer a global view of distributive justice theories to later proceed to a meta-normative analysis of discourses of justice in the legislative framework.

Subsequent chapters deal with health care law and policy making in the United States and the United Kingdom. Chapter three ('For-Profit Stakeholders in American Health Care Policy') is dedicated to the presentation of the history and developments of main policy trends in American health care. Attention is given to the role of leading actors in the construction of this unique system. The part played

---

[55] D Ibbetson, 'Comparative Legal History: A Methodology' in A Musson and C Stebbings (eds), *Making Legal History: Approaches and Methodologies* (Cambridge, Cambridge University Press, 2012) 134.

by employers in the creation of risk-pooling systems, by insurers in the creation of third-party payer schemes and by the medical profession in the consolidation of the privately run health services are explained with a historical narrative. This brief panorama is most useful in understanding issues of cost and access affecting health care in the United States and the solutions that have been so far provided in an effort to manage and contain these problems.

Chapter four ('Locating Ideas of Justice in American Health Care Reforms') brings to light major reforms for the financing and provisions of health care services in the United States. It begins with the enactment of a law for the indigent aged, the Kerr–Mills Act (1960) and finishes with the most recent change brought to the system with the ACA (2010), without omitting the amendments to the Social Security Act (1965) that created the federal programmes of Medicare and Medicaid, and the Republican Health Maintenance Organization (HMO) initiative established through the enactment of the Health Maintenance Organization and Resources Development (HMO) Act 1973. The analysis of the language and discourses used by actors belonging to the medical profession, insurance industry and corporate employers brings forward the existing overlap between concrete policy-making choices and theoretical normative patterns.

Similarly, for the United Kingdom, chapter five ('For-Profit Stakeholders in British Health Care Policy') introduces the historical foundation of the NHS. From its inception in 1948 to the present, the role played by the for-profit sector, more particularly the medical profession, in the creation of the first publicly run health care system in the world is highlighted. The focus of this presentation is on the NHS and the evolving role of the private sector in the delivery of health care services and its impact on the organisation of the national system of care. The private partnership initiatives to finance and provide health care in England are also highlighted.

This historical tour d'horizon leads to the presentation in chapter six ('Locating Ideas of Justice in British Health Care Reforms') of key health care reforms in the United Kingdom. Attention is given to the indirect participation of the medical profession, through its dialogue and confrontation of various governments' health care policy, in the elaboration of the following legislation: the NHS Foundational Act (1946), the reform brought by Margaret Thatcher with the NHS and Community Care Act (1990) and the most recent overhaul of the system brought by the Health and Social Care Act (2012). The chapter also presents the importance of foundational ideas of justice at the core of the NHS that instilled path dependency in British health care law and policy.

Finally, the analysis led in previous chapters invites a conclusion on the role of distributive justice theory in the law-making process. The conclusion, chapter seven, therefore reiterates the crucial need for prioritising resources in health care and on the influence of path dependency leading the American and British health care systems to more recently adopt converging health care policies.

# 2

# Understanding Health Care as a Question of Justice

'Justice is the first virtue of social institutions, as truth is of systems of thought'[1]

John Rawls

## I. Introduction

Two fundamental questions are at the heart of health care policy debates in the United States and the United Kingdom. Should health care services be provided based on a person's needs rather than their ability to pay? And if so, what constitutes the appropriate level of care to be provided in a universal health care system? Answers to both questions are often pragmatic but also appeal to broader ideas of justice that theorise the distribution of scarce resources.[2] This polarising discussion can also be taken as an opportunity to reflect more deeply on the role of justice in health care, as claims made in favour or against a universal system help contextualise the methods preferred for a just allocation of resources.

For instance, egalitarianism, and in some respects, utilitarianism and communitarianism have argued that universal health care constitutes a requirement for the attainment of justice. Indeed, egalitarian theories prescribe either equality in life opportunities, equality in capabilities or prudential equality in treatment to achieve justice in health care. All three of these goals can only be reached through a universal system of care. Utilitarianism, on the other hand, aims at providing individuals with tools to maximise society's utility and this often translates into providing universal health care to all members of society. Finally, the collection of thoughts and theories that form the communitarian justice focuses on a balanced allocation of health care resources taking into account the patient's illness and the needs of the local community to achieve just health care outcomes for society as a whole. Conversely, libertarianism and neoliberalism prioritise freedom and self-ownership, as they posit that a just health care system can only

---

[1] J Rawls, *A Theory of Justice* (Cambridge, MA, Harvard University Press, 2005) 3.
[2] K Patel and ME Rushefsky, *Healthcare Politics and Policy in America*, 4th edn (Armonk, NY, ME Sharpe, 2014) 235–74.

be achieved through a free market and the decentralisation and privatisation of services. Thus, in theory, each of these distributive models offers principles and patterns of allocation that aim to achieve justice in health care.

Organising principles also influence the allocation of resources in Western welfare systems. Mainly, the principles of solidarity and subsidiarity inform discussions on the universal provision of health care services. Both principles were foundational to the elaboration of welfare theories in Europe during the nineteenth and twentieth centuries. These concepts also raise additional queries: what are the responsibilities and the level of commitment expected from individuals towards their peers in health care? And, what is the appropriate level of central government involvement in the provision of health care services? These questions should therefore also be examined when considering the allocation of health care resources as a question of justice.

Theories of a right to health care or an absolute human right to health, are also of interest as they introduce a link between the theory of moral political philosophy and the theory of health care organising principles. This formalistic approach offers a picture of what constitutes a just health care right and a pathway to produce more just health care laws.

Interestingly, in spite of the knowledge we have of these theoretical frameworks, health care systems continue to struggle and are unable to tackle scarcity and access issues. Perhaps these underwhelming outcomes in health care can be explained by welfare states' incapacity to mitigate ideas of justice with the reality of the legislative process; or could it be explained by health care key stakeholders' unwillingness to inform policy decisions with these theoretical frameworks? Addressing more specifically these questions requires surveying all three theoretical approaches (moral philosophy, organising principles and legal theory of health care rights) because only a complete view of the theory can help determine whether for-profit actors in the United States and the United Kingdom have appealed to ideas to discuss or negotiate major health care reforms.[3]

Thus, after having analysed why the allocation of health care resources is a worthy question of justice, this chapter fleshes out five theoretical approaches to the allocation of health care resources starting with the theoretical debate around universality of care as a requirement for the attainment of justice. The third part of the chapter focuses on principles of solidarity and subsidiarity, which transcend all theories of moral philosophy presented in the second part of the chapter. Finally, the chapter closes with a discussion of theories of health and health care rights.

## II. Justice and the Allocation of Health Care Resources

Justice is concerned with human relationships in the social order and issues of distribution. It balances the needs and desires of individuals with the claims of the

---

[3] See appendix for the detail of textual occurrences analysed in the primary sources.

community. According to Aristotle's definition, justice is what everyone is due. It mandates that we treat those who are alike equally and those who are different in proportion to their differences.[4] Political philosophers have therefore outlined principles to connect property with morally justifiable allotments of burdens and benefits to achieve just distributive outcomes. Their theories create rules of social cooperation to allocate rights and responsibilities.[5]

Some academics have also been critical of health care policy outcomes and found health care laws to be deprived of moral foundations, even though, in theory, all health care reforms directly or indirectly consider elements of justice.[6] Unlike moral systems that apply to individual actions, these distributive principles apply to institutions. They provide guidelines for the organisation of political, social and economic life.[7] In reality, institutional policies, including policies for the distribution of health care resources, are influenced or framed by principles derived from a combination of these models. They accept and/or reject one or more conception of justice.

As mentioned in the introduction of the book, it is the importance of health care in our modern societies, the contribution these resources make to a population's health status and the potential they have to alleviate pain and suffering, that make them stand out from any other good. For these reasons health care resources are worthy subjects of justice. Health care policy-making mandates a reflection on the most appropriate process to determine 'what everyone is due' in health care. In other words, asking whether health care resources should be universally available automatically frames the debates in terms of justice.[8] This fundamental query also encloses other underlying considerations. What should be the basic entitlement in health care? Should resources be allocated based on a patient's, a community's or a population's needs? Should we aim at providing individuals with greater life opportunity by satisfying their health care needs?

The concept of need is indeed intimately linked to discussions of justice in health care. It is somewhat infinitely expandable given our ageing societies.[9] We tend to need what is available and this may become limitless as we try to expand life, increase wellbeing and as we successfully achieve advances in medical technology. Universal health care systems embracing need as a benchmark for the attainment of justice propose to increase wellness or reduce illness. This may

---

[4] See generally, HH Joachim and DA Rees (eds), *Aristotle: The Nicomachean Ethics* (Oxford, Clarendon Press, 1953).

[5] S Fleischacker, *A Short History of Distributive Justice* (Cambridge, MA, Harvard University Press, 2009) 1–17.

[6] N Daniels and JE Sabin, *Setting Limits Fairly: Learning to Share Resources for Health* (Oxford, Oxford University Press, 2008) viii.

[7] GR Almgren, *Health Care Politics, Policy and Services: A Social Justice Analysis*, 2nd edn (New York, Springer Publishing Company, 2012) 16.

[8] TL Beauchamp and JF Childress, *Principles of Biomedical Ethics* (Oxford, Oxford University Press, 2001) 243.

[9] RD Lamm, 'Rationing of Health Care: Inevitable and Desirable' (1992) 140 *University of Pennsylvania Law Review* 1511, 1511–15.

translate in having patients with equivalent health care needs treated alike and other patients treated differently. However, this also brings about the question of differentiating factors.[10]

Another underlying consideration relating to the universal provision of health care services is whether these resources ought to be distributed on the basis of acquisitions of private property rather than imposing the financial burden on society as a whole through general taxation. Advocates in favour of a universal health care system propose to provide a core of publicly financed health care services and to have peripheral treatments left in the hands of patients. Opponents of the universal system are adamant that all health care services should be independently purchased by patients, providing them with more choice and autonomy. This indirectly leads to discussion on individual responsibility in the allocation process. In this respect, it is important to note that many diseases and medical conditions are exacerbated or even caused by individual behaviour. Therefore, should patients bear the cost when their lifestyle or reckless behaviour has contributed to their illness? Alternatively, should they be given lower priority in the system?[11]

Many are the questions at the heart of health care policy-making in Western welfare states. The answers provided by political philosophy are complex as are those given by organising principles such as solidarity and subsidiarity, and interesting is the response of legal frameworks to these doctrines.

## III. Moral Political Philosophy and Universality of Care

### A. Claims in Support of Universality of Care

Liberal egalitarianism posits that the allotment a person receives at birth creates fundamental inequalities between individuals. Even though every individual should be put on an equal footing and treated fairly, the 'life lottery' produces unjust outcomes. Redistribution must therefore correct these discrepancies to achieve justice. A person's health status also depends heavily on conditions present at birth; however, no amount of redistribution can eradicate particular inequalities linked to health. In order to achieve justice in health care, systems should not aspire to equalise health status, but allocate resources following principles of equality.[12]

---

[10] See generally, A Gutmann, 'For and Against Equal Access to Health Care' in R Bayer, AL Caplan and N Daniels (eds), *In Search of Equity* (Boston, MA, Springer, 1983).

[11] See generally, HM Evans, 'Do Patients Have Duties?' (2007) 33 *Journal of Medical Ethics* 689.

[12] R Hoedemaekers and W Dekkers, 'Justice and Solidarity in Priority Setting in Health Care' (2003) 11 *Health Care Analysis* 325, 327–28.

## i. Liberal Equality

Egalitarian theorists conceptualise equality in health care as embedded in a larger understanding of justice.[13] To achieve their equalising goals, they prioritise different objectives: equality in life opportunities, equality in capabilities or prudential equality in treatment.[14] All of which ultimately lead to a system supporting universal health care. All three equalising goals are presented in this section, as well as the components required for each of these trends to achieve a just health care system.

### a. Equality in Life Opportunities

John Rawls' philosophical work was pioneering in theorising a model of justice based on fairness and individual freedom. For Rawls, justice requires that all be treated equally and that inequalities be repaired with a system of distribution based on morally relevant factors.[15] Rawls imagines a state of nature in which individuals are unaware of their social status (fortune, class position, etc) or any assets received at birth (abilities, intelligence, strengths, etc). Personal talents and attributes are considered irrelevant to calculations that could lead to a just outcome because of their randomness and a person's inability to control these factors.

In this fictional state, individuals are rational agents driven by the desire to establish a process for the fair allocation of resources through contract. According to Rawls, the absence of bias and the necessity to reach a unanimous decision will automatically lead actors to freedom and equality.[16] The rhetorical device helps to identify morally relevant factors for the allocation of resources and to provide an objective answer to what constitute essential elements of justice.[17] In the initial position, individuals are inclined to shape and elect principles that secure the best possible outcome for everyone and indirectly for themselves. In a way, the hypothetical state turns selfishness into altruism.

The social contract is binding on all individuals, and even though consent is not fundamental, unanimity of consensus legitimises the agreement.[18] The fundamental principles identified under the veil of ignorance lead to the ranking of five essential goods: (i) basic liberties; (ii) freedom of movement and choice of occupation; (iii) powers and prerogatives of offices and positions of responsibility; (iv) income and wealth; and (v) social bases of self-respect. All of which are the object of the social contract.[19]

---

[13] See generally, A Sen, 'Why Health Equity?' (2002) 11 *Health Economics* 659.
[14] Hoedemaekers and Dekkers, above (n 12) 327–28.
[15] Rawls, *A Theory of Justice*, above (n 1) 303.
[16] ibid, 12.
[17] ibid, 14–15.
[18] ibid, 515.
[19] ibid, 62, 93.

In a just world, the distribution of these primary goods should follow two fundamental principles: the liberty principle that establishes that individuals are entitled to basic liberties as long as they do not infringe on another person's freedom; and the difference principle that states that social and economic inequalities are permissible as long as they provide the greatest benefit to the least advantaged, and that attached offices and positions are open to everyone under conditions of fair equality of opportunity.[20] Thus, liberal egalitarianism promotes equality and individual freedom but also tolerates inequality as long as it benefits the least favoured. In practice, these principles can be used as a metric to assess the fairness of a policy outcome.

Rawls chooses to focus on the equality of resources to achieve equal life opportunities rather than focusing on the equality of welfare because, unlike resources, personal levels of wellbeing cannot be objectively assessed and therefore appropriately equalised.[21] For him, the benefit that individuals may derive from resources or their capacity to better achieve their life plans are also irrelevant to the allocation process. Individuals are responsible for their choices. Primary goods are helpful in the selection of life plans but only because they provide individuals with equal opportunities.[22]

Thus, in order to guarantee the equality of opportunities, resource egalitarianism requires that governments intervene in the allocation of the resources that are the most crucial for the achievement of life plans. The state, as a neutral actor, will not subsidise or penalise the use of resources, but it ought to oversee that the distribution process remains fair and equal.[23] As health care resources participate in the production of many primary goods and are fundamental to the achievement of good health, their allocation should take place under state supervision. Governments should ensure that the allocation of health care resources follows the liberty and difference principles.

In an influential interpretation and extension of Rawls' theory, Norman Daniels also argues that a just health care system should be based on the fair equality of opportunity.[24] Although Daniels offers no explicit defence of the principle, to edify his theory, he relies implicitly on the importance of fair opportunity and health in the achievement of life plans.[25] Daniels does not blindly support an orthodox account of equality that potentially could lead to bad health care for all. Rather, he argues that since it is inevitable for some individuals to fall sick and for others to remain healthy, universal access to care represents the only logical solution to guarantee that all health care needs be met equally.[26]

---

[20] ibid, 302–03.

[21] ibid.

[22] JE Roemer, *Theories of Distributive Justice* (Cambridge, MA, Harvard University Press, 1998) 192–93.

[23] Beauchamp and Childress, above (n 8) 247–48.

[24] Almgren, above (n 7) 35–36.

[25] Beauchamp and Childress, above (n 8) 247–48.

[26] N Daniels, 'Justice and Access to Health Care' [2008] *Stanford Encyclopedia of Philosophy*, available at: plato.stanford.edu/archives/spr2013/entries/justice-healthcareaccess.

As with Rawls, for Daniels health inequalities result from an unjust distribution of health determinants at the original position and they should not be tolerated.[27] It is therefore incumbent on institutions governed by Rawlsian principles of justice to enforce a right to health care to guarantee equal opportunities.[28] Social benefits should not be distributed on the basis of undeserved or advantageous property; on the contrary, the distribution of health care resources should follow the priority rule: 'those who suffered the greatest reduction in their opportunity range, as the result of health problems, should receive the highest priority in the allocation of health care resources'.[29] Evidently, the rule caters for a minimal level of care to the worst off patients.[30] Put differently, Daniels argues that inequality can be rectified if the needs that interfere the most with 'normal species functioning' are tackled first. He explains that 'it will be more important to prevent, cure, or compensate for those disease conditions which involve a greater curtailment of normal opportunity range'.[31] Unfortunately, the scope and the nature of 'normal species functioning' remain debatable since they also heavily depend upon the availability of decent health care services. This therefore implies some form of circularity in the benchmark used to allocate health care resources.[32]

Ultimately, welfare states that embrace resource egalitarian principles invest in governmental institutions with the mission to promote just distribution of health care resources and to provide individuals with equal opportunities to achieve their life plans.[33] Ill health and the impossibility of perfecting one's health status because of inadequate social arrangements are negatively relevant to social justice.[34] Thus, health care systems must meet the needs of all patients and strive to prevent diseases, illnesses and injuries regardless of patients' choices post-allocation. The resource egalitarian doctrine also advocates a right to universal health care and prescribes that health care services be provided based on needs rather than means. Whether an individual takes the responsibility to seek treatment or reverts to unhealthy habits after treatment is irrelevant to the initial distribution. Thus, resource egalitarian policies promote personal autonomy and prioritise the least favoured and vulnerable groups in the allocation process.[35]

---

[27] N Daniels, 'Broken Promises: Do Business-Friendly Strategies Frustrate Just Healthcare?' in DG Arnold (ed), *Ethics and the Business of Biomedicine* (Cambridge, Cambridge University Press, 2009).

[28] ibid.

[29] Mark Stein restating Norman Daniels' rule in MS Stein, *Distributive Justice and Disability: Utilitarianism Against Egalitarianism* (New Haven, CT, Yale University Press, 2008) 185.

[30] Hoedemaekers and Dekkers, above (n 12) 327–28.

[31] See generally, N Daniels, 'Health-Care Needs and Distributive Justice' (1981) 10 *Philosophy & Public Affairs* 146.

[32] E Jackson, *Medical Law: Text, Cases, and Materials*, 3rd edn (Oxford, Oxford University Press, 2013) 49.

[33] Beauchamp and Childress, above (n 8) 248.

[34] Sen, above (n 13) 660.

[35] Beauchamp and Childress, above (n 8) 341–43.

### b. Equality of Capabilities

The welfare egalitarian doctrine principally draws on the work of Amartya Sen, developed in reaction to John Rawls' justice theory.[36] Welfare egalitarians, in contrary to resources egalitarians, are concerned with the benefits a person derives from resources and strive to find solutions that give individuals better and equal access to advantages.[37] Welfare egalitarianism seeks equality of capabilities to achieve functionings (ie, states of being and doing). Mobility, happiness, self-respect, adequate nutrition and the escape of morbidity rank high among these objectives.[38]

However, resource egalitarians have argued that the offensive and expansive tastes that could jeopardise the allocation of resources imply that justice cannot be achieved through the equality of welfare. According to Rawls, conceptions of welfare are as diverse as they are incommensurable and therefore cannot be satisfied. Despite this fundamental opposition, Sen proposes a discussion on the impact resources have on individual lives. He consciously chooses not to focus on equalising primary goods.[39]

Instead of seeking equality in the means to achieve wellbeing, welfare egalitarianism gives priority to the ends, the capabilities that allow individual freedom to attain wellbeing.[40] Welfare egalitarianism is more content with providing equal access to all available health care resources rather than committing to the unreachable goal of providing every patient with equal health care resources.[41] Thus, health care policies committing to a welfare egalitarian idea of justice see universality of care as providing individuals with the capacity to improve their health status.[42]

A distinction should nevertheless be drawn between health achievements and the ability to achieve good health.[43] If we consider, for example, two individual foregoing medical visits, one avoiding medical screening out of fear, and the other because of financial incapability and lack of insurance, the difference becomes more apparent. The welfare outcome of these two individuals is essentially the same. Nonetheless, the insured person is at an advantage compared with the uninsured. She holds more options and disposes of a greater capability. This is why welfare egalitarianism emphasises equality of real freedom commensurate with equality of condition. The ability to choose between options is instrumental and reflects a person's capability to achieve life plans. Thus, capabilities must be equalised in order to achieve justice.[44]

---

[36] Almgren, above (n 7) 4.
[37] Stein, above (n 29) 6.
[38] Roemer, above (n 22) 192–93.
[39] Human definition of maximisation mechanisms.
[40] Roemer, above (n 22) 192–93.
[41] ibid.
[42] Hoedemaekers and Dekkers, above (n 12) 327–28.
[43] Roemer, above (n 22) 192–93.
[44] R Arneson, 'Egalitarianism' [2002] *Stanford Encyclopedia of Philosophy*, available at: plato.stanford. edu/archives/sum2013/entries/egalitarianism.

Welfare egalitarianism, however, does not appear to account for the signifi-cance of personal responsibility. It posits that individuals are strictly responsible for their life choices and not for opportunities based on their abilities. This may be problematic if an individual with socially determined life plans precludes them from taking responsibility.[45] Under this conception of justice, responsibil-ity is placed on political, economic and social structures advancing or impeding a person's capacity to achieve wellbeing.[46] Welfare egalitarian policies therefore aim at creating a minimum level of capabilities. No social or political institution should be given preference over another and this applies to health care systems. Although universal health care should be available it should not be prioritised over other governmental policies providing individuals with the capacity to achieve their life plans.[47]

### c. Prudentially Defined Equality

Another variation to the Rawlsian egalitarian theory emerges from the work of Ronald Dworkin on prudentially defined equality. Dworkin suggests providing individuals with a universal opportunity to access health care. His proposal builds on the assumption that rational and prudent individuals would, under specific circumstances, purchase insurance to yield events of bad health.[48] He imagines a world in which rational agents are under a thin veil of ignorance. Conscious of their talents and preferences, they are however unaware of their handicaps. At this point, every agent is given the opportunity to purchase coverage to hedge the risk associated with potential misfortunes. Thus, it is expected that once the veil is lifted, some handicapped and fully-abled individuals will have purchased cover-age. Others, having decided against the purchase, will be responsible for their own preferences.[49]

The fiction of the thin veil of ignorance produces just and fair results. It reflects perfectly an individual's degree of aversion to risk and justly levels the playing field. Dworkin favours this ambition-sensitive solution to a resolution leading to endowment-sensitive outcomes.[50] For him, insurance markets transform events of brute luck into events of option luck.[51] Prudential egalitarianism requires individuals to be compensated for the situational disadvantages hampering their

---

[45] Roemer, above (n 22) 192–93.

[46] Almgren, above (n 7) 4.

[47] See generally, MC Nussbaum, 'Aristotle, Politics, and Human Capabilities: A Response to Antony, Arneson, Charlesworth, and Mulgan' (2000) 111 *Ethics* 102.

[48] Daniels, 'Justice and Access to Health Care', above (n 26).

[49] ibid.

[50] Roemer, above (n 22), for other discussions on responsibility and an 'opportunity-egalitarian' distribution of resources focusing on inputs rather outputs, see R Hockett, 'Justice in Time' (2008) 77 *George Washington Law Review* 1135.

[51] Roemer, above (n 22) 248.

achievement and the disadvantages for which they are not responsible. Individuals must, however, take an active role in the allocation process. Dworkin distinguishes tastes, ambitions and circumstances. Individuals are responsible for their preferences as long as they identify with them.[52] The importance this doctrine ascribes to responsibility in distributive justice is unique.[53]

According to Dworkin, not giving the means and social benefits necessary to level the playing field constitutes the greatest injustice. Not providing individuals with the same opportunity to achieve life plans is fundamentally unjust. Thus, offering an opportunity to access health care resources, regardless of a person's initial endowments, is not only reasonable, but is a requirement of justice. This egalitarian doctrine contends that individuals should be given a fair chance to prevent disadvantages that are not the result of their wrongdoings. Thus, no one should be held responsible for his or her bad health.[54]

Health care policy aiming at prudential equality would lead to the implementation of solidary systems of risk sharing. Individuals would be encouraged to perform reciprocal duties, for example, paying taxes to finance health care services, while respecting the collective right to access these resources.[55]

## B. Alternative Claims in Support of Universality of Care

Under both egalitarian and utilitarian justice theories the worst off in society are the greatest beneficiaries of the allocation process. However, goals and methods differ. Egalitarians are concerned with providing the means to equalise resources or capabilities, whereas utilitarians are preoccupied with helping those in need in order to maximise utility. This translates to the promotion of a universal health care system but under different conditions.[56]

The communitarian doctrine, on the other hand, emerges from a collection of thoughts on recurring themes, namely, the critique of liberal theories and individualism, the politics of the community and the importance of shared values.[57] With regard to the distribution of resources, communitarianism proposes a contextualised approach focusing on conventions, traditions and loyalties within

---

[52] ibid, 192–93.

[53] C Knight, *Luck Egalitarianism: Equality, Responsibility, and Justice* (Edinburgh, Edinburgh University Press, 2009) 1.

[54] See generally, R Dworkin, 'What is Equality? Part 2: Equality of Resources' (1981) 10 *Philosophy & Public Affairs* 283.

[55] See generally, R Houtepen and R ter Meulen, 'The Expectation(s) of Solidarity: Matters of Justice, Responsibility and Identity in the Reconstruction of the Health Care System' (2000) 8 *Health Care Analysis* 355.

[56] Stein, above (n 29) 6.

[57] See eg, MJ Sandel, 'The Procedural Republic and the Unencumbered Self' (1984) 12 *Political Theory* 81; M Walzer, *Spheres of Justice: A Defense of Pluralism and Equality* (New York, Basic Books, 2008).

the community.[58] Access to health care should not be based on an individual's right or wealth. This has also led communitarian philosophers to argue in favour of a universal health care system, even though health care resources must be allocated in proportion to illness and at the local and community level to benefit society as a whole.[59]

## i. Utilitarianism

Utilitarians theorists believe that society must provide schemes to maximise the common good (ie, utility). The standard of justice that derives from this postulate creates the most important obligation under the doctrine.[60] However, the process of utility maximisation has to be performed by doing the least harm to the fewest people, and by preventing the most harm for the greatest number.[61]

Moral rules and norms of allocation are tested for their capacity to maximise the aggregate level of utility.[62] Therefore, an act is just only if it maximises the sum of all individual pleasures, satisfaction, happiness, wellbeing or absence of pain.[63] Some utilitarian theorists have argued that the maximisation should go beyond happiness to encompass knowledge, health, success, understanding, enjoyment and personal relationships.[64] Utility is therefore measured in terms of the intrinsic value certain actions can produce. Contrarily, other utilitarian philosophers have argued that the intrinsic good lies within the preferences of the greatest number and that aggregate utility is only an optimal benchmark for allocation.[65]

Regardless, the utility maximisation rule can lead to extreme consequentialism since actions are solely assessed based on their potential of increasing utility.[66] Extreme instances of deprivation or abundance are acceptable if the greatest good for the greatest number is guaranteed. Also objectionable is utilitarianism's tolerance for unequal distribution. The interests of the majority can potentially override the rights of the minority. For example, an already prosperous group could be given priority over resources that would also benefit an indigent group if the prosperous group's aggregate utility is greater than the utility the poorer group could derive from these resources.[67] Thus, utilitarian justice has the potential to

---

[58] See generally, RH Robbins, *Global Problems and the Culture of Capitalism* (Boston, MA, Pearson Allyn and Bacon, 2005).

[59] See generally, G Mooney, '"Communitarian Claims" as an Ethical Basis for Allocating Health Care Resources' (1998) 47 *Social Science & Medicine* 1171.

[60] See generally, J Bentham, *An Introduction to the Principles of Morals and Legislation* (Oxford, Clarendon Press, 1879).

[61] See generally, Bentham, ibid; see generally, Almgren, above (n 7).

[62] See generally, Bentham, above (n 60).

[63] Hoedemaekers and Dekkers, above (n 12) 328–29.

[64] J Griffin, *Well-Being: Its Meaning, Measurement, and Moral Importance* (Oxford, Oxford University Press, 1986) 67.

[65] See eg, Griffin, ibid.

[66] JE Crimmins, 'History of the Utilitarian Social Thought' in J Wright (ed), *International Encyclopedia of the Social & Behavioral Sciences*, 2nd edn (Oxford, Elsevier, 2015) 981–82.

[67] Beauchamp and Childress, above (n 8) 342.

create a 'tyranny of the majority'. The majority's preferences may override those of a minority group if an increase in aggregate utility justifies those preferences. This is because utilitarianism is indifferent to oppressive distribution. It validates the empowerment of the majority to see its preferences fulfilled while potentially crushing the minority. Just distribution does not imply fair distribution but only a utility maximising process.[68]

In the realm of health care, utilitarian policies that aim at maximising the population's welfare are likely to include the implementation of a universal health care system. Universal access to services creates greater wellbeing and greater productivity for the greatest number. However, as resources are limited utilitarian health care policy may also lead to rationalistic calculation to assess which patient derives the greatest utility for a treatment. Since utilitarianism grants equal footing to all preferences, the choice of treatment to be publicly financed should be the result of a general consultation. The interests of all affected parties should have equal weight and all preferences should be externally and impartially considered.[69] Even if a preference produces negative externalities or has morally questionable outcomes it cannot be discredited. Individuality does not carry weight in the achievement of justice. Individuals are the only relevant variants in utility's calculus.[70]

Utilitarian policies may also create systems where priority access is given to patients who have the most potential to improve society's aggregate health status. Utilitarian policies in health care justify the maximisation of the aggregate utility and the ranking of patients' needs to establish prioritisation processes. An assessment of the burden that a disease creates is irrelevant.[71] The only objective of utilitarian health care systems is to provide cost-efficient health services. This implies empirically testing treatments and health care services for their utility. For instance, the Quality-Adjusted Life Year (QALY) provides a measure of quality and quantity of life lived through treatment. The greater the QALY as a result of the treatment, the higher it will rank on the priority list. Treatment and health care services bearing high costs or benefiting only a small group of individuals are likely to be relegated to the bottom of the priority list. Consequently, individuals requiring the lowest-priority treatments receive the least care.[72]

Although, in practice, utilitarianism may raise controversial ethical questions, it should not be interpreted as managerial or technocratic doctrine. Social programmes for the protection of public health and the equal and universal distribution of basic health care are a crucial requirement for the attainment of justice under this theory.[73]

---

[68] W Kymlicka, *Contemporary Political Philosophy: An Introduction* (Oxford, Oxford University Press, 2002) 27.

[69] RM Hare, 'Ethical Theory and Utilitarianism' in A Sen and B Williams (eds), *Utilitarianism and Beyond* (Cambridge, Cambridge University Press, 1982) 26.

[70] ibid, 23–39.

[71] Beauchamp and Childress, above (n 8) 340.

[72] Hoedemaekers and Dekkers, above (n 12) 328–29.

[73] Kymlicka, above (n 68) 9.

## ii. Communitarianism

The communitarian doctrine rejects the liberal social models based on interpersonal relationships, rights and contracts.[74] Liberalism, be it liberal egalitarianism or libertarianism, is deemed to be individualistic and abstract because of its insensitivity to collective goals and its disregard for the relevance of a person's history as a product of a communal life.[75] Individualism cannot be developed without common structures especially not outside the bounds of a family. Communitarian theorists therefore argue that the opportunity to make life choices and autonomy are factitious.[76] This explains why in the communitarian mindset, liberty and equality are subordinate to the needs of the community. Alongside the idea of justice, solidarity is fundamental. Individuals are responsible for the community that has and continues to forge them, and respectively, the community is accountable to each of its individuals.[77]

Essentially, the doctrine calls for the recognition of human dependence on society and the obligation of individuals to sustain the common good. Unlike liberal societies where the common good is tailored to fit individual ideas of good, in communitarian societies it provides a benchmark to assess individual preferences and defines the community's way of life.[78] Communitarianism's view establishes that health care is important not only because it is an atypical good but also because it contributes to the achievement of a greater common good for society.

Communitarianism also argues that liberalism's quest for a universal theory of justice applicable to all societies is somewhat misguided since an objective and removed perspective from our community can never be attained. No single theory of justice can apply to all societies, as justice is also the product of a common understanding of ideas and shared values. According to Michael Walzer,

> a society is just if it acts in accordance with the shared understanding of its members, as embodied in its characteristic practices and institutions. Hence identifying principles of justice is more a matter of cultural interpretation than of philosophical argument.[79]

Principles for the governance of each community evolve with their history and are rooted in concrete, unique cultural attributes. In fact, the communitarian justice theory embraces cultural and moral relativism.[80]

---

[74] Walzer, above (n 57) 86–94.

[75] MJ Sandel, *Liberalism and the Limits of Justice*, 2nd edn (Cambridge, Cambridge University Press, 1998) 1–13.

[76] See generally, C Taylor, 'Cross Purposes: The Liberal-Communitarian Debate' in NL Rosemblum (ed), *Liberalism and the Moral Life* (Cambridge, MA, Harvard University Press, 1989).

[77] ibid.

[78] See generally, Walzer, above (n 57).

[79] ibid.

[80] JP Ruger, *Health and Social Justice* (Oxford, Oxford University Press, 2010) 25–26.

To achieve justice, resources must be employed to fulfil community-endorsed social goals.[81] Attending to the needs of the community supersedes the realisation of personal achievements or the satisfaction of individual needs for liberty or equality.[82] Shared practices and their understanding within a community are the essential underpinnings of a just distribution of resources.[83] Acts, rules or policies expressing and reinforcing the values of the community will be given priority over individual needs.[84] Communitarian theorists believe that the idea of community precedes the idea of justice. Justice is a tool to achieve greater solidarity. Justice is simply a vehicle that enables individuals to make genuine voluntary decisions by providing them with an appropriate structure to construct loving relationships free of domination, subordination and corruption.[85]

Identity does not need to be built *de novo*. To the contrary, justice from values of social goods already ingrained within the community must naturally emerge. Communitarians define the community as a small group of individuals or institutions with set goals, roles and obligations. The community exists in the form of common social practices, cultural traditions and shared social understanding.[86] The smallest communal unit is the family, in which parents and children join together in the realisation of their goals, roles, obligations, social practices and traditions.[87] Members of the community must appreciate their shared history, culture and common attitude towards welfare in order to establish principles for the just allocation of communal resources.[88]

However, the unanimous consensus that is required for the achievement of the common good seems virtually unattainable. Therefore, despite its critique of liberalism, communitarianism has had to make a moderate shift towards liberal dynamics. For the doctrine to endure and to achieve the just allocation of resources for the community, distribution has been addressed with some novelty.[89] In recent years a new form of communitarianism has emerged that combines a liberal and more individualist conception of justice with the idealistic goals of communitarianism.[90] In this revised theory, the community is an active participant in the upbringing of self-governing individuals and provides sufficient resources for individuals to function and develop as independently as possible from its boundaries.[91]

---

[81] Beauchamp and Childress, above (n 8) 337–99.
[82] Kymlicka, above (n 68) 210–11.
[83] ibid, 209.
[84] Beauchamp and Childress, above (n 8) 356.
[85] ibid, 199–210.
[86] ibid, 357–58.
[87] Kymlicka, above (n 68).
[88] Beauchamp and Childress, above (n 8) 357.
[89] Hoedemaekers and Dekkers, above (n 12) 329–30.
[90] P Selznick, 'Foundations of Communitarian Liberalism' in A Etzioni (ed), *The Essential Communitarian Reader* (Lanham, MD, Rowman & Littlefield, 1998).
[91] ibid.

Health care systems adopting a communitarian approach for the allocation of resources emphasise the role of primary care medicine at the community level. The systems monitor and cater to the health care needs of populations located in secluded, rural areas and promote the decentralisation of health care services. In some Western welfare states, medical homes emerged in the 1960s taking a communitarian approach to the practice of medicine.[92] Medical offices were slowly transformed into small clinics and started to centralise medical records, which made it easier to provide primary care services at the community level. During this time, the importance of serving children and families in an environment that encouraged deeper relationships between health care providers and their patients was recognised. The innovative idea of medical homes reflected a bottom-up, grassroots approach to the delivery of care. Today, they still provide primary care services and promote wellness and early prevention.[93]

Ultimately, in order to achieve justice, distribution of resources should not be based on individual needs but should reflect the community's idea of what constitutes necessary health care. Public consultations are often used to survey the community and to set goals in these health care systems. Thus, within a single communitarian health system, different allocation processes might emerge to palliate different conceptions of need.[94]

## C. Claims Against Universality of Care

Libertarianism presents the state as a single dominant, effective and protective association. With its exclusive exercise of force on the territory, it is in charge of defending the population against foreign and domestics threats and protecting property and personal autonomy.[95] Although the cost of protection offered by the 'minimal state' is borne by the entire population it does not involve compulsory payments for any other benefits. Exactions are a direct interference with the protection of individual rights and therefore cannot be levied by a libertarian government.[96] This, of course, translates into the realm of health care. Libertarianism argues patients' autonomy and the power to choose the appropriate level of care for one's condition. The allocation of resources must therefore be left outside the public sphere and put into the hands of the free market.

Neoliberalism follows in these footsteps and, although it is not a stand-alone theory of justice, it proposes that health care systems be privately run free of

---

[92] C Sia et al, 'History of the Medical Home Concept' (2004) 113 (Supplement 4) *Pediatrics* 1473, 1473.

[93] ibid.

[94] Hoedemaekers and Dekkers, above (n 12) 329.

[95] R Nozick, *Anarchy, State, and Utopia* (New York, Basic Books, 1974) 15–17.

[96] J Penner et al, *McCoubrey & White's Textbook on Jurisprudence* (Oxford, Oxford University Press, 2012) 237.

state regulation. Its principles have inspired policies for the allocation of resources and are often interpreted as relying on libertarian ideals. Under both models of allocation, meeting the population's health care needs is not a duty that has to be carried out by the state and the achievement of justice does not encompass universality of care.

## i. Libertarianism

In *Anarchy, State, and Utopia* Robert Nozick offers a libertarian response to Rawls' theory. He explains that libertarianism does not focus on the allocation of benefits but on the just acquisition of individual holdings, whatever they may be. The process of acquiring property must be irrespective of whether or not it leads to just outcomes. Justice should be evaluated according to three principles: justice of acquisition, justice in transfer and just rectification in the case of unjust holdings.[97] Only the market can perform a just distribution of resources by providing a platform for the transfer of legitimately acquired property. Rectification of these exchanges only arises if the property was taken illegitimately from its owner or if an illegitimate interference obstructed market exchanges.[98]

Public powers should not be involved in the distribution of wealth.[99] Libertarianism considers that individuals hold a moral right to grant or deny any aspect of their person and to dispose freely of any legitimately acquired property or profits derived from these holdings.[100] Individuals are protected against any non-consensual loss of their moral right to self-ownership, as long as it does not violate the rights of others. Therefore, publicly financed policies promoting welfare or social rights, including claims to universal health care, cannot exist.[101] State interference through taxation would force individuals to dispose of their holdings for the benefit of the community and constitute a violation of their intrinsic moral rights.[102]

From a libertarian standpoint, individuals having purchased insurance coverage to finance their health care needs have acquired a property right over health care services. Physicians, as any other individuals, have a moral intrinsic right to liberty and therefore cannot be coerced into providing services through a socially sponsored scheme.[103] Furthermore, individuals are considered to be responsible for their own circumstances including the improvement and protection of

---

[97] Nozick, above (n 95) 150–53.

[98] See generally, HT Engelhard Jr, *The Foundations of Bioethics*, 2nd edn (New York, Oxford University Press, 1996).

[99] Nozick, above (n 95).

[100] Almgren, above (n 7) 5–6.

[101] Penner et al, above (n 96) 238.

[102] B van der Vossen and P Vallentyne, 'Libertarianism' [2002] *Stanford Encyclopedia of Philosophy*, available at: plato.stanford.edu/archives/fall2014/entries/libertarianism.

[103] ibid.

their health.[104] Illness and old age are risks inherent to the human condition; free individuals are therefore expected to plan for protection by purchasing insurance coverage. At the very least, they will have to pay out of pocket for health care services or rely on the participation of their family and close networks to finance their health care needs.[105]

With regard to the delivery of health care services, again, individuals should contribute to the system without resorting to the help of higher-level authorities. Governmental intervention is unnecessary because human relationships alone are capable of satisfying health care needs. This explains the importance given to charity in the achievement of justice under the libertarian doctrine. Justice does not create a duty to support the sick and the needy. These responsibilities fall within the ambits of charitable institutions.[106] Considering that resources dedicated to health care are becoming scarcer in Western welfare states, libertarian theorists have claimed that charity will play a bigger role in the delivery of care. For lack of profit some services may no longer be available through the market and the population will have to rely on charitable institutions for treatments.[107]

Ultimately, no inherent right or claim to health care exists under the libertarian theory of justice. Personal autonomy and liberty are the only necessary foundations of a just health care system and the privatisation of health care services is an utmost protected value.[108] Health is valuable and justifies action against those who are trying to harm or interfere with the health of others, but it remains a negative interest. It requires protection but does not imply any duties to be actively carried out. Health care systems based on libertarian principles are therefore 'individual-oriented' and focus on personal necessities rather than on collective health care needs.[109]

## ii. Neoliberalism

In the eighteenth and nineteenth centuries a new class of merchants and industrials, that vigorously opposed public involvement with their commercial dealings, started promoting ideas of economic laissez-faire. Contemporary neoliberalism is the revival of their vision. It proposes to use cost-efficient solutions, available through an unregulated market, free from the intervention of central government. In health care, this translates into the privatisation, deregulation and decentralisation of services.[110]

---

[104] Beauchamp and Childress, above (n 8) 245.
[105] Almgren, above (n 7) 32–33.
[106] Hoedemaekers and Dekkers, above (n 12) 325.
[107] Beauchamp and Childress, above (n 8) 245.
[108] ibid, 360–61.
[109] Hoedemaekers and Dekkers, above (n 12) 326–27.
[110] M Terris, 'The Neoliberal Triad of Anti-Health Reforms: Government Budget Cutting, Deregulation, and Privatization' (1999) 20 *Journal of Public Health Policy* 149, 151–52.

Essentially, the doctrine is based on the assumption that individuals always put their personal needs first, and that they can have only limited concerns for others and their environment. Neither the public good nor the community are central elements of the model. Social policies are considered irrelevant and even detrimental as they hinder the market's good functioning and create discrimination among individuals. Some will benefit from social programmes while others will finance these structures without gaining any assistance. Thus, the ideology focuses on the individual, their family and their responsibility.[111] Ethics, morality and social ideals that reflect personal preferences are dealt with independently of state supervision. The market is seen as the utmost democratic institution as it allows everyone to participate and provides a vehicle for individuals to express choices. The government's role is therefore limited to the safeguard of market efficiency.[112]

Neoliberals consider that health care is a commodity. Therefore, individuals and patients as consumers need to be provided with optimal purchasing opportunities.[113] Governments cannot universally finance or provide health care resources because these services belong in the private sector. Like any other private good, the distribution of health care is most efficiently performed on a platform that is free from interference and that allows power to be decentralised.[114] Health care is a source of profit, and medicine is a moneymaking instrument, therefore, markets can create enough incentives to generate an optimal level of competition, leading to better performing and more efficient systems.[115]

The doctrine also claims that the laws of supply and demand help patients be more responsible in their consumption of health care services as the cost of treatment performs an indirect rationing function and thereby optimises the allocation of resources.[116] The market also provides individuals with more choice, autonomy and better quality services.[117] Personal freedom therefore supersedes the need for equity in health care. With regard to the delivery of services, neoliberalism advocates a system tailored to the needs of the local population. Ideally, the decentralisation and close proximity of facilities would help patients be more involved in their treatment. Services could potentially be streamlined, costs lowered and inequalities among the population reduced.[118]

The fundamental principles of the neoliberal doctrine are in direct opposition to the principles of sharing risk and financial burden, as well as delivery of public

---

[111] M Rösch, 'What Does Neoliberalism Mean?' (1998) *Eberhard Karls Universität Tübingen* tiss.zdv. uni-tuebingen.de/webroot/sp/barrios/themeA2a.html.

[112] ibid.

[113] S McGregor, 'Neoliberalism and Health Care' (2001) 25 *International Journal of Consumer Studies* 82.

[114] Robbins, above (n 58).

[115] D Callahan and AA Wasunna, *Medicine and the Market: Equity v Choice* (Baltimore, MD, Johns Hopkins University Press, 2006) 20.

[116] ibid, 29–30.

[117] McGregor, above (n 113) 85.

[118] ibid, 86–87.

health services based on needs.[119] Ultimately, a market-led, individualised, privatised and decentralised model to finance and deliver health care services may be more economically efficient but it does not allow the implementation of a universal health care system.

# IV. Organising Principles for Health Care Systems

A philosophical and moral discussion on universal health care as a requirement for justice naturally leads to a discussion on the just organisation of health care systems. On either side of the issue, two additional queries ought to be answered to better allocate health care resources. First, what are the responsibilities and the level of commitment expected from individuals towards their peers in health care? And, what is the appropriate level of central government involvement in the provision of health care services?

The complementary but distinct principles of solidarity and subsidiarity provide answers to these queries as they transcend all the models presented for the allocation of health care resources. In a nutshell, solidarity refers to a benevolent attitude towards weaker social groups that implies the fair distribution of health services for society as a whole.[120] Subsidiarity refers to the power of individuals and non-state institutions to provide and finance health care needs and deems local authority the most competent institution to address these issues.[121] Both organising principles refine the normative schemes used for the distribution of health care resources as they provide additional guidelines to help design more just health care systems.

## A. The Principle of Solidarity

The idea of solidarity in social policy stems from Émile Durkheim's conception of justice.[122] For the sociologist, the observance of charity in traditional societies had led to just outcomes and the strong kinship present in these environments had helped foster feelings of empathy and a benevolent attitude among individuals. Thus, modern societies should strive to achieve this level of morality and to cultivate reciprocal feelings of sympathy to build a sense of mutual responsibility among its members.[123]

---

[119] See generally, McGregor, ibid.
[120] Houtepen and Ter Meulen, above (n 55) 355–56.
[121] H-M Sass, 'The New Triad: Responsibility, Solidarity and Subsidiarity' (1995) 20(6) *Journal of Medicine and Philosophy* 587, 591.
[122] See generally, WD Halls (trans) and E Durkheim, *The Division of Labour in Society* (London, Macmillan, 1984).
[123] See generally, E Schoenfeld and SG Meštrović, 'Durkheim's Concept of Justice and its Relationship to Social Solidarity' (1989) 50 *Sociological Analysis* 111.

As Europe was facing social challenges in the 1930s, models to organise welfare systems were developed based on Durkheim's innovative idea. His conception of solidarity provided Western democracies with the underpinning for two welfare systems: the German Bismarkian model of social insurance and the European public service model. The Bismarkian system proposed a rights-based approach focusing on the provision of services at the local level. The public service model, on the other hand, focused on the duty of public authorities to universally provide public goods. The latter inspired the creation of the United Kingdom's social system.[124] Under both models, solidarity takes the form of a vertical relationship, where the 'strong' help the 'weak' through the redistribution of burdens and benefits, or of a horizontal relationship, in which the 'strong' and the 'weak' join forces and share risks to jointly contribute to welfare.[125]

Western welfare states have now organised their social systems according to a variety of other structures, however the prominent role of the state and mandatory social health insurance remain common characteristics of solidary welfare systems.[126] In the realm of health care, solidarity possesses different redistributive dimensions. On the one hand, risk solidarity implies that individual contributions to health care be unrelated to health risk. All members of society are given equal access to services irrespective of their health status. Any type of risk selection on the part of insurers or the public sector is prohibited.[127] The risks and costs associated with illness are spread among the entire population. Simply put, the healthy and the sick, the young and the old, all contribute in a solidary manner to the edification of a just health care system. On the other hand, income solidarity implies that contributions to health care financing be proportional to an individual's income or to the ability to pay. Solidarity therefore also implies the redistribution of resources.[128] Both dimensions transform interdependence into solidarity.[129]

This organising principle is also fundamental to discussions on global health care packages and prioritisation processes involving the creation of social programmes for the aged, the chronically ill, the disabled, the poor, and other vulnerable groups.[130] However, its principles collide with the notions of freedom of choice and responsibility, which also come into play when reforming health

---

[124] R Klein, *The New Politics of the NHS: From Creation to Reinvention*, 7th edn (London, Radcliffe Publishing, 2013) 4–5.

[125] W Arts and J Gelissen, 'Welfare States, Solidarity and Justice Principles: Does the Type Really Matter?' (2001) 44 *Acta Sociologica* 283, 285.

[126] See generally, WA Glaser, *Health Insurance in Practice: International Variations in Financing, Benefit, and Problems* (San Francisco, CA, Jossey-Bass Publishers, 1991).

[127] See generally, Arts and Gelissen, above (n 125).

[128] H Maarse and A Paulus, 'Has Solidarity Survived? A Comparative Analysis of the Effect of Social Health Insurance Reform in Four European Countries' (2003) 28 *Journal of Health Politics, Policy and Law* 585, 589–90; DA Stone, 'At Risk in the Welfare State' (1989) 56 *Social Research* 591.

[129] See generally, Pope John Paul II, *On Social Concerns* (Boston, MA, St Paul Edition, 1987).

[130] Hoedemaekers and Dekkers, above (n 12) 329–30.

care systems. It is the need to account for differences in life goals, risk aversion and lifestyle choices impacting individuals that leads to the ideological confrontation and sometimes to the advent of 'hybrid' distributive outcomes.[131] Social policy experts have also argued that solidarity in health insurance may be eroded because of successive reforms and the growing emphasis on cost-control, efficiency and market competition.[132]

## B. The Principle of Subsidiarity

Subsidiarity suggests that individuals should solve issues with the help of the lowest and least centralised competent authority. Social institutions should therefore operate as close to the local population as permitted.[133] The principle also involves a personal commitment to life goals thanks to the services of others. Individuals should seek to execute their plans without significant supervision from governing bodies and mostly with the support of means provided by the community.[134] The state's involvement should be marginal to preserve scarce resources and to allow individuals to preserve their autonomy.[135] Centralised powers are neither absent nor exempt from intervening to protect the weak and the poor, however subsidiarity calls for a bottom-up approach. Top-down actions should be confined to exceptional circumstances and to helping achieve the common good.[136] Subsidiarity also grants a central role to associations and active social interaction. Charities and other associations actively participate in society by promoting voluntary interaction among individuals and by helping their members develop greater dignity. Those with lesser means are assisted with their plan and their finding of individual social roles.[137]

In a subsidiary health care system, instead of delegating choices to centralised authorities, decisions for the allocation of resources assign maximum responsibility to individuals or the smallest group. However, depending on the allocation model and the health care system's structure, the unit in charge of the process may vary. For example, both egalitarianism and utilitarianism vest the state and public institutions with the duties to universally distribute health care services. Under both models these institutions are deemed to be the smallest, most competent

---

[131] See generally, Sass, above (n 121); Maarse and Paulus, above (n 128) 589.

[132] See generally, JA Morone, 'Citizens or Shoppers? Solidarity Under Siege' (2000) 25 *Journal of Health Politics, Policy and Law* 959.

[133] See generally, Pope John Paul II, *Centesimus Annus* (1991).

[134] A Føllesdal, 'Survey Article: Subsidiarity' (1998) 6 *Journal of Political Philosophy* 190, 190.

[135] See generally, Sass, above (n 121).

[136] D Golemboski, 'The Flip Side of Subsidiarity: Sometimes It Takes More Than a Village' (2012) 139 *Commonweal* 9, 9.

[137] Føllesdal, above (n 134) 198–99; *See generally*, I Bode, 'The Welfare State in Germany' in C Aspalter (ed), *Welfare Capitalism Around the World* (Hong Kong, Casa Verde, 2003).

authority that can justly distribute health care among individuals. Communitarianism, on the other hand, dictates that the community responds to local needs and demands, as it is closest and therefore most aware of health care issues affecting the population. Similarly, libertarianism and neoliberalism, consider that individuals are the lowest and least centralised unit capable of justly allocating health care resources. It is possible for them to do so through the market or by appealing to charity.

More concretely, in the United States, questions of subsidiarity are often discussed to determine the role of the federal and state governments in health care. Policymakers favouring a subsidiary approach for the delivery of care suggest that states should take the lead on the provision of services as they are closer and more in tune to the needs of their population.[138]

Although the idea of solidarity is still prominent in discussions relating to health care allocation issues in most Western welfare states, policymakers also focus on the importance of a subsidiary means of allocation. Across Western welfare states, distribution choices are made according to both principles, and above all greater importance is given to patient choice and autonomy at a systemic level.[139]

# V.  Theories of a Right to Health and a Right to Health Care

The philosophical claims and organising principles fleshed out in the second and third parts of this chapter are the basis for theoretical propositions of just health care rights. Indeed, theories of distributive justice provide different appraisals of the needs covered by legal entitlements.[140] Legal claims are also justified by normative structures, and health care rights have, at times, underpinned their value with philosophical and moral claims.[141]

In theory, health and health care legal claims are categorised as either negative rights, (ie, legal claims providing the bearer with the prerogative of being able to enjoy the state of affairs free from interference), or positive rights, (ie, entitlements providing the rights bearer with a positive action or benefit).[142] Thus, negative health and health care rights require the state's or public powers' protection, whereas positive health and health care rights require that resources be attributed

---

[138] Golemboski, above (n 136) 9.

[139] Sass, above (n 121) 593.

[140] K Hessler and A Buchanan, 'Specifying the Content of the Human Right to Health Care' in R Rhodes, MP Battin and A Silvers (eds), *Medicine and Social Justice: Essays on the Distribution of Health Care* (Oxford, Oxford University Press, 2002).

[141] Beauchamp and Childress, above (n 8) 359–61.

[142] See generally, TL Beauchamp and RR Faden, 'The Right to Health and the Right to Health Care' (1979) 4 *Journal of Medicine and Philosophy* 118.

to the provision of specific entitlements.[143] In reality, health care legal claims are more complex and contain both negative and positive entitlements.[144] Each distributive model theorises these claims as either absolute or specific and places individual entitlement to health care within the negative/positive right dichotomy as illustrated below.

Therefore, before diving into the analysis of specific reforms in subsequent chapters, discussions on the existence, nature and content of health care rights should be examined. The final part of this theoretical presentation explores the different answers each normative model and organising principle have yielded on the existence of a right to health care, and concludes with a discussion on the existence of a broader and absolute right to health.[145] This presentation will be most useful in determining whether theoretical approaches on the right to health care were instrumental to the negotiation of health care laws.

## A. The Egalitarian Perspective on a Right to Health Care

Liberal equality conceives justice as fairness and as a norm of cooperation that equalises and liberates human beings to make them active members of society.[146] Even though the theory rests mainly on Rawls' fiction of the *original position*,[147] the philosopher had initially not provided for a right to health care. Health was absent from the list of basic rights and primary goods. It is only in his later work, *Justice as Fairness: A Restatement*, that Rawls argues medical care as a primary good. He mentions:

> Provision for medical care, as with primary goods generally, is to meet the needs and requirements of citizens as free and equal. Such care falls under the general means necessary to underwrite fair equality of opportunity and our capacity to take advantage of our basic rights and liberties, and thus to be normal and fully cooperating members of society over a complete life.[148]

However, transposed into the legal sphere, equality may lead to unattainable or unorthodox outcomes. Scarce resources do not allow limitless entitlements to care and strict equality in bad health should never be the goal of just health care policy.[149] Egalitarian theory therefore understands health care rights as providing individuals or groups with a baseline: a 'decent', 'reasonable', 'basic', 'essential'

---

[143] Almgren, above (n 7) 33–34.
[144] See generally, Beauchamp and Faden, above (n 142).
[145] See generally, AE Buchanan, 'The Right to a Decent Minimum of Health Care' (1984) 13 *Philosophy & Public Affairs* 55.
[146] Beauchamp and Childress, above (n 8) 339–41.
[147] N Daniels, *Just Health Care* (Cambridge, Cambridge University Press, 1985) 35.
[148] J Rawls, *Justice as Fairness: A Restatement* (Cambridge, MA, Harvard University Press, 2001) 174.
[149] Stein, above (n 29) 57.

or 'adequate' level of care. A minimum entitlement avoids committing to open-ended financing programmes and is essential in elaborating a right to care for all.[150] Unfortunately, defining the content of this baseline has proven to be challenging, as illustrated by the constitutional and international legislation on a right to health (see section E below).[151]

Egalitarian rights to health care are also often defined in collectivist or individualist terms, which produce different outcomes.[152] Both trends agree that equality in health care is an entitlement, but collectivists posit that social institutions and the state, on the basis of solidarity, should provide a standard package of care to the entire population irrespective of one's ability to pay for such services. The content of the health care package is fixed and provides equal resources to all individuals. Individualist egalitarians, however, conceive social institutions and the state as minimal insurers guaranteeing the 'plain vanilla' or a 'bog standard' of health care services. Each individual can supplement the minimum guarantee with the purchase of additional health care services. This trend is more preoccupied with equality in outcome than equality in treatment.[153] Thus, health care policies adopting an individualist right to health care usually propose voucher systems supplemented by private insurance schemes.

A right to health is also instrumental in resolving inequalities through a fair allocation process. Health is one of the most important equalisers of opportunity and it encompasses an array of social entitlements and resources.[154] Equality in health may however be unrealisable considering the wide range of determinants that may impact an individual or a population status, be it the environment, education, nutrition and health care.[155]

## B. The Utilitarian Perspective on a Right to Health Care

The existence of a utilitarian right to health care is contingent on the group that will claim entitlements under this right. Allen Buchanan explains and illustrates this point with a striking example:

> The chief difficulty with utilitarian arguments is that they are not capable of providing a secure foundation for a right to a decent minimum for everyone. Consider, for example, the class, of Down's syndrome new-borns. These [mentally impaired] individuals, who often suffer from various physical defects as well, require a large expenditure of social

---

[150] E Elhauge, 'Allocating Health Care Morally' (1994) 82 *California Law Review* 1449, 1465–92.

[151] See generally, Gutmann, above (n 10).

[152] R Dworkin, *Sovereign Virtue: The Theory and Practice of Equality* (Cambridge, MA, Harvard University Press, 2002) 1–11.

[153] Almgren, above (n 7) 33–34.

[154] ibid.

[155] N Daniels, *Just Health: Meeting Health Needs Fairly* (Cambridge, Cambridge University Press, 2007) 143.

resources over a lifetime. And relative to these costs the contribution these individuals make to social utility is not large, at least as far as we must work with a conception of contribution that is in some way quantifiable. If this is so, then Utilitarianism will justify excluding these infants from even the most minimal health care provided to others as a matter of right. It is important to see that individuals in this class are capable of various enjoyments and would greatly benefit from the services from which they are excluded. Thus Utilitarianism may require that, even for the most basic services, what is guaranteed for one individual may not be available to another, even though their needs are equal and both would benefit greatly from the service.[156]

Thus, a universal right to health care producing the highest level of health outcome for the general population could be unachievable because of individual differences in health status and health care needs.

However, it may still be possible to develop a utilitarian derivative right to a decent minimum of health care for a set group. This entitlement would have to be the product of the group's consensus and give equal weight to individual preferences, as well as prioritising the treatments leading to the greatest utility outcomes.[157] Conversely, if a right to health care was unable to yield maximal utility, only a more selective and limited set of entitlements would be provided to the set group. Utilitarianism does not necessarily mandate a basic right to health care to achieve justice; however many utilitarian policies are instrumental in the organisation of universal health care systems in Western welfare states.[158]

## C. The Communitarian Perspective on a Right to Health Care

The communitarian philosophy does not explicitly establish the existence of a right to health care but encourages the protection of these entitlements with collective and consensual rights. Since individual claims may impede the community's goal of achieving justice through consensus, equality and liberty should be subordinate to the community's needs and the protection of the common good.[159] However, individual participation in the elaboration of communal rights to health care is not only just in itself, it is instrumental to the achievement of the common good.[160]

The content of communitarian rights to health care should reflect the needs of a specific community. As a basis, members set priorities together and relay their aspirations to policy-making entities that are in charge of formulating the health

---

[156] Buchanan, above (n 145) 60.
[157] See generally, N Rescher, *Distributive Justice: A Constructive Critique of the Utilitarian Theory of Distribution* (New York, Bobbs-Merrill, 1966).
[158] Almgren, above (n 7) 38–40.
[159] Kymlicka, above (n 68) 209–73.
[160] Mooney, above (n 59) 1176.

care agenda. In contrary to liberal conceptions of health care rights, the allocation of resources is not based on individual needs, preferences or health status but on collective claims. The community is in the best position to judge the amount of resources it requires and how to most efficiently deploy them to achieve just health care. Furthermore, the empathic attitudes of many individuals towards health problems are likely to be conducive to a more integrated society.[161]

## D. The Libertarian Perspective on a Right to Health Care

Liberty and property are cornerstones of the libertarian doctrine. Not only are they essential to the achievement of justice they should be understood as natural rights, decrees of nature. Individuals are free to dispose of their holdings and may not derive benefit from the holdings of their peers. Conversely, entitlements to health care are understood as social rights and incompatible with these natural rights.

A right to health care would put unjustifiable strains on the state's authority and resources and a universal right to health care would hinder individual autonomy and right to self-ownership. Thus, the libertarian assumption is that nature takes priority over society.[162] More practically, free individuals should be able to decide whether to seek support from associations, charity or commercial providers to fulfil their health care needs. Libertarianism also expects individuals to independently mitigate health risks without relying on a claim to health care.

## E. Health as an Absolute Right

The aftermath of the Second World War saw the emergence of a movement recognising an international right to health. The World Health Organisation (WHO) pioneered, as it first defined the entitlement in those terms. In its Constitution, the WHO described health as a state of 'complete physical, mental and social well-being, and not merely the absence of disease or infirmity'[163] and expressed that 'the enjoyment of the highest attainable standard of health is one of the fundamental rights of every human being'.[164]

Two years later, in 1948, the Universal Declaration of Human Rights[165] gave a fundamental value to the right to health through a broad interpretation of the right to life and Article 25 establishing that

---

[161] Mooney, above (n 59) 1176.

[162] A Rand, *The Virtue of Selfishness* (New York, Signet, 1964) ch 14.

[163] Preamble to the Constitution of the World Health Organization as published in World Health Organization, *Basic Documents*, 41st edn, (Geneva, 1996). The WHO Constitution was signed in 1947 and entered into force on 7 April 1948.

[164] ibid.

[165] Universal Declaration of Human Rights (adopted 10 December 1948 UNGA Res 217 A(III)).

everyone has the right to a standard of living adequate for the health and well-being of himself and his family, including food, clothing, housing and medical care and necessary social services.[166]

The right was then elaborated upon and many international and regional treaties and conventions were incorporate in its core.[167] Most importantly, under the International Covenant on Economic, Social, and Cultural Rights (ICESCR), which constitutes one of the three pillars of the UN International Bill of Rights, and subsequently enacted in Article 12:

Everyone has the right to a standard of living adequate for the health and well-being of himself and of his family, including food, clothing, housing and medical care and necessary social services, and the right to security in the event of unemployment, sickness, disability, widowhood, old age or other lack of livelihood in circumstances beyond his control.[168]

Even though the definition is not limited to medical care, health services' input become a central component of the right to an adequate standard of living. Article 2 of the Covenant also implies that states can realise the right 'progressively' and with 'the maximum of the available resources'.[169] The broad wording of these provisions allows some flexibility in its implementation. However, the UN Committee on Economic, Social and Cultural Rights (CESCR) also provided some specifics on 'minimum core obligations' to ensure that economic, social and cultural rights did not become an unattainable standard.

The minimum core makes each state a party to the Covenant responsible for at least fulfilling the minimum essential levels of each right. Bearing in mind potential limitations in resources, the Committee nevertheless requires that priority be given to satisfy the basic needs of the people.[170] The requirement may become an impediment to the rationing of health care resources at the national level since no clear guideline is offered regarding its content. It is difficult to precisely define the obligations and the amount of resources to be dedicated to fulfilling the minimum core.

---

[166] ibid, art 25.

[167] The International Convention on the Elimination of all forms of Discrimination Against Women, the Convention on the Rights of the Child and conventions adopted within the context of the International Labour Organisation. On a regional level, the European Social Charter, the African Charter on Human and Peoples' Rights and the Additional Protocol to the American Convention on Human Rights in the Area of Economic, Social and Cultural Rights. Reference should also be made to the European Convention on Human Rights and Biomedicine which proclaims a right to equitable health care.

[168] International Covenant on Economic, Social and Cultural Rights (adopted 16 December 1966, entered into force 3 January 1976) 993 UNTS 3 art 2.

[169] ibid.

[170] UN Committee on Economic, Social and Cultural Rights (CESCR), General Comment No 3: The Nature of States Parties' Obligations (Art 2, Para. 1, of the Covenant), 14 December 1990, E/1991/23.

The United States (1977)[171] and the United Kingdom (1968)[172] are both parties to the ICESCR and therefore implicitly acknowledge the special status of health in their societies. More remarkably, some countries have elevated the human right to health to the ranks of a constitutional entitlement. France, for example, based on the values of human dignity and the right to life has included the right to health in the preamble of its Constitution, giving 'to all, notably to children, mothers and elderly workers, protection of their health, material security, rest and leisure'.[173]

South Africa, forerunner in the domain of socio-economic rights, also guarantees a 'minimum level of human dignity' with a justiciable right to health care.[174] Its Constitutional Court has, however, rejected the minimum core approach in its adjudication of socio-economic rights cases. In both *Government of the Republic of South Africa and Others v Grootboom and Others* (2000)[175] cases, the Court refused to specify the content of the 'minimum core' as it believed it lacked the institutional capacity to do so. It nonetheless explained that the 'minimum core' helped determine whether a governmental measure was 'reasonable' or responded adequately to the needs of those in desperate circumstances.[176] The Court reinterpreted the concept in the light of a higher moral principle of human dignity and the right to a minimum standard of decency in life.

The 'minimal level of health' will inevitably vary from country to country and it may be perilous to set an international/global benchmark to realise a right to health. It is governments' duty to respect the human right to health care and to try to achieve it, but clearer guidelines may need to be more clearly set at a national level.

Ultimately, a human and constitutional right to health indicates the importance of health care at a national and more global level. Conceptualising health as a right and health care as a necessary element for the achievement of justice is a first

---

[171] Status of Treaties Chapter IV: Human Rights (*United Nations Treaty Collection*, 2017), available at: treaties.un.org/Pages/ViewDetails.aspx?src=IND&mtdsg_no=IV-3&chapter=4&clang=_en#EndDec.

[172] ibid.

[173] Constitution De 1946, IVe République.

[174] See generally, N Haysom, 'Constitutionalism, Majoritarian Democracy and Socio-Economic Rights' (1992) 8 *South African Journal on Human Rights* 451.

[175] *Minister of Health and Others v Treatment Action Campaign and Others (no 2)* (CCT8/02) [2002] ZACC 15, 2002 (5) SA 721, 2002 (10) BCLR 1033 (5 July 2002); *Government of the Republic of South Africa and Others v Grootboom and Others* (CCT11/00) [2000] ZACC 19, 2001 (1) SA 46, 2000 (11) BCLR 1169 (4 October 2000).

[176] In *Grootboom* the Court mentions that 'A society must seek to ensure that the basic necessities of life are provided to all if it is to be a society based on human dignity, freedom and equality. To be reasonable, measures cannot leave out of account the degree and extent of the denial of the right they endeavour to realise. Those whose needs are the most urgent and whose ability to enjoy all rights therefore is most in peril, must not be ignored by the measures aimed at achieving realisation of the right'. It further clarifies in *TAC* that 'This minimum core might not be easy to define, but includes at least the minimum decencies of life consistent with human dignity. No one should be condemned to a life below the basic level of dignified human existence. The very notion of individual rights presupposes that anyone in that position should be able to obtain relief from a court'.

step in taking a broader and more objective philosophical perspective on health care allocation issues.

## VI. Conclusion

The debate on universality of care as a requirement of justice reveals how political philosophy has theorised allocation processes that can be applied to the realm of health care. These philosophical frameworks can be applied at two levels. They inform discussions on the preferred methods to finance health care systems and the discussions on the preferred models for the provision of health care services.

Arguing in favour of universality of care, egalitarianism conceives justice in terms of redistribution to palliate initial inequalities and suggests that health care resources be distributed equally for a fair and just system. Equality in opportunity or capacity leads liberal egalitarians to prefer a universal health care system where treatment is provided on the basis of need and following either Rawls' difference principle or Dworkin's prudentially defined equality principles.

Utilitarianism provides an interesting middle ground in this discussion. It proposes to rank patients' health care needs to ration and justly allocate scarce resources. It advocates in favour of a universal system, as it is most likely to maximise utility in health care by reducing pain and suffering for a majority of patients. Communitarianism, for its part, offers a collection of thoughts that conceives health care in relation to the needs of the community. A universal health care system should emerge as a product of a collective consultation and services should be provided based on collective and local needs.

On the other hand, libertarianism understands justice in relation to freedom and property and it refuses to adopt a top-down approach to health care. This doctrine argues that universal health care financed through general taxation is oppressive and violates individual freedom to dispose of property without public interference. Similarly, neoliberalism proposes to reduce the role of the state in health care by decentralising and privatising the financing and provision of services.

The complementary but distinct principles of solidarity and subsidiarity also contribute to the organisation of health care systems. Each welfare state ought to determine the level of responsibilities and commitment that it expects from individuals towards their peers, as well as the appropriate level of central government involvement in the provision of health care. The moral, philosophical and organisational perspectives that have been laid out in this chapter all translate into the theory of a right to health and health care. Each distributive justice theory has articulated a legal approach to health care.

All the theoretical approaches explored in this chapter are therefore used as a grid reading to analyse American and British health care reforms in chapter four and chapter six. This analysis however makes no claims of inside information with regard to the motivation that led the key actors to use these theoretical frameworks to formulate their desire to reform health care systems. Claims of justice are claims of compliance or a desire to comply with a set benchmark of attainment. Therefore, actors involved in the development of health care laws maybe have hoped, with their discourses, to endow the process with the aura of an external standard. It may not be that these actors intended to create morally just laws. Discourses might have been instrumental in achieving self-motivated goals. However, this also does not rule out the possibility that justice may have made its way in the law-making process.

# 3

## For-Profit Stakeholders in American Health Care Policy

'Unless we put medical freedom into the Constitution the time will come when medicine will organize itself into an undercover dictatorship.'[1]

Benjamin Rush

## I. Introduction

Ever since the foundation of the American Republic interest groups in the United States have had a central role in law and policy making. They have been able to either curb initiatives or advance causes to their advantage. Some academics have gone as far as to argue that interest groups' engagement has robbed the United States of its democracy and of a universal health care system.[2] In many ways for-profit actors have stood to gain or lose from health care reforms because of the place they have carved out for themselves at the heart of the health care system.[3]

Indeed, during the nineteenth century doctors institutionalised their power with the creation of the American Medical Association (AMA) and ever since, the professional group has, to a greater or lesser extent, been involved in the elaboration of major health care reforms. For the most part, the medical profession has stood firm against universal health care and the socialisation of medicine. American employers, for their part, have had to offer attractive benefits to their employees to defy the powerful unions that threatened their managerial power after the Second World War. The fear of losing control over their workforce, along with the tax incentives provided by the government, encouraged them to offer health care coverage to their employees and organise themselves as a powerful lobbying group. Finally, American insurance, that first developed as a not-for-profit

---

[1] Benjamin Rush, signer of the Declaration of Independence (1787).
[2] See eg, P Navarro, *The Policy Game: How Special Interests and Ideologues Are Stealing America* (New York, Wiley, 1984); JT Bennett and TJ Di Lorenzo, Destroying Democracy: How Government Funds Partisan Politics (Washington DC, Cato Institute, 1985).
[3] See generally, JG Smith, *Political Brokers: People, Organizations, Money and Power* (New York, Liveright, 1972).

enterprise, transformed into a commercial venture because of the substantial gains the industry could yield from the health care market. Essentially, with the help of the medical profession, medical insurers have become the main 'managers' of the public–private sector relationship in health care. Thus, by and large, throughout the twentieth century the expansion of medical technology prompted a shift in the American population's expectations and an increase in the provision of health care services. Simultaneously, social relations became more deeply embedded and the physician-dominated insurance plans crystallised vested interests.[4]

The first section of this chapter therefore proposes to further explore the overlapping history of the for-profit sector in American health care policy to understand its role in the edification of a mostly privately run system.[5] In turn, the part played by the medical profession in the creation of a private system of health care delivery, of employers in the structuring of employees risk pools and of insurers in the development of third-party payer schemes is analysed. The for-profit's reaction to elements of a broader social context throughout this period and beyond certainly help elucidate how for-profit stakeholders have been able to influence reformative efforts and instil path dependency in American health care policy.

Issues resulting from policy's path dependency are also introduced and analysed throughout the chapter to conclude that over time American providers (health care professionals and hospitals) as well as purchasers of care (employers and insurers) have in concert participated in the enactment of an incremental system of care that has prevented the development of a universal health care system in the United States. The piecemeal organisation of health care services is therefore a direct product of the stakeholders' history and the more recent issues affecting the health care system. Indeed, the United States is also confronting a series of related conflicting, yet distinct, problems flowing directly from policy path dependency.[6] The country remains politically divided not so much because of the nature of these issues but because of the controversy surrounding the solutions.[7] The last part of the chapter therefore examines these issues in greater detail and the policies developed in response by recent governments. The analysis focuses mostly on cost-containment policies and policies reducing access barriers, both of which have led to some of the elaboration of major health care reforms analysed in chapter four. This historical and contemporary presentation is equally helpful in assessing the place of justice and profit in American health care law.

[4] K Patel and ME Rushefsky, *Healthcare Politics and Policy in America*, 4th edn (Armonk, NY, ME Sharpe, 2014) 29.

[5] P Pierson, 'Not Just What, But When: Timing and Sequence in Political Processes' (2000) 14 *Studies in American Political Development* 72, 83.

[6] GJ Annas, *American Health Law* (Boston, MA, Little Brown, 1990) 2.

[7] See eg, DA Cortese and RK Smoldt, 'Healing America's Ailing Health Care System' (2006) 81 *Mayo Clinic Proceedings* 492; R Downing, *Suffering and Healing in America: An American Doctor's View from Outside* (Seattle, WA, Radcliffe Publishing, 2006); TR Reid, *The Healing of America: A Global Quest for Better, Cheaper, and Fairer Health Care* (New York, Penguin Press, 2009).

# II. The Overlapping History of American For-Profit Actors

Over the course of the nineteenth century and the first part of the twentieth century, the American health care system evolved in the absence of any strong role of government. Medical professionals, employers and insurers had mostly tasked themselves with the financing and provision of health care services. The medical profession began to institutionalise the practice of medicine according to its interests and established a framework that the health insurance industry and American employers helped sustain.[8]

Medical professionals had regrouped and claimed legitimacy through the AMA and vigorously opposed compulsory and publicly sponsored health care. They also advocated free enterprise in medicine and therefore the private provision of health care services.[9] The profession consistently had a significant impact on health care policy but seemed to have lost some of its stamina at the beginning of the new millennium. At the financing level, American employers have been most instrumental. During the 1940s they established work-based risk pools in which low-risk and healthy employees sponsored the higher-risk employees' health care costs.[10] In some aspects this pooling system has now been jeopardised by recent reforms, specifically in relation to the coverage offered by small businesses. Nevertheless, it remains one of the most fundamental underpinnings of the American health care system. As the following section illustrates, commercial insurers with third-party payer schemes have also helped further consolidate the medical profession and employers' position in the health care system.[11] They have taken advantage of coverage gaps and have benefited the most from the incremental nature of the health care system. Visibly, the history of all these stakeholders intersects in many instances although they remain distinct in many other aspects as illustrated in the following section.

## A. Medical Professionals

From the pre-Civil War era up until the late nineteenth century, the medical profession was unlicensed and unregulated. The lack of technological advances

---

[8] S Giaimo, *Markets and Medicine: The Politics of Health Care Reform in Britain, Germany, and the United States* (Ann Harbor, MI, University of Michigan Press, 2002) 148–64.

[9] GR Almgren, *Health Care Politics, Policy and Services: A Social Justice Analysis* (New York, Springer Publishing Company, 2012) 61–62.

[10] See generally, D Blumenthal, 'Employer-Sponsored Health Insurance in the United States: Origins and Implications' (2006) 355 *New England Journal of Medicine* 82. According to survey of the US Department of Health & Human Services the population of uninsured in 2010 was 49.9 million: aspe. hhs.gov/basic-report/overview-uninsured-united-states-summary-2011-current-population-survey.

[11] P Starr, *The Social Transformation of American Medicine* (New York, Basic Books, 1982) 290–335.

in medicine limited the treatment options physicians had at their disposal.[12] Consequently, the demand for health care was small, and insurance needs were non-existent. Life expectancy had remained low although infectious diseases had slowly been tackled with better hygiene and the discovery of antibiotics. Doctors were paid only a small fee by the government and received little compensation for treating patients. In 1847, as the sole dispensers of care, along with pharmacists, apprenticeship trained physicians decided to unite and form the AMA.[13] After the Civil War the professional group established its authority with important scientific achievements. Its expertise and new-found sovereignty also helped to consolidate its economic and political power into social privilege.[14]

At the beginning of the twentieth century the AMA was promoting a specific policy agenda that opposed any form of prepayment system. Groups of independent doctors that had not joined the ranks of the AMA were pressurised by the association not to engage in this practice. Organised physicians who were sitting on a majority of regulatory and hospital boards would threaten to revoke the licences or hospital privileges of the dissident doctors who were challenging the AMA's line of conduct.[15] In the 1920s, the association even engaged in a battle with the Committee on the Costs of Medical Care that comprised of academics, physicians and private interest groups, because of its project of voluntary insurance for group medicine.[16] In the end nothing substantial came out of the media war, but the AMA had to fight any financing experiments as it stood to protect the economic interests of its members.[17]

After the Second World War, President Franklin D Roosevelt made a major health care policy proposal: an increase of federal funds to finance a national health insurance and achieve universal coverage. Roosevelt was unsuccessful but his successor, President Harry Truman, supported a similar initiative. He suggested amending the Social Security Act (1935)[18] in order to establish a federally managed insurance fund. The scheme would provide individuals with coverage in exchange for a monthly contribution. Indigent Americans would also benefit from the fund's coverage, as public agencies would be covering for their premiums.[19] Of course the AMA mobilised considerable effort to fight the reform.

---

[12] KM Ludmerer, *Time to Heal: American Medical Education from the Turn of the Century to the Era of Managed Care* (Oxford, Oxford University Press, 1999) 4.

[13] JS Hacker, 'The Historical Logic of National Health Insurance: Structure and Sequence in the Development of British, Canadian, and US Medical Policy' (1998) 12 *Studies in American Political Development* 57, 66–70.

[14] Starr, above (n 11) 5.

[15] CF Chapin, 'The American Medical Association, Health Insurance Association of America, and Creation of the Corporate Health Care System' (2010) 24 *Studies in American Political Development* 143, 146.

[16] C Gordon, *Dead on Arrival: The Politics of Health Care in Twentieth-Century America* (Princeton, NJ, Princeton University Press, 2004) 410.

[17] Starr, above (n 11) 198–220, 290–334.

[18] Social Security Act Pub L 74–271, 49 Stat 620 (1935).

[19] Starr, above (n 11) 283–84.

It spent over $1 million on an opposition campaign to contract a publicity firm and have its members directly lobby legislators.[20] The medical profession was particularly militant claiming that the adoption of a federally sponsored system would lead to lower quality services. Obviously, the project would have undermined the profession's authority and stifled its autonomy. It could have even resulted in the collapse of the free enterprise model. However, the international political climate of the Cold War was also favourable to the professional group's campaign. Reformers were being accused of engaging in a Soviet conspiracy to attack the heart of the federal government with 'socialised medicine'.[21]

Ultimately the AMA stopped the reformative efforts. This accomplishment represented an important milestone for the association. It had defeated the universal project and established a trajectory for American health care policy. Thereafter, AMA leaders were determined to fight every battle with the same enthusiasm and to vocalise their opposition to numerous health care policies.[22] The medical profession also had control over the supply and demand of services thanks to illness diagnosis and prescribed treatments. As it was easy for the AMA to influence patterns for the allocation of health care resources an incremental universal coverage became the only pursuable alternative.[23]

Thanks to a constellation of factors the AMA consolidated its political power during the Eisenhower Administration.[24] First, its scientific expertise continued to establish doctors as a dominant profession and provided AMA leaders with some leverage and autonomy from the state. Second, the association was able to considerably increase its membership because of its role in occupational development. The licensing laws, school accreditation activities and ethical guidelines put considerable power in the hands of the association. In fact, it became difficult for doctors outside the organised group to obtain hospital privileges or malpractice insurance.[25] Finally, its great number of members also helped yield considerable amounts of money to make it a prosperous group.[26]

The AMA was therefore highly confident in its power to sway health care policy and counter any efforts to develop a universal system. It had also rallied the commercial insurers to its cause and to exercise more pressure on the government.[27] Ironically, it was the AMA's domineering and overconfident

---

[20] Chapin, above (n 15) 152.

[21] B Hoffman, 'Health Care Reform and Social Movements in the United States' (2003) 1 *American Journal of Public Health* 75, 77.

[22] Chapin, above (n 15) 152.

[23] Almgren, above (n 9) 64.

[24] See eg, R Harris, *A Sacred Trust* (New York, New American Library, 1966); JG Burrow, *AMA: Voice of American Medicine* (Baltimore, MD, The Johns Hopkins Press, 1963).

[25] See generally, D Wilsford, *Doctors and the State: The Politics of Health Care in France and the United States* (Durham, NC, Duke University Press, 1991).

[26] Chapin, above (n 15) 152.

[27] ibid, 144–45.

attitude that eroded its power and alienated some of its supporters. As it system-atically rejected reformative efforts, the profession was losing the support of the population.[28] Social movements were also in favour of a plan to provide coverage for the elderly so it was difficult for the AMA to 'engage in open warfare' against the project of a federal health care system.[29] Ultimately, doctors had to give in. They had lost some autonomy with the advent of Medicare and Medicaid (1965) and more crucially some of their political clout. From the 1950s to the 1960s, concerns had shifted from access to health care service to the cost and quality in the health care sector.[30]

And so, as Richard Nixon became president in 1968 the Democrats' liberal mandate in health care came to an end. Health care policy had to show some restraint because the cost of the Medicare and Medicaid programmes had skyrock-eted during the first decades of their creation. According to Nixon a considerable amount of resources was invested without substantial benefits being provided to the American population.[31] This had a ripple effect on the medical profession as it had to embrace and participate in the HMO project to realise a more cost-effi-cient system. As further explored in chapter four, although fee-for service had not been abolished prepayment for health care service became a new trend. Ironically, a few years later President Jimmy Carter had the ambition to revive the project of a comprehensive national health insurance programme. As he came into office in 1977, however, budgetary constraints put a damper on the initiative. Carter had also proposed to control hospital costs, another proposal that never materialised and was highly unpopular with the medical profession.[32]

The 1980s brought the Republicans back into power with a conservative agenda for health care. President Ronald Reagan was promoting managed care and competition and suggested that these health care resources be treated like any other commodity. Doctors therefore began to behave like business provid-ers reaching out to patients as if they were customers.[33] At the end of the decade, however, international conflicts and the Persian Gulf War occupied most of the political space, which essentially meant that President George HW Bush's health care policy had to be put on the back burner despite the surging number of uninsured.[34] But as the presidential electoral campaign unravelled in 1992, health care reform emerged again as a central political issue.

Democratic candidate Bill Clinton promised to deliver a comprehensive reform that would provide all Americans with universal health care.[35] After the election,

---

[28] ibid, 152.

[29] Hoffman, above (n 21) 78.

[30] Chapin, above (n 15) 146–52.

[31] Richard M Nixon, 'Message to Congress' in *Weekly Compilation of Presidential Documents* (Washington DC, Office of Federal Register, 1971).

[32] See generally, JK Iglehart, 'The Carter Administration's Health Budget: Charting New Priorities with Limited Dollars' (1978) 56 *Milbank Memorial Fund Quarterly* 51.

[33] See generally, SP Wallace and EL Carroll, 'Health Policy for the Elderly' (1989) 26(6) *Society* 66.

[34] Hoffman, above (n 21) 78.

[35] Patel and Rushefsky, above (n 4) 63.

because he was wary of insurers and businesses, he drafted a 'for-profit friendly' detailed proposal. To execute his vision, he thought of a system of health alliances to preserve the employer-based coverage and the commercial insurance market. The medical profession's reaction to the plan was positive but some advocates of universal health care coverage thought the proposal gave all-encompassing powers to the private sector and took away patients' choice.[36] Thus, as the debate intensified, many more alternatives were put before Congress, but no option successfully mobilised a majority.[37]

At the beginning of the millennium, universal coverage ambitions had therefore vanished. The medical profession, however, welcomed President George W Bush's plan to reform the law on medical malpractice. In 2003, he suggested that awards for pain-and-suffering be capped at $250,000 to control rising health care costs. Doctors' medical malpractice insurance premiums were on the rise because of potential liability, which created a general inflation of health care services prices. In spite of the profession's support, Congress failed to pass the reform.[38] Finally, 10 years later, President Barack Obama also obtained the support of medical professionals, but this time for the most comprehensive health care reform in American history. Surprisingly, the AMA wanted to be part of a project that aimed at expanding health care coverage, reducing costs, improving the quality of services, reforming government programmes and the payment and delivery system.[39] The Affordable Care Act (ACA) was eventually enacted after a series of tumultuous debate and became law in 2010.

In light of this chronology, it is apparent that the AMA has fostered path dependency in American health care policy. As analysed in chapter four, these trends have also been relayed in the drafting of the laws that regulate the allocation of health care resources. Doctors and the AMA did support some initiatives promoting the public good and better care for the disenfranchised, but only as long as their authority and autonomy were not compromised. They have also hammered in their vision of the system, painting universal health care as radical socialism and the doctor–patient relationship as sacrosanct. Interestingly, this has led the practice of medicine to become subordinate to the bureaucracy of the private health insurance system as discussed further in this section.[40] In the words of sociology and public affairs Professor Paul Starr:

> The failure to rationalize medical services under public control meant that sooner or later they would be rationalized under private control. Instead of public regulation, there will be private regulation, and instead of public planning, there will be corporate planning.[41]

---

[36] Hoffman, above (n 21) 78.
[37] Patel and Rushefsky, above (n 4) 64.
[38] ibid, 65.
[39] JH Tanne, 'Obama asks AMA to support his healthcare reform package' (2009) 338 *BMJ* 1522, 1522.
[40] Giaimo, above (n 8) 148–64.
[41] Starr, above (n 11) 449.

## B. Employers

In the 1940s, as the economy was moving towards full employment, manufacturing methods improving and urbanisation was accelerating, the Internal Revenue Service established insurance benefits as taxable services to be repaid with pre-tax dollars to corporations. Tax savings thereby reduced the cost of private coverage and led employers, in the span of a decade, to increasingly provide their employees with health insurance. In order to keep costs low, insurance premiums were based on the employee group's use of health care services.[42]

Two decisive tax laws enacted during wartime also contributed to an increase in employer-sponsored insurance. The 1942 Revenue Act[43] required the taxing of excess profits made on corporate earnings to prevent profiteering. Only profits higher than pre-war levels were taxable, therefore employer contributions to health insurance were not levied. The purpose of the law was to create an incentive to provide employees with fringe benefits while reducing excess profits. The National War Labor Board's 1943 decision[44] to make employers' contributions to employee-benefit plans a substitute for an increase in wages also significantly participated in making employers pooling and financing entities.[45]

Post-war, it was the risk of lung disease and work accidents weighing heavily on miners and their families that forced unions to take action. John L Lewis, President of the United Mine Workers, played a compelling role in improving workers' health coverage. In 1946 he led a strike to urge mine owners to contribute to their workers' medical costs. Successful in their action, miners were given the assurance that they would receive compensation in the event of death or a work accident thus providing their family with a stable source of income. Employees from other sectors also required greater protection but the unions' political averseness led them to negotiate health and accident coverage as part of collective bargaining benefits instead of seeking help from the government. President Truman had reached out to union leaders but had failed to secure their support for his national health insurance project. That same year, the Congress of Industrial Organizations, a federation of unions of organised workers in Canada and the United States, passed the 'Security Through Bargaining' resolution. Health benefits would then be established through the negotiation of collective bargaining contracts.[46]

---

[42] RR Bovbjerg, CC Griffin and CE Carroll, 'US Health Care Coverage and Costs: Historical Development and Choices for the 1990s' (1993) 21(2) *The Journal of Law, Medicine & Ethics* 141, 145–46.

[43] United States Revenue Act 1942, Pub L 753, Ch 619, 56 Stat 798 (21 October 1942).

[44] The National War Labor Board was created in 1917 to improve labour relations during the First World War and issue decisions in cases of conflicts between employees and employers.

[45] J Quadagno, *One Nation, Uninsured: Why the US Has No National Health Insurance* (Oxford, Oxford University Press, 2005) 50.

[46] ibid, 48–51.

Although the federal government was forced to ration goods during the Great Depression, factories ramped up production and needed more workers. In an era characterised by labour–management struggles, collectively bargained health benefits gave leverage to employers to recruit and retain unionised employees. Trade unions failing to obtain higher wages and bound by no-strike pledges were nevertheless able to negotiate health and pension benefits through collective agreements.[47] As noted by Jacob Hacker, employers were proactively pre-empting the creation of a public health system rather than being forced into concessions.[48]

Simultaneously, commercial insurers aggressively marketed group health insurance policies. The plans became popular with employers. They allowed them to provide benefits to employees while building their corporate identity independently from the unions.[49] Employers also offered coverage to dissuade employees from joining the ranks of a union that would provide them with health benefits. Similarly, in non-unionised firms, employers purchased insurance packages on large scales to keep unions at bay.[50] Thus, from 1940 to 1966, the number of privately insured people increased from six to more than 75 million.[51]

The Employee Retirement Income Security Act (ERISA, 1974)[52] was another significant addition to the edification of the employer-sponsored insurance system. ERISA's primary purpose was to offer protection to employees against benefit investors and pension funds. However, it also helped self-insuring employers bypass state mandates that required that particular health care services be covered.[53] Employers had the opportunity to design insurance packages free of regulatory approval.[54] Unfortunately, the law compromised the insurance equilibrium and gave rise to adverse selection. Healthy and better-paid employees were taken out of the mainstream insurance pools because of large employers' insurance schemes. Prices rose and small employers struggled to participate in the insurance system.[55]

The economic downturn triggered by the oil-shock of the 1980s also increased insurance prices. Large employers sought more autonomy from private insurers.[56]

---

[47] ibid, 49.

[48] JS Hacker, *The Divided Welfare State: The Battle over Public and Private Social Benefits in the United States* (Cambridge, Cambridge University Press, 2002) 299.

[49] Quadagno, *One Nation, Uninsured*, above (n 45) 52.

[50] ibid, 49.

[51] ibid.

[52] Employee Retirement Income Security Act 1974 (ERISA) Pub L 93–406, 88 Stat 829, enacted 2 September 1974, codified in part at 29 USC ch 18.

[53] DW Moran, 'Whence and Whither Health Insurance? A Revisionist History' (2005) 24 *Health Affairs* 1415, 1418; *See generally*, Sylvester J Schieber, 'The Future of Retiree Health Benefits in Higher Education in the United States' (2005) *Recruitment, Retention and Retirement in Higher Education: Building and Managing the Faculty of the Future* 101.

[54] Blumenthal, above (n 10) 84.

[55] Moran, above (n 53) 1417–18.

[56] JR Gabel and AC Monheit, 'Will Competition Plans Change Insurer–Provider Relationships?' (1983) 61 *Milbank Memorial Fund Quarterly/Health and Society* 614, 617–21.

They independently developed cost-containment solutions entering into negotiations with hospitals and physicians. As self-insurance lowered the rates and administrative costs, it became a more general trend in health care financing.[57] Throughout the end of the century and entering into the new millennium, businesses continued to be a cornerstone of the American health care system. A majority of Americans are still covering their health costs through employer-sponsored insurance.[58] In fact, according to the Health Reform Monitory Survey (2016),[59] 83.1 per cent of American workers age 18 to 64 were offered employer-sponsored insurance. The decline in employer-sponsored insurance expected with the enactment of the ACA has yet to materialise.

The trajectory of employer-sponsored insurance in the United States is the product of a series of accidents of history. On the one hand, the syndicates' pressure on factory and mine owners, and on the other, the employers' counter-pressure forcing unions to ultimately fall within the ranks. Interestingly, because of this narrative, employers are not a consolidated group. Large employers have different concerns from their smaller counterparts. At times, they may even have been sitting at opposite ends of the negotiating table especially when it came to mandated health care coverage. With the exception of some differences across industries, larger employers absorb insurance premium expenses through labour costs and thus are less sensitive to mandated health care coverage initiatives. Conversely, smaller structures, represented by the National Federation of Independent Businesses and the Chamber of Commerce, oppose mandated employer health care coverage.

Despite their diverging points of view, employers have always been part of the legislative discussions on health care representing one of the most important sources of financing.[60] Regardless of the decline this form of coverage has suffered since its peak in the 1980s, health benefits of millions of Americans remain closely tied to their employment.[61] Employer-sponsored insurance was built around an outdated vision of employment that saw individuals as lifetime employees of a single entity. Benefits were to provide protection against risk of unemployment, poor health and old age. Even though the job market is now dramatically different – employees often have multiple employers throughout their active life – this method of insurance never effectively adapted to this new reality.[62]

---

[57] J Quadagno, 'Why the United States has no National Health Insurance: Stakeholder Mobilization Against the Welfare State, 1945–1996' (2004) (Extra Issue) *Journal of Health and Social Behavior* 25, 34.

[58] Patel and Rushefsky, above (n 4) 49.

[59] F Blavin et al, 'Employer-Sponsored Insurance Stays Strong, with No Signs of Decay under the ACA: Findings through March 2016' (2016) *Urban Institute: Health Policy Centre*: hrms.urban.org/briefs/employer-sponsored-insurance-aca-march-2016.html.

[60] Almgren, above (n 9) 128–29.

[61] ME Smyrl, 'Beyond Interests and Institutions: US Health Policy Reform and the Surprising Silence of Big Business' (2014) 39 *Journal of Health Politics, Policy and Law* 5, 7–10.

[62] Quadagno, *One Nation, Uninsured*, above (n 45) 53.

## C. Insurers

Prior to the end of the nineteenth century the lack of medical advances accounted in great part for the absence of medical insurance schemes in the United States. Treatments were mostly dispensed at patients' homes and hospitals that acted as charitable institutions were only used as a last resort. The patients that were unable to pay for a doctor's private services sought treatments in houses organised as medical dispensaries. These alms houses were financed on the basis of charitable contributions. Thus, until the beginning of the new century, American medicine remained privately funded with an informal system based on a fee-for-service model. An increase in immigration and the rise of literacy along with a boom in the industrial sector left patients wanting more from medical professionals and less from the medical charities that made arbitrary judgements on the course of treatments.[63]

In 1912, an alternative to the traditional model of private financing emerged as Theodore Roosevelt's Progressive Party called for a national health insurance plan. Unsurprisingly, the AMA voiced its discontent and formed a strong opposition to the proposal. Hostility towards the idea of socialised medicine had a rallying effect on the medical profession.[64] Nevertheless, decades later, Franklin D Roosevelt (FDR) had wanted to revive the universal health care plan. He proposed a prepaid voluntary insurance scheme to finance the provision of medical services by physician practice groups. He and the New Dealers believed that the traditional system of private insurance financing the solo practice of medicine had to be replaced to provide more affordable health care to Americans.[65] Regrettably he was forced to abandon the project soon after his election in 1932. FDR simply could not afford to turn his back on the medical profession. Just like at the beginning of the century, the AMA was determined to preserve its interests and its autonomy, and would blockade any project of socialised medicine. He understood that not letting go of his health care policy plan would doom the passage of the entire 1935 Social Security Act.[66]

It is in this context that the American Hospital Association (AHA) developed a 'business model' to promote conservative insurance. The AHA essentially wanted to provide means to finance the services hospitals were increasingly providing to American patients.[67] Even though sources of income had to be stabilised to deal with the financial challenges brought by the Great Depression, the AHA did not allow external forces to have any sort of control over the delivery of services.

---

[63] Almgren, above (n 9) 61.
[64] TJ Litman and LS Robins, *Health Politics and Policy*, 2nd edn (New York, Delmar, 1991) 4.
[65] Quadagno, *One Nation, Uninsured*, above (n 45) 21–22.
[66] See generally, Harris, above (n 24).
[67] Litman and Robins, above (n 64) 116; L Shi and DA Singh, *Delivering Health Care in America*, 2nd edn (Gaithersburg, MD, Aspen, 2001) 113–15.

Thus, the AMA found an ally in the AHA. They both fought to maintain the voluntary insurance system and had the desire to steer clear of any socialised insurance model.[68] Insurance premiums based on community ratings distributing the cost of health care among most of the population were also created during this period.

Until the 1940s, the indemnity insurance market was not profitable because of unpredictable actuarial losses and moral hazard risks. After the war, however, employer-sponsored coverage had changed the face of the insurance industry and enabled commercial insurers to participate in a new market.[69] Insurance gradually became a vehicle for funds between the patient and health care service providers, but it was not yet used as an instrument to oversee or manage the patient–provider relationship.[70] During that period, most American middle-class health care coverage was bought through a combination of private action and public programmes in the form of tax subsidies. This was a prosperous period for American medicine as competition was controlled and support for medical education came from philanthropic sources and the public.[71]

Eventually, advances in medical technology led to an increase in health care costs.[72] Private insurers, which until that point had been reluctant to enter the health market for fear of moral hazard and adverse selection, started offering alternative forms of coverage.[73] Thus, the AHA and the AMA developed the 'Blue' insurance plans. Blue Cross took on the provision of hospital insurance coverage and Blue Shield offered coverage of physician services.[74] The plans were basic but efficient: in exchange for a small monthly fee, Blue Cross would provide its subscribers with coverage for the cost of hospital care, and in the event of hospitalisation, the insurer would pay hospitals for their services without any limitations, irrespective of the price of treatment.[75] As subscribers were given the opportunity to choose their hospital and physician, single-hospital plans disappeared. The AHA had carefully drafted the Blue Cross guidelines to guarantee that competition among treatment facilities was reduced to a minimum. Notably, Blue Cross insurers were awarded the status of non-profit corporations because of their charitable purpose and the benefits they provided to American society. Indeed, thanks to the 'Blues', low-income individuals were freed from the burden of hospitalisation costs.

---

[68] Patel and Rushefsky, above (n 4) 38.

[69] Annas, above (n 6) 20–21.

[70] DW Light, 'The Restructuring of the American Health Care System' (1997) *Health Politics and Policy* 46, 49.

[71] Bovbjerg, Griffin and Carroll, above (n 42) 146.

[72] See generally, CE Rosenberg, *The Care of Strangers: The Rise of America's Hospital System* (Baltimore, MD, John Hopkins University Press, 1995).

[73] MA Thomasson, 'From Sickness to Health: The Twentieth-Century Development of US Health Insurance' (2002) 39(3) *Explorations in Economic History* 233, 234.

[74] Litman and Robins, above (n 64) 48–51; see generally, Shi and Singh, above (n 67).

[75] Annas, above (n 6) 20.

Thus, Blue insurers were offered tax relief through state legislation excluding them from the traditional insurance regulation.[76] The Blue Cross insurance plans were advantageous for the insured and mostly for the service providers. Hospitals were finally getting a fixed and constant source of income, and subscribers were able to afford hospital care.[77] Blue Cross plans spread rapidly. In 1938 only 100,000 out of 1.4 million patients had indemnity coverage but nearly one in five Americans were enrolled in a services-benefit plan by the end of 1946.[78]

Physicians were initially opposed to third-party financing schemes. The AMA believed that the economic advantages generated by this insurance system could not offset a potential loss of control or autonomy. Later, acceptance of private prepayment schemes to cover hospitalisation costs resulted from a compromise as well as the assurance that the traditions and the ideology of American medicine would remain carefully protected.[79] This explains why the initial Blue Cross plan included no provision regarding the role or duties of physicians. Physicians also organised a network of prepaid plans to safeguard their independence and keep the Blue Cross insurers out of the practice of medicine. Under the AMA's supervision, the Blue Shield voluntary health insurance was designed to cover doctors' service fees and to maintain price discrimination privileges (ie, the practice of charging different rates to different customers based on their ability to pay).[80] The AMA also adopted guidelines preventing Blue Cross hospital service plans from underwriting physician services.[81] Physician dominance also ensured that competitive providers remain excluded from the market of outpatient care. For their part, commercial insurers began aggressively pursuing alternative markets to compensate for their losses.[82] Targeting groups of young and healthy individuals, they quickly understood the opportunity these insured represented: great profit without risks of adverse selection.[83] Decades later, commercial insurers continued their pursuit of profit and forced employers into complex negotiations with providers to impose managed-care plans. They promoted physician networks and health maintenance organisations to further increase their sales.[84]

The 'Blues' opened the door to commercial health coverage and proved that the insurance market had a lucrative potential. Overall, the limited scope of the Blue Cross and Blue Shield plans and their non-profit status contributed to the

---

[76] See generally, RD Eilers, *Regulation of Blue Cross and Blue Shield Plans* (Homewood, IL, SS Huebner Foundation for Insurance Education, 1963).

[77] Thomasson, above (n 73) 237.

[78] Annas, above (n 6) 19.

[79] ibid, 15.

[80] Thomasson, above (n 73) 244; see generally, Shi and Singh, above (n 67); Starr, above (n 11) 306–10.

[81] FR Hedinger, *The Social Role of Blue Cross as a Device for Financing the Costs of Hospital Care: An Evaluation* (Graduate Program in Hospital and Health Administration, 1966); Almgren, above (n 9) 63–64.

[82] See generally, T Bodenheimer, 'Should we Abolish the Private Health Insurance Industry?' (1990) 20 *International Journal of Health Services* 199.

[83] Thomasson, above (n 73) 240.

[84] Quadagno, 'Why the United States has no National Health Insurance, above (n 57) 29.

rise of commercial insurers. Blue insurers were tied to community ratings, charging a flat fee to all the insured irrespective of their medical history or risk factors. Commercial insurers, on the contrary, were free from this status and could engage in experience rating, charging higher premiums to sicker applicants or the customers they believed represented a great health risk. As a result, they offered more competitive prices to healthy groups and took a fair share of the Blue insurers' market. Third-party payment schemes provided a new and more efficient means of reimbursement and contributed to the AMA's and AHA's efforts to prevent the socialisation of medicine.[85] The medical profession and the insurance industry had also demonstrated the value of voluntary insurance to the American public. Patients' expectations had been heightened. The population was no longer satisfied with the local family physician; they wanted modern medicine and the possibility to choose from a wide range of treatments. This, of course, implied having the means to finance interventions offered by specialists.[86]

During the 1960s, more state and federal moneys were spent on public health services, welfare medicine, research and hospital construction.[87] Two major public insurance programmes were also created, Medicare, for the elderly, and Medicaid, for the poor. These initiatives indirectly benefited the insurance sector that had secured its role as an intermediary between the government and the service providers and established itself as the manager of the public–private system.[88] Essentially, both programmes only became safety nets for vulnerable groups of Americans that remained uninsured or uninsurable.[89] The following decade, on the other hand, brought more significant advances in private coverage. To reduce costs, large enterprises opted for self-funding or self-insurance. Corporate funds were used to pay the costs of their employees' health care coverage and thereby reduce the insurers' role to mere administrative functions. Narrower insurance pools slowly led to a price increase and began to constitute a substantial threat to the entire system's stability. Many self-insured employers feared the financial consequences of having chronically ill employees. Risk-spreading was limited to a small category of individuals who could neither bear nor dilute the costs. A shift towards a wider pool of insurance was imminent.[90]

In the 1980s, the Acquired Immune Deficiency Syndrome (AIDS) epidemic touched the United States; a decade later the country became aware of the disease's impact on the insurance system.[91] Although health insurance schemes

---

[85] Thomasson, above (n 73) 240.

[86] Chapin, above (n 15) 150.

[87] Quadagno, *One Nation, Uninsured*, above (n 45) 94–107.

[88] Chapin, above (n 15) 145.

[89] See generally, RA Peters, 'The Social Security Amendments of 1960: Completing the Foundations of Medicare and Medicaid' (2004) 26 *Journal of Health and Human Services Administration* 438.

[90] Chapin, above (n 15) 145.

[91] See generally, RA Padgug and GM Oppenheimer, 'AIDS, Health Insurance, and the Crisis of Community' (1991) 5 *Notre Dame Journal of Law, Ethics & Public Policy* 35.

have dramatically and negatively affected seropositive and chronically ill people, AIDS and chronic illnesses associated with the infection have posed only a minor threat to the health insurance industry. There has always been an inevitable and irresolvable contradiction between society's need to establish equity in the provision of health care and the insurance industry's need to safeguard its profitability and efficiency.[92] And although Clinton was most concerned with the overhaul of the health care system during the 1990s, he also focused on more incremental changes in the realm of health care insurance. In 1996, the Health Insurance Portability and Accountability Act became law. The inclusion of a provision limiting insurance companies' ability to deny coverage or to impose pre-existing conditions exclusions, and of provision guaranteeing portability of insurance coverage with employment, marked an important turning point for the health insurance sector.[93]

Today, private insurers largely operate health care financing in the United States. Their capacity to reduce liability and to increase their profit margins by applying drastic underwriting rules guides health policy and still leaves a great portion of the population in the hands of publicly funded programmes that exhaust governmental budgets.[94] Paradoxically, the not-for-profit origins of American health care insurance drove it to become a highly lucrative corporate enterprise giving insurance companies paramount powers and a platform to voice their opinions on health care policy in the United States.[95]

This industry continues to epitomise the lobbying power of for-profit groups in American health care. Just like medical professionals, insurers have a lot to gain with the preservation of a weak and fragmented system of coverage where public and private financing arrangements do not overlap. The industry had, and will, continue to fight the expansion of public programmes to guarantee that the most lucrative share of the market is always within its reach and that its role does not become accessory to the main form of coverage. The incremental approach preserves an 'unhealthy' status quo, undercutting any effort to achieve universal health care in the United States. The latest health care reform has nonetheless tried to destabilise the insurance's hegemony by forcing the industry to accept higher risk insured and applicants with pre-existing conditions in order to relieve the government safety net programmes.[96]

---

[92] See eg, B Schatz, 'The AIDS Insurance Crisis: Underwriting or Overreaching?' (1987) 100 *Harvard Law Review* 1782; AA Terl, 'Emerging Issues of AIDS and Insurance' (1987) 12 *Nova Law Review* 1291.

[93] Health Insurance Portability and Accountability Act Pub L 104–191, 100 Stat 2548 (1996).

[94] In 2011, together Medicare and Medicaid represented 49% of the total National Health Expenditure, leaving only 33% of the spending on private care and many uninsured, 'NHE Fact Sheet' (Centers for Medicare & Medicaid Services, 2017), available at: www.cms.gov/research-statistics-data-and-systems/statistics-trends-and-reports/nationalhealthexpenddata/nhe-fact-sheet.html.

[95] Almgren, above (n 9) 63–64.

[96] See generally, JP Hall and JM Moore, 'The Affordable Care Act's Pre-Existing Condition Insurance Plan: Enrollment, Costs, and Lessons for Reform' (2012) *The Commonwealth Fund* 5.

## III.  Contemporary Dynamics in Health Care Policy

Cost, access and quality of care form a rigid 'iron triangle' constraining the development of health care policy in the United States. A 2004 report of the Federal Trade Commission and Department of Justice explained that 'increasing the performance of the health care system along any one of these dimensions [could] compromise one or both of the other dimensions, regardless of the amount that is spent on health care'.[97] Although in theory optimising these parameters is possible, in practice cost reduction in public programmes would endanger the quality and access to health care services.[98]

With regard to financing, many Americans pay for the health care services they utilise with a variety of sources. Most often, it is a mix of out-of-pocket payments and employment-based insurance. For the past decades, however, the lion's share of health care expenditure has come from the federal government. Programmes such as Medicaid for low-income individuals and other eligible, Medicare for individuals over 65 and their dependants, veteran health care services, and children health care needs via the Children Insurance Program (CHIP) are all publicly financed.[99]

This explains why since the Second World War and well into the 2000s health care costs have rapidly increased and arguably affected the competitiveness of American businesses supporting the health insurance needs of their employees. Already in the 1970s automobile executive Lee Iacocca complained that his company was spending more on employees' health care costs than on raw materials to make its products.[100] The National Business Group on Health has even contended that excessive health care costs have had an impact on the price tag of American consumer goods.[101] Big businesses have made a point to express their discontent with rising costs. According to large employers, health care has affected the corporate bottom line and costs have had a spillover effect on job creation and investment in new technologies. Unfortunately, the passage of the ACA has only mildly lowered health care costs for American businesses.[102] These are arguments that have captured the attention of decision-makers in Washington and guaranteed that employers' interests are heard as part of the health care policy-making process.[103]

---

[97] Federal Trade Commission and Department of Justice, *Improving Health Care: A Dose of Competition* (2004).

[98] MA Hall, MA Bobinski and D Orentlicher, *The Law of Health Care Finance and Regulation*, 3rd edn (New York, Wolters Kluwer Law & Business, 2014) 158–69.

[99] Patel and Rushefsky, above (n 4) 25.

[100] Smyrl, above (n 61) 7.

[101] See generally, National Business Group on Health, *Principles for National Health Care Reform: The View of the National Business Group on Health* (Washington DC, NBGH, 2008).

[102] See generally, National Association of Manufacturers, *ManuFacts: Health Care Reform* (Washington DC, National Association of Manufacturers, 2011).

[103] JS Hacker and P Pierson, 'Business Power and Social Policy: Employers and the Formation of the American Welfare State' (2002) 30 *Politics & Society* 277, 280.

Cost, access and quality issues continue to occupy most policy debates and tend to indirectly involve discussions on universal health care or the lack thereof. Therefore, before turning to the successive reforms that have attempted to tackle these issues, it is important to understand the growing concerns around health care expenditures in the United States. Historically, the for-profit sector has tried to respond to these issues with a range of cost-containment measures. Among which, the Health Maintenance Organizations (HMO), Health Savings Accounts (HAS) and co-insurance schemes that are unable to yield any long-term results. Existing management and containment policies in health care are nonetheless worth examining as part of a complete picture of American health care policy.

## A. The Issues: Costs and Other Barriers to Access Health Care

Polls on the American public's perception of its health care system during the 1980s and 1990s were showing great dissatisfaction with the provision of health care services.[104] More recent surveys expose the population's desire for better services financed by the government. In fact, prior to 2010, Americans were mostly favourable to an overhaul of the system even though they were ambivalent about the exact policy options.[105] The discontent with the past and current system comes from the pressure high costs and coverage barriers have put on the American population. Furthermore, previous public spending was construed as having no real impact on the quality of care.

In 2017, the annual cost of health care for a household of four had reached $26 994. This significant portion of income was used to cover contributions to insurance premiums and out-of-pocket costs such as co-payments, deductibles and additional amounts not covered under a private insurance policy.[106] From an international vantage point, the United States also ranks first for health care expenditure and last for coverage in the Organisation for Economic Co-operation and Development's (OECD) report.[107] Uniquely, it is the only nation with a mature health care system that does not provide universal health care services to its population.[108]

In fact, problems of access to care in the United States obviously stem from the cost of services but also the structure and organisation of the system.

---

[104] RJ Blendon et al, 'Satisfaction with Health Systems in Ten Nations' (1990) 9 *Health Affairs* 185, 185.
[105] Patel and Rushefsky, above (n 4) 34.
[106] C Girod, S Hart and S Weltz, '2017 Milliman Medical Index' *Milliman* (2017), available at: www.milliman.com/uploadedFiles/insight/Periodicals/mmi/2017-milliman-medical-index.pdf.
[107] L Lorenzoni, A Belloni and F Sassi, 'Health-Care Expenditure and Health Policy in the USA Versus Other High-Spending OECD Countries' (2014) 384(9937) *The Lancet* 83, 83.
[108] See eg, Light, above (n 70); TS Jost, *Disentitlement?: The Threats Facing our Public Health-Care Programs and a Rights-Based Response* (New York, Oxford University Press, 2003).

*Affordability*, or the relationship between prices of services and patients' ability to pay, is only one of four dimensions affecting Americans' ability to access health care. *Accommodation*, the manner in which health care is supplied; *availability*, the volume of existing health care supplies for the population's needs; and *acceptability*, encompassing non-financial barriers to health care, also constitute significant barriers,[109] all of which are linked directly or indirectly to the distribution of health care resources in a largely fragmented system.

The partnership between insurers, hospitals, medical professionals, employers and the unions is at the origin of this disjointed organisation. It has also led to the rise of employment-based coverage.[110] Today, 49 per cent of American employees and their dependants are financing their health care costs with insurance secured through employment.[111] However, the rampant inflation and ineffective measures to control costs implemented during the 1980s only drove employers to engage in risk pooling within their structures instead of adopting health care plans based on community risk ratings. To this day, employers are still embracing various forms of risk selection, finding ways to push higher risk employees out of their labour force. With ERISA, tax and labour law offers a legal basis for self-insuring employers who engage in risk selection despite the state law prohibition to engage in such practices.[112]

Employer-based coverage also varies according to the sector, the employer's size, the number of hours worked and wages received by the insured employees. Large employers, of 200 employees or more, typically offer generous benefits and pay a significant share of health care coverage. In the past, these larger employers provided insurance to their retired employees; unfortunately, as they struggle with costs, health benefits for their current or future retirees have been dropped.[113] The system is under pressure: what was once offered as a reward and benefit in lieu of higher wages is now insufficient to cover excessive health care expenses. American employers have voiced their concerns in and outside political institutions and continue to do post-ACA.

The lack of universal coverage in the United States has fostered a two-tier system, where on one side, some Americans are able to secure coverage at a high price, and on the other, the most vulnerable part of the population depends on charity and inadequate public subsidies.[114] Public insurance programmes are financing the health care needs of those unable to secure coverage privately. Thus, the federal government has become the largest and most strained purchaser of

---

[109] JT Kullgren, CG McLaughlin, N Mitra and K Armstrong, 'Nonfinancial Barriers and Access to Care for US Adults' (2011) 47(1) *Health Services Research* 462, 465.

[110] Almgren, above (n 9) 118.

[111] 'Health Insurance Coverage of the Total Population' (2016) *The Henry J Kaiser Family Foundation*, available at: www.kff.org/other/state-indicator/total-population.

[112] *DiFederico v Rolm Company* 201 F 3d 200 (3rd Cir 2000); *Owens v Storehouse, Inc* 984 F 2d 394 (11th Cir 1993).

[113] Patel and Rushefsky, above (n 4) 32–33.

[114] Almgren, above (n 9) 163–64.

health care in the United States.[115] Similarly, for most out-of-pocket patients payments exceed any reasonable limits and for many, health care bankruptcy has become a reality.[116] However, as a result of the ACA's policies targeting health care costs, the situation is currently not as bleak as it was over the past decades. The rate of uninsured Americans has been significantly reduced and reached an unprecedented low.[117] Despite the significant progress, problems of access have not entirely been eradicated. Millions of Americans still struggle to obtain coverage in part because of the ACA's inability to relieve non-financial barriers.[118] In fact, two-thirds of Americans who are unable to cope with health care costs also experience a range of non-financial barriers.[119]

Mostly affected are adults in low-income communities with cultural and language barriers.[120] Young adults, as well as patients with a chronic condition and individuals in rural areas, also have a higher prevalence of being affected by these barriers.[121] These groups cite their inability to reach a doctor's office outside work hours and great distances between the different points of delivery as the most common reasons for not accessing medical services.[122] Indeed, low-income patients cannot afford to take time off work to visit their family doctors, and patients in rural areas face long commutes to reach hospitals or other health care facilities that often only provide them with a limited range of services.[123]

Private underwriters play a more indirect but equally important role in access to care. They govern and safeguard a system in which the insured have only limited power. The overreliance on the private insurance model as a means to finance health care services has led patients and their physicians to make irrational decisions when it comes to treatment options and related costs. Third parties acting as intermediaries have led doctors to be desensitised to the costs associated with the treatment and procedure they prescribe to their patients.[124]

The overutilisation of resources is also often cited as a participating factor in unaffordable health care in the United States.[125] Advances in medical technology

---

[115] Hacker, *The Divided Welfare State*, above (n 48) 71–84.

[116] See generally, P Krugman and R Wells, 'The Health Care Crisis and What to do About It' (2006) 53(5) *The New York Review of Books* 1.

[117] The law requires private health insurance plans to allow young adults to remain as dependants on their parents' plans and eliminate cost-sharing for evidence-based clinical preventive services. It will also expand eligibility for Medicaid and provide lower income individuals with subsidies for health insurance premiums and cost-sharing.

[118] BD Sommers et al, 'The Impact of State Policies on ACA applications and Enrollment Among Low-Income Adults in Arkansas, Kentucky, and Texas' (2015) 34 *Health Affairs* 1010, 1010; see generally, BD Sommers, 'Health Care Reform's Unfinished Work: Remaining Barriers to Coverage and Access' (2015) 373 *New England Journal of Medicine* 2395.

[119] Kullgren et al, above (n 109) 469.

[120] Sommers, 'Health Care Reform's Unfinished Work', above (n 118) 2395.

[121] Kullgren et al, above (n 109) 462.

[122] Kullgren et al, above (n 109) 467.

[123] 'Healthcare Disparities and Barriers to Healthcare' (Stanford eCampus Rural Health, 2010), available at: ruralhealth.stanford.edu/health-pros/factsheets/downloads/rural_fact_sheet_5.pdf.

[124] Krugman and Wells, above (n 116) 4.

[125] Patel and Rushefsky, above (n 4) 59.

have led medical professionals to explore costly treatment options for more savvy and demanding patients. However, it is the cost of defensive medicine that has, along with increasing insurance prices, led to the demise of the American system.[126] Moral hazard has also had an equally important impact on the private insurance market in the United States and has contributed to the prominence of employer-based insurance and the overutilisation of resources. Moral hazard creates situations where coverage provides the insured with an incentive to seek health care as it alters their risk behaviour. Individuals with coverage are also inclined to act more recklessly with their health knowing that the cost of treatment will be picked up by their policy.[127] The ripple effect on health care prices is considerable. Providers are more inclined to offer services at a higher price to the extent that they are guarantee a profitable return from insurers' payments.[128]

Conversely, employers always look for ways to reduce prices of health care and find solutions for their employees to reduce their utilisation of services to cut down overall expenses.[129] Employers' concerns over rising costs and the inability of the public sector to cope with health care expenses has led to trade-offs and a search for practical cost-containment solutions.[130]

The following section unpacks some of these propositions starting with the manner in which the contemporary structure of employer coverage has had to adapt. It also provides a survey of the management and cost-containment measures that have been put forward since the 1970s.

## B.  The Failed Solutions: Management and Cost-Containment

Issues precluding adequate access to care in the United States have led to numerous policy proposals. Most solutions target health care costs, even though some propositions have been formulated to remove other barriers to care.[131] The following section, however, focuses solely on cost-containment solutions because of the for-profit sector's central role in the creation and implementation of these proposals. Employers, insurers, and at times doctors, have had much to gain from these policies and have often used them as part of their profit-maximising strategies.

From a commercial standpoint, insurers and employers share similar motivations to reduce health care costs and have put forward different propositions to fulfil this goal. First on the list is reducing liability by limiting the number of high-risk individuals in their insurance pool. Over the last decade, the retention of healthier employees has thereby become a priority for American employers.

---

[126] Krugman and Wells, above (n 116) 3–4.
[127] Thomasson, above (n 73) 234.
[128] Almgren, above (n 9) 131.
[129] ibid, 128–29.
[130] Patel and Rushefsky, above (n 4) 283–313.
[131] eg, the Affordable Care Act (2010) proposes to tackle pre-existing conditions and insurance prices.

Primary preventive care and health promotion aiming at the eradication of the consumption of tobacco products, or to encourage weight loss, exercise and stress management, have ranked high on the list of business objectives.[132] In certain settings, particularly in the case of large employers, incentives to change employees' behaviour have significantly helped reduce expenditures.[133] The ACA has also helped propel this movement with its promotion of corporate wellness programmes.[134] These programmes are, for example, incentivising workers to enrol in gym and fitness clubs or even to undergo biometric testing for cholesterol or blood sugar levels.[135] Some companies have even gone as far as reducing their 'unhealthy' employees' benefits or using lifestyle choices as reference points for their hiring and firing process. These policies have become highly controversial and health experts have become wary of these trends. More particularly, the American Civil Liberties Union has been most vocal in insisting that the management of human resources based on an employee's personal life is greatly encroaching on one's wellbeing.[136] The picture is also often more complex than a history of poor lifestyle and bad health habits. Most often, bad health stems from a chronic condition associated with an environmental, hereditary or socio-economic factor that is beyond the employee's control.[137]

Interestingly, American employers have also looked to raise health care consumers' awareness hoping that the insured will become more risk averse and less inclined to seek health care services. They have also imposed penalties for health care utilisation. The premise is that Americans consume more health care than they actually need because of the third-party payment system. It is true that over time the system's incentive structure has created important inefficiencies. Employers are under the impression that consumers are less involved and sensitive to costs because only insurers deal directly with health care bills.[138] Medical professionals and the fee-for-service system are also partly to blame. Aware of their patients' employer-based insurance coverage, they will often provide a greater number of services to trigger higher charges. Patients and doctors rarely have concerns since the insurer will pay most of, if not all, the fee.[139]

These perverted incentives were the rationale that pushed the Bush Administration to develop a policy encouraging a consumer-directed health care system.

---

[132] See generally, S Fleming, 'Wellness Programs Lighten Health Costs' (2005) 120(3) *American City & County* 8.

[133] See eg, JF Fries et al, 'Reducing Health Care Costs by Reducing the Need and Demand for Medical Services' (1993) 329 *New England Journal of Medicine* 321; Smyrl, above (n 61) 5.

[134] Patient Protection and Affordable Care Act, 42 USC § 18001 (2010) s 4303.

[135] J Appleby, 'Employers Tie Financial Rewards, Penalties to Health Tests, Lifestyle Choices' *Kaiser Health News* (2 April 2012), available at: khn.org/news/employers-financial-rewards-penalties-health-tests/.

[136] See generally, American Civil Liberties Union, *Legislative Briefing Kit: Lifestyle Discrimination in the Workplace* (Washington DC, American Civil Liberties Union, 1998).

[137] Appleby, above (n 135).

[138] See generally, Krugman and Wells, above (n 116) 10.

[139] Patel and Rushefsky, above (n 4) 286.

The Medical Savings Accounts (MSA), more recently known as Health Savings Accounts (HSAs), were introduced in the early 2000s as cost-management tools to aggressively reduce health care costs and give more autonomy to consumers.[140] Another underlying rationale behind the policy initiative was to have consumers pay more out of pocket to be directly involved in health care decisions. Essentially, HSAs are comprised of two parts: a high deductible insurance plan meant to cover the patient's most expensive health care needs; and a tax-sheltered savings account to pay for elective procedures or smaller medical interventions. Employees can debit their accounts to pay for health care and at the end of the financial year roll-over any remaining funds free from federal tax.[141] Patients are therefore expected to act more diligently and compare health care prices before purchasing any treatment. The Republican Administration preferred to cut taxes on out-of-pocket health care spending instead of relying on solidarity and redistribution of income to finance health care services through general taxation.[142]

Unfortunately, these accounts have been shown to be problematic and financially inefficient. Patients rarely make rational decisions when it comes to health care. In fact, studies have found that even though patients do cut back on treatment when paying out of pocket, they are also incapable of making sensible choices between necessary and futile treatments.[143] HSAs could therefore indirectly create additional barriers to care, providing insured with a perverse incentive not to utilise services. On the whole, HSAs benefit the wealthy but not the low-income patient who is unable to set aside the maximum amount to benefit from the tax relief on unspent funds. These accounts also encourage adverse selection and jeopardise employers' community risk-pools because healthier employees are willing to opt out from the company plan to gain more tax-free wages.[144]

Employers have also attempted to reduce, or at least reverse, the incentives that lead providers to promote overutilisation of health care services.[145] Negotiations with providers to reduce costs have also led to the redesign of a portion of the health care delivery system in the United States.[146] Managed care organisations emerged in the 1970s. Ever since, employers have encouraged their workforce to enrol and use these organisations to cut down their health care costs.[147] Initially they were designed to offer an alternative to the traditional fee-for-service insurance model.

---

[140] ibid, 296.
[141] Almgren, above (n 9) 124–25.
[142] Krugman and Wells, above (n 116) 3–4.
[143] ibid.
[144] See generally, ibid, 4.
[145] See generally, AE Buchanan, 'Managed Care: Rationing Without Justice, But Not Unjustly' (1998) 23 *Journal of Health Politics, Policy and Law* 617.
[146] See generally, MA Baily, 'Managed Care Organizations and the Rationing Problem' (2003) 33(1) *Hastings Center Report* 36.
[147] See generally, Patel and Rushefsky, above (n 4).

Today, these organisations continue to deliver services to employees enrolled in prepaid group plans.[148]

There are three types of structure available: the HMOs, the Preferred Provider Organizations (PPOs) and the Point of Services (POS) providers.[149] In PPO structures the large number of members allows employers or insurers to negotiate with medical professionals to provide their services at a discounted rate. PPO consumers are free to use providers outside their network.[150] Contrarily, POS customers are limited to the providers within their network. However, out of these three structures, only HMOs constitute a single integrated system that combines the financing, underwriting and delivery of health care services within its structure.[151]

HMOs deliver a comprehensive set of health care services to their members in exchange for a predetermined monthly capitation fee.[152] Unlike traditional insurance plans, HMOs do not insure against the cost of episodes of care. They provide coverage regardless of incidents of bad health affecting their insured. Since insurance risk is more easily shared and spread through a larger pool of insured, these managed care organisations have been able to offer lower premiums and expand benefits to their members. These managed care organisations are also keen on keeping their members healthy to reduce costs and retain a maximum of the leftover money.[153] HMOs have also actively sought to reduce costs by keeping utilisation and number of treatments delivered low. For this, physicians servicing these structures are paid a monthly fee in order to neutralise the perverse incentives (overtreatment) of the fee-for-service system. HMOs have also channelled health services utilisation by centralising all health care services into one structure. Customers have access to doctors, hospitals and nursing homes within their HMO insurance group.[154]

Unfortunately, these structures may also create some important barriers to access. The 'lock-in' feature of the organisation mandates that patients seek medical care solely from providers within their HMO's closed network. This may limit patients' choice and access to health care services.[155] More generally, with regard to health care financing, HMOs were expected to generate pressures on the traditional coverage and delivery system. The competitive impact has nonetheless been

---

[148] See generally, MA Hall and WS Brewbaker (eds), *Health Care Corporate Law: Managed Care* (Gaithersburg, MD, Aspen, 1996).

[149] JC Robinson, 'The Future of Managed Care Organization' (1999) 18(2) *Health Affairs* 7.

[150] G Preston, 'Preferred Provider Organization (PPO)' in MJ Stahl (ed), *Encyclopedia of Health Care Management* (Thousand Oaks, CA, Sage Publications, 2004) 439–40.

[151] See generally, Hall and Brewbaker, above (n 148).

[152] KG LaFrance, 'Preferred Provider Organization (PPO)' in MJ Stahl (ed), *Encyclopedia of Health Care Management* (Thousand Oaks, CA, Sage Publications, 2004) 265–66.

[153] ibid.

[154] JL Falkson, 'Market Reform, Health System, and HMOs' (1981) 9 *Policy Studies Journal* 213, 213.

[155] See generally, Hall and Brewbaker, above (n 148).

questionable. Traditional fee-for-service providers have not felt the need to revisit their cost structures because of the presence of managed care organisations on the market.[156]

Furthermore, widely used by the for-profit sector to reduce its health care expenditure are cost sharing and cost-shifting strategies. Cost sharing can be achieved with multiple tools. Sometimes coverage involves a deductible that requires patients to pay a fixed amount before the insurance benefit can begin. Co-insurance can also shift some of the cost to the insured. It involves the use of co-payments that require a percentage or fixed contribution from patients once they have exceeded their deductible.[157]

Regrettably, the multiple cost-containment solutions engaging insurers and employers presented in this chapter have thus far been unable to successfully tackle issues associated with the costs of health care services. Even though stakeholders have the power to create more justice in health care, their motivation to increase profits seems to go against the eradication of barriers to access. Solutions to improve issues affecting the American health care system are ultimately under the control, and strictly within the reach, of the for-profit sector.

# IV. Conclusion

The overlapping history of the for-profit sector reveals how medical professionals, employers and insurers have constructed and instilled a mostly privately run health care system in the United States. A series of accidents in history have enabled for-profit stakeholders to consolidate their position at the heart of the system and has allowed them to oppose any shift towards universal health care. Right at the inception, the trust that political elites and the American public had put in the profession has helped physicians gain significant clinical, economic and political power.[158] The profession also became more legitimate with the creation of the AMA. Institutionalisation eventually translated into a monopolistic position in health care.[159] In fact, the AMA's stance against governmental involvement has had more impact on health care policy in the 1940s and 1950s than the opposition formed by American businesses.[160] Nonetheless, American employers have also played a major role in the edification of the system. As risk-pooling entities and main providers of employee coverage, employers have had a significant impact on major reforms affecting the financing of health care services in the United States.

---

[156] Patel and Rushefsky, above (n 4) 299–300.

[157] ibid, 301.

[158] See generally, MA Peterson, 'From Trust to Political Power: Interests Groups, Public Choice, and Health Care' (2001) 26 *Journal of Health Politics, Policy and Law* 1145.

[159] Starr, above (n 11) 90–92.

[160] Smyrl, above (n 61) 7–11.

The opposition of union forces along with the incapacity of successive governments to cope with employees' demands also participated in cultivating a system of employer-based coverage.

Insurers have also contributed to the incremental system of care by fostering a close relationship with the medical profession. The Blue insurers and later the commercial industry have help ingrain path dependency in health care policy in the United States.[161] The development of the third-party financing system and the fee-for-service reimbursement method planted the seeds for long-lasting cost issues. Not apparent in the 1960s, health care financing problems became critical in the 1980s. Perhaps the insured were at first more concerned with the extent of their coverage than with the rising cost of their premiums and out-of-pocket payments. Nonetheless, these practices created incentives to provide marginally beneficial or even unnecessary treatments to patients.[162] During this period, insurers successfully shifted policy discourse away from clinical professionalism to a 'market-consumer' philosophy.[163]

Thus, the United States has, and continues to be, an outlier in the realm of health care. However, the atypical setup of the system does not stem from a failure to adequately redistribute resources but from an inability to control costs and non-financial barriers.[164] Unlike any other Western welfare state, the American government relies heavily on the private sector (employers and insurers) to finance some of the population's health care services. Small and large corporations are extensively involved in sponsoring substantial health care insurance bills. Health care has become the most expensive employer-sponsored benefit.[165] Research also shows that industries with the highest levels of employer-sponsored coverage have the slowest growth.[166] These swelling figures have placed some financial constraints on businesses and have created competitive disadvantage on the international scene. Despite the difficult reality that a large number of Americans still face issues to access care, no sustainable solutions have been offered by the insurance industry or American employers. The organisation and the functioning of the system therefore continue to be under the influence of the for-profit's 'undercover dictatorship'.

---

[161] See generally, M Laugesen and TH Rice, 'Is the Doctor In? The Evolving Role of Organized Medicine in Health Policy' (2003) 28 *Journal of Health Politics, Policy and Law* 289.

[162] Annas, above (n 6) 33–40.

[163] See generally, DA Stone, 'The Doctor Businessman: The Changing Politics of a Cultural Icon' (1997) 22 *Journal of Health Politics, Policy and Law* 533.

[164] J White, 'The 2010 US Health Care Reform: Approaching and Avoiding How Other Countries Finance Health Care' (2013) 8 *Journal of Health Economics, Policy and Law* 1, 10–12.

[165] LH Teslik and T Johnson, 'Healthcare Costs and US Competitiveness' (2007) *Backgrounder*, available at: www.cfr.org/publication/13325/healthcare_costs_and_us_competitiveness.html?breadcrumb=%2Fpublication%2Fby_type%2Fbackgrounder.Act

[166] N Sood, A Ghosh and JJ Escarce, 'Employer-Sponsored Insurance, Health Care Cost Growth, and the Economic Performance of US Industries' (2009) 44(5) *Health Services Research* 1449, 1461.

# 4

# Locating Ideas of Justice
# in American Health Care Reforms

'If you always do what you always did, you'll always get what you always got.'[1]

Henry Ford

## I. Introduction

Opinions on what constitutes the greatest challenge to health care in the United States vary across the political spectrum. Conservative policymakers point the finger at growing federal health care expenditures, whereas liberal politicians focus on inequalities in the provision of health care services in the country.[2] These differences in outlook however go beyond political divergence.[3]

Over the past 70 years American health care policy has constantly oscillated between two perspectives with regard to the most appropriate distribution of health care resources. On the one hand, proponents of a market approach have argued that the allocation of health care resources, just like the allocation of any other commodity, should be left to an unsupervised competitive market.[4] The 'laisser-faire strategy', they claim, is most efficient and provides the best value for money.[5] Since any positive outcome derived from governmental regulation has thus far been defied by structural and incentive problems,[6] greater control from public powers can only lead to an increase in health care costs and curb technological advances in medicine.[7]

---

[1] Quote attributed to Henry Ford, American Captain of Industry founder of Ford Motor Company.

[2] D Mechanic, *The Truth About Health Care: Why Reform is not Working in America* (London, Rutgers University Press, 2006) 22–23.

[3] K Patel and ME Rushefsky, *Healthcare Politics and Policy in America*, 4th edn (Armonk, New York, ME Sharpe, 2014) 35.

[4] AC Enthoven and SJ Singer, 'Markets and Collective Action in Regulating Managed Care' (1997) 16(6) *Health Affairs* 26, 27–28; *See generally*, D Goldhill, *Catastrophic Care: How American Health Care Killed My Father – and How We Can Fix It* (New York, Alfred A Knopf, 2013).

[5] N Daniels, 'Broken Promises: Do Business-Friendly Strategies Frustrate Just Healthcare?' in DG Arnold (ed), *Ethics and the Business of Biomedicine* (Cambridge, Cambridge University Press, 2009).

[6] See generally, W McClure, 'Structural and Incentives Problems in Economic Regulation of Medical Care' (1981) 59 *Milbank Memorial Quarterly/Health and Society* 107.

[7] See eg, S Davidson, *Still Broken: Understanding the US Health Care System* (Stanford, CA, Stanford University Press, 2010); JC Goodman, *The Regulation of Medical Care: Is the Price Too High?*

Conversely, advocates favouring the reduction in health care inequalities support strong governmental oversight and the universal provision of health care services.[8] They suggest that the market is incapable of achieving perfect competition, and therefore public powers should intervene as a second-best solution.[9] Other market deficiencies such as information asymmetry between medical professionals and their patients, and the opacity of the third-party financing system also mandate the regulation of the allocation process.[10] Without government's involvement and the universal provision of health care services, the distribution of these resources would lead to excessive expenditure, an increase in access barriers and the inefficient delivery of services.[11]

These contrasting perspectives certainly have a degree of influence on the law-making process even though health care reforms are more nuanced because they are the product of complex negotiations and drafting.[12] These ideologies also echo the frameworks of moral political philosophy and organising principles presented in chapter two. For instance, the laisser-faire competitive market approach conveys many tenets of libertarian justice and neoliberalism, whereas the governmental regulatory approach relays principles of the liberal egalitarian doctrine. Nevertheless, it is not possible to infer strictly from these observations that ideas of justice have made their way into American health care law.

Reforming the health care system in the United States is also particularly intricate because it involves the participation of many actors[13] and, as a federal system, the coordination of multiple levels of government and authority.[14] Thus, this chapter largely focuses on the role played by American for-profit actors, namely medical professionals, insurers and employers, in the elaboration of four federal health care reforms in the United States: the Kerr–Mills Act (1960), the Amendments to the Social Security Act (1965), the Health Maintenance Organization and

(San Francisco, CA, Cato Institute, 1980); JC Goodman, *Priceless: Curing the Health Care Crisis* (Oakland, CA, Independent Institute, 2012).

[8] GJ Annas, *American Health Law* (Boston, MA, Little Brown, 1990) 33–40; see generally, McClure, above (n 6).

[9] KJ Arrow, 'Uncertainty and the Welfare Economics of Medical Care' (1963) 53 *American Economic Review* 851, 945–46; SH Altman and SL Weiner, 'Regulation as a Second Best Choice' in US Federal Trade Commission and W Greenberg (eds), *Competition in the Health Care Sector: Past, Present, and Future* (Washington DC, Government Printing Office, 1978) 421–27.

[10] Arrow, above (n 9) 946–47.

[11] JA Morone and LR Jacobs, *Healthy, Wealthy and Fair: Health Care and the Good Society* (New York, Oxford University Press, 2005) 19–37.

[12] See eg, JC Banaszak-Holl, SR Levitsky and MN Zald, *Social Movements and the Transformation of American Health Care* (Oxford, Oxford University Press, 2010); RI Field, *Mother of Invention: How the Government Created 'Free-Market' Health Care* (Oxford, Oxford University Press, 2013).

[13] See generally, P Starr, *Remedy and Reaction: The Peculiar American Struggle Over Health Care Reform* (New Haven, CT, Yale University Press, 2013).

[14] PR Lee and CL Estes, 'New Federalism and Health Policy' (1983) 468 *Annals of the American Academy of Political and Social Science* 88, 89–91; S Sirpal, 'The Affordable Care Act and Incentivized Health Wellness Programs: A Tale of Federalism and Shifting Administrative Burden' (2014) 37 *Journal of Health and Human Services Administration* 327, 329.

Resources Development (HMO) Act (1973) and the Affordable Care Act (2010). Although the analysis mainly pertains to the discourse of these actors during Congressional hearings leading up to the enactment of the laws, key interventions from other stakeholders are also analysed.[15] This chapter thereby establishes that ideas of justice have informed the initial stages of the law-making process and the final draft of each Act. The historical context that gave rise to these reforms is also presented to further demonstrate that the American for-profit sector has, over time, instilled path dependency in health care policy.

The first part of the chapter opens with the decades after the Second World War, during which the American government worked towards achieving a quasi-universal system by complementing the already established workers' employer-based coverage. The Kerr–Mills Act was the first (failed) attempt to provide coverage to retirees through the Medical Assistance to the Aged Program. The Amendments to the Social Security Act (1965), presented in the second part of the chapter, build on the Kerr–Mills precedent to combine social insurance with coverage for retired citizens through Medicare, and for the poor and children through Medicaid.

Unfortunately, the expansion of public programmes that aimed at bridging the gap left by the for-profit sector triggered inflation and put a significant strain on public funds. Thus, a decade later, health care policy had to shift towards cost-containment. Nonetheless, the private system of coverage would be preserved with competitive strategies that were elaborated in partnership with the for-profit sector. The HMO Act (1973), analysed in the third part of the chapter, marks the start of this new policy approach. Decades later, a myriad of other cost-containment policies were put forward with limited success.[16] Finally, in 2008, the Obama Administration took an unprecedented stance on health care and proposed a reform to tackle at once health care expenditure and inequality issues. The latest health care reform in the United States presented in the last part of the chapter therefore proposed an expansion of public entitlements and a reform of the insurance sector to achieve universal health care. The ACA (2010) aimed to bring the American system closer to an international standard set by its Western welfare states counterparts.[17]

All things considered, contrary to politicians and academics who suggest that health care legislation in the United States is solely the result of pragmatic and market-driven choices,[18] this chapter demonstrates that the allocation of health care resources also draws from elements of justice.

---

[15] See appendix for the detail of textual occurrences analysed in the primary sources.

[16] GR Almgren, *Health Care Politics, Policy and Services: A Social Justice Analysis* (New York, Springer Publishing Company, 2012) 65–66.

[17] J White, 'The 2010 US Health Care Reform: Approaching and Avoiding How Other Countries Finance Health Care' (2013) 8(3) *Health Economics, Policy and Law* 1, 21.

[18] DP Carpenter, KM Esterling and DMJ Lazer, 'The Strength of Weak Ties in Lobbying Networks: Evidence from Health-Care Politics in the United States' (1998) 10 *Journal of Theoretical Politics* 417, 418.

# II. The Kerr–Mills Act (1960)

During the 'New Deal' era the federal government extended its social and economic guarantees by introducing the Social Security Act (1935).[19] The American Medical Association (AMA) had, however, successfully lobbied against the inclusion of health insurance in the legislation. This exclusion left the elderly in a precarious situation, as they required more medical attention than any other group. Retirees were also particularly vulnerable as they fell outside the scope of employer coverage and struggled to enrol in group insurance schemes. High health care costs and high individual insurance rates had crippled their finances.[20]

Thus, in the early 1960s, the recently merged American Federation of Labor and the Congress of Industrial Organizations, forming the union of the AFL–CIO, helped the elderly become an organised group and voice their concerns on the political scene. In response, the government formulated the Kerr–Mills Act.[21] Enacted on 13 September 1960, the legislation created the Medical Assistance to the Aged Program (MAA). The aim of the initiative was twofold. First, to provide complementary benefits in addition to the aid already available through the Old Age Assistance (OAA) programmes that were created under the Social Security Act. The second aim of the Act was to provide assistance for a new welfare category: the 'medically indigent elderly'. These new beneficiaries were defined as elderly persons capable of providing for their ordinary needs but unable to pay for health care services.[22]

## A. The Means Test and the New Welfare Category

The MAA provided federal funds to all 42 states based on their income per capita, a method later used under Medicaid.[23] Compared with the OAA, the programme offered a greater range of medical services and extended coverage beyond hospitalisation costs.[24] The MAA also had to ease the retirees' financial burden caused by health care costs.[25] As resources were limited, a means test was design to proceed with the allocation. Governmental assistance was to be granted to persons under

---

[19] Social Security Act Pub L 74–271, 49 Stat 620 (1935).

[20] Patel and Rushefsky, above (n 3) 56.

[21] J Quadagno, *One Nation, Uninsured: Why the US Has No National Health Insurance* (Oxford, Oxford University Press, 2005) 58.

[22] S Fine, 'The Kerr–Mills Act: Medical Care for the Indigent in Michigan, 1960–1965' (1998) 53 *Journal of the History of Medicine and Allied Sciences* 285, 292–93.

[23] JD Moore and DG Smith, 'Legislating Medicaid: Considering Medicaid and its Origins' (2005) 27(2) *Health Care Financing Review* 45, 46–47; Almgren, above (n 16) 73.

[24] Fine, above (n 22) 285.

[25] Staff of S Comm on Health of the Elderly, 88th Cong, Rep on Medical Assistance for the Aged the Kerr–Mills Program 1960–1963 (Comm Print, 1963) 3.

a precise income threshold to leave the self-sustaining part of the population in the hands of the private sector. The policy echoed the medical profession's and the AMA's position on resource allocation. The applicants' financial status became a focal point and although the programme was federally funded, states were given the responsibility to determine who, among their over-65 medically needy residents, was to receive the funds.[26]

The concept of medical indigence had emerged after the Second World War and was picked up by craftsmen of the Kerr–Mills Act. Persons 'who could provide for their ordinary daily needs but [that] could not afford to pay for sizable personal health services'[27] consisted of a more substantial portion of the population in the 1960s. Although the medically indigent applicants could have been re-grouped under existing public assistance programmes, politicians felt it would have been unjust to have them seek welfare benefits because of hefty medical bills. Nonetheless, a negative consequence of the categorisation was the inevitable meshing of medical assistance for the poor with general public assistance. The social stigma associated with welfare programmes was transposed onto medical assistance.[28] Clearly, too much emphasis was placed on the means and not enough on the medicine.[29] By using the same assessment process as other welfare assistance programmes, the MAA was not sufficiently distinguishing the 'medically indigent' from the 'indigent'. Applicants had to demonstrate their inability to provide for their health care needs to be shrouded in the welfare cloak.[30]

Applicants' income and assets had to be scrutinised.[31] Embarrassed by the queries, many elderly people elected not to seek assistance despite their medical needs. In most states, the test became a deterrent.[32] Politicians and a significant part of the American population also bitterly received the assessment method. Despite the general discontent, 12 states decided to adopt a family responsibility provision that also imposed the means test on an applicant's relatives. This procedure disrupted family relationships and further dissuaded applicants from seeking assistance. Most elderly people worried about the hardship the scrutiny might cause their families.[33]

---

[26] ibid.

[27] OW Anderson and H Alksne, *An Examination of the Concept of Medical Indigence* (Health Information Foundation, 1957) 1–2, 4.

[28] Moore and Smith, above (n 23) 45–46.

[29] Staff of S Comm on Health of the Elderly, 88th Cong, above (n 25).

[30] ibid, 29.

[31] 'So that the county board of assistance can decide as fast as possible whether you are eligible for MAA, be ready when you apply to give them the facts on your age, residence, amount of income, and value of property. It may help if you bring papers that give this information. Also have with you the names and addresses of your husband or wife, your sons and daughters', Commonwealth of Pennsylvania, Department of Public Welfare, Informational Leaflet No 8, 'If You Need Medical Assistance for the Aged' (1962).

[32] Staff of S Comm on Health of the Elderly, 88th Cong, above (n 25) 4.

[33] ibid.

In fact, the MAA was harshly criticised for fostering an alliance between welfare and medical care. Protecting only a small portion of the elderly population, the Act failed to meet the demand for a social insurance programme for the aged. The labour market had been excluded, and only the vulnerable were covered: the aged, the blind and women with dependent children.[34] In the end, only 1 per cent of the elderly population secured coverage with the MAA. However, despite its limited success, the Act had laid an important foundation for its successor, Medicaid.[35]

## B.  Ideas of Liberal Equality

Legislative preparatory work on the Kerr–Mills Act relays the intent of Congress and different stakeholders involved in the elaboration of this unprecedented piece of legislation. The interactions between political actors during the 1958 Social Security Legislation Hearings before the Committee on Ways and Means of the House of Representatives (Committee Hearings of 1958)[36] and the 1960 Hearings before the Committee on Finance of the Senate (Committee Hearings of 1960)[37] reveal discussions on the just allocation of health care resources in the United States. During both consultations, politicians[38] and key witnesses asked questions and presented their points of view to the Committee. The hospital associations,[39] nurses[40] and medical associations,[41] as well as charities[42] were represented. Lobbies in favour of many vulnerable groups,[43] such as the blind[44] and the aged,[45] and those representing the for-profit sector (employers[46] and insurers)[47] were also present.

Although their comments on the substance of the Bill were limited, the impact that insurers and employers had on the negotiations was considerable. The health

---

[34] Moore and Smith, above (n 23) 46–47; US Health Resources Administration, *Health in America: 1776–1976* (Rockville, US Department of Health, Education, and Welfare, 1976).

[35] Annas, above (n 8) 29.

[36] Social Security Amendments of 1958: Hearing on HR 13549 Before the H Comm on Ways and Means, 85th Cong 2288 (1958).

[37] Social Security Amendments of 1960: Hearing on HR 12580 Before the S Comm on Finance, 86th Cong 2288 (1960).

[38] Senators (Sen McNamara, Kennedy, Javits, Leverett), governors (Gov Rockfeller), congressmen (Cong Forand, Fino, Engle, Byrd, McDonough, Stephens, Jennings, Van Zandt, Ullman, Hosmer), representatives of the Social Security Department (Mr Volpan, Mr. Cruikshank).

[39] The University of Minnesota Hospitals (Dir Amberg).

[40] The American Nurses Association (Ms Thompson).

[41] The American Medical Association (D Larson), The Texas Medical Association (Mr Tez), The Medical Society of North Carolina (M Grogan).

[42] The National Conference of Catholic Charities (Rev O'Grady).

[43] The American Public Welfare Association (Dr Winston).

[44] The National Federation of the Blind (Pres Tenbroek and Mr Schloss).

[45] The National League of Senior Citizen (Pres McLain).

[46] The National Association of Manufacturers (Mr Culin).

[47] The American Life Convention, Health Insurance Association of America and Life Insurance Association (Mr Faulkner), Blue Shield Medical Care Plans (Chair Stubbs).

insurance gap left in the Social Security Act was the product of the for-profit sector's pressures. The MAA had to help bridge coverage discrepancies for a specific group no longer eligible for employer-sponsored insurance. Ultimately, the government had to take action and intervene in the allocation of health care resources. A discussion on society's duty to protect vulnerable groups[48] had become dominant. The egalitarian undertone of these discourses denotes a meeting of the minds on the need for a social contract to protect the medically indigent elderly. At least 16 statements directly refer to a 'vulnerable group' that ought to be protected under a new law.

Democratic Congressman Engle argued that the elderlies' life opportunities could be affected if the federal government did not change the allocation of health care resources. He stated that 'unless we make some basic changes in our social security law most of our older citizens in a few short years will be consigned to an economically and socially underprivileged group'.[49] Inequalities in health care were to lead to long-term inequality in opportunity and this could no longer be tolerated in American society. The chairman of the Senate Finance Committee, Senator Byrd, equally acknowledged that that the elderly constituted a least favourable group inviting members present at the hearing to

> recognize that senior citizens of this State and Nation, as a group, have recognized health and medical care needs which are substantially greater that those of younger age groups, and which, in terms of cost, far exceed the financial means of our aged population.[50]

During the Committee Hearings of 1958, Republican Congressman McDonough stressed the importance of providing all Americans with equal opportunities. He explained that '[the American] wants the opportunity to choose his own profession, to make his own decisions as they regard his own welfare and that of his family'.[51] The Treasurer of the National Insurance Plan, Robert C Townsend, of course, supported this view and stated that 'these benefits [would] affect everybody, giving greater opportunity to all, no matter what their ages or positions may be'.[52]

The 'medically indigent'[53] had been identified as a group and, out of a sense of 'equity',[54] society had to provide for their medical needs. Byrd, among others, recognised senior citizens as a least advantaged group. The unequal distribution of health care resources in their favour was thereby justified, in the same way as

---

[48] See Social Security Amendments of 1958: Hearing on HR 13549, above (n 36) 63, 72, 76, 105, 211, 322, 323, 366, 482, 775, 848, 879, 947; Social Security Amendments of 1960: Hearing on HR 12580, above (n 37) 56, 202, 343, 383, 417, 420, 426.

[49] Social Security Amendments of 1958: Hearing on HR 13549, above (n 36) 482.

[50] Social Security Amendments of 1960: Hearing on HR 12580, above (n 37) 343.

[51] Social Security Amendments of 1958: Hearing on HR 13549, above (n 36) 676.

[52] ibid, 298.

[53] Social Security Amendments of 1958: Hearing on HR 13549, above (n 36); Social Security Amendments of 1960: Hearing on HR 12580, above (n 37) 343.

[54] Social Security Amendments of 1958: Hearing on HR 13549, above (n 36) 261, 1001.

Rawls' *difference principle*, encouraged divergence from an orthodox egalitarian allocation. Inasmuch as the inequality was to make the least advantaged in society materially better off, it had to proceed. In the presented case the medical indigent elderly were the most unequal and least favoured, and the Act had to make an acceptable change favouring this group. In this sense, the 'means test' illustrates the roles of luck and responsibility in economic life. It translated the priority rule into practice. Those who suffer the greatest reduction in their opportunity range as a result of health care costs had to receive the highest priority and the most resources in the allocation process. The test was instrumental in identifying those who suffer the greatest detriment.

The liberal egalitarian rhetoric present in the discourse of many stakeholders naturally led to a critique of the libertarian approach to the provision of health care services. Ideas against a subsidiary system of care and conversely ideas in support of solidarity in health care financing were discussed. The concept of 'charitable care'[55] was particularly under attack. Townsend, contended that

> charity, whether public or private, can be tolerated only when it is clear that it is a necessary evil. But here in America it is not necessary. It is within the power of this Congress to create a system of insurance which would cover all Americans as a matter of right.[56]

Townsend's intervention implied a need and the importance of a benevolent attitude towards weaker social groups, and a commitment to fairer distribution of health care resources. Subsidiarity could no longer be a rule or a fallback position. The United States had to cultivate a more solidary system. Similarly, Democratic Senator Bob Barlett also pointed out that 'a country which prides itself on self-reliance and initiative should be a country where men and women need not to rely on charity or doles to meet medical needs in old age'.[57] Similarly, a majority of the testimonies during the Committee Hearings of 1958 and the Committee Hearings of 1960 evoked principles of liberal equality, some of which informed the final version of the Kerr–Mills Act.[58] Although not prominent, a cluster of instances also relayed ideas of communitarianism[59] and utilitarianism.[60]

---

[55] Social Security Amendments of 1958: Hearing on HR 13549, above (n 36) 127, 260, 290, 325; Social Security Amendments of 1960: Hearing on HR 12580, above (n 37) 128, 197, 211, 394, 395, 438, 44.

[56] Social Security Amendments of 1958: Hearing on HR 13549, above (n 36) 290.

[57] Social Security Amendments of 1960: Hearing on HR 12580, above (n 37) 438.

[58] At least 13 instances refer directly to the concept of equality of opportunities, Social Security Amendments of 1958: Hearing on HR 13549, above (n 36) 204, 217, 211, 298, 398, 410, 474, 560, 676; Social Security Amendments of 1960: Hearing on HR 12580, above (n 37) 213, 298, 368, 371.

[59] Social Security Amendments of 1958: Hearing on HR 13549, above (n 36) 173, 260, 261, 479, 618, 856, 941, 1019, 1095, 1209; Social Security Amendments of 1960: Hearing on HR 12580, above (n 37) 201, 212, 238, 293, 143, 428.

[60] Social Security Amendments of 1960: Hearing on HR 12580, above (n 37) 236, 297, 382, 400, 728, 778, 1024, 1042.

After the passage of the Act and its enactment, Democrats looked back on the initiative as an inadequate but necessary piece of legislation.[61] Republicans, for their part, were concerned about the cost-management aspect of the programme and reluctantly accepted the Kerr–Mills Act as 'something they had to do'.[62] Although the final version of the Act does not explicitly appeal to ideas of justice, it makes a proposition that hopes to level the playing field in health care and provide resources for the least favoured in society, the 'medically indigent elderly'. The intent of the Act and the MAA was to identify through the 'means test' a particular vulnerable group in order to allocate, in priority, additional health care resources to provide them with the same opportunities as other more fortunate Americans.[63]

## III. Medicare and Medicaid (1965)

The underwhelming outcomes produced by the MAA and the Kerr–Mills Act in the 1960s left policymakers in search of a more efficient solution to solve the elderly health care cost issue.[64] The civil rights movement had gained popularity and the general public was starting to perceive access to care as an essential element in the fulfilment of life opportunities.[65] Adding to these societal pressures, other political elements propelled health care reform to the top of the federal government's agenda. For instance, the lack of motivation and the inability of the for-profit sector to provide coverage for the most vulnerable part of the population, the elderly and the poor, most certainly called for central government's action.

Employer-based coverage also could not meet the demands of the elderly. At the beginning of the century, unions had successfully claimed health insurance as a fringe benefit for their workers; nonetheless their retired members lacked coverage for their leisure years. Collectively bargained plans were unable to sustain this form of coverage because of the excessive concession on workers' wages that the cost of insurance would require.[66] And, despite the active work force's concerns about its benefits and its desire to be acknowledged, it was equally important for unions to satisfy their pensioners' needs. Union leaders were therefore determined to have the government finance a programme for the elderly to absorb part of the retirees' health care costs and allow more room for negotiations on the active workforce's wages and benefits.[67]

---

[61] See generally, MC Bernstein and JB Bernstein, *Social Security: The System That Works* (New York, Basic Books, 1988).
[62] Quadagno, *One Nation, Uninsured*, above (n 21) 60.
[63] Staff of S Comm on Health of the Elderly, 88th Cong, above (n 25) 3.
[64] ibid.
[65] Patel and Rushefsky, above (n 3) 235.
[66] Quadagno, *One Nation, Uninsured*, above (n 21) 56.
[67] ibid, 57.

The insurance sector also had to deal with the elderlies' precarious situation as Blue insurers were losing business to the price-cutting private insurers. Commercial underwriters were basing their actuarial calculations on risk and experience and abandoned community-rating insurance plans. They were thereby able to offer lower rates to attract the younger and healthier insured. Blue insurers were therefore left with the elderly and the other high-risk applicants.[68] Nevertheless, insurers knew that any health care policy that could potentially tackle these issues would require the medical profession's stamp of approval and the full cooperation of the AMA. Unfortunately, doctors had thus far been opposed to any national health insurance system initiatives.[69]

With the start of the presidential campaign in 1960, political rivals were compelled to formulate plans for health care policy. The northern Democrats, with John F Kennedy, together with the American Federation of Labor and Congress of Industrial Organization (AFL–CIO) and senior citizens, supported the Democratic Party's platform and promoted a new public programme for the elderly named 'Medicare'. On the other side, the Republicans, with their candidate Richard Nixon, the AMA, the Health Insurance Association of America, the business community and some southern Democrats, directly opposed a government-sponsored programme for the aged.[70] Ultimately victorious, Kennedy made the enactment of Medicare his top priority and as he had the support of the general public he pushed for the swift passage of his new proposal: the King–Anderson Act. Indeed, by 1962, 69 per cent of Americans were in favour of the legislation to create Medicare.[71]

Ultimately unsuccessful with the King–Anderson Act, President Kennedy made recommendations for protection against the cost of serious illness and further promoted his Medicare programme as an initiative that would help meet the health care needs of the American elderly during a 'Special Message on Aiding Our Senior Citizens' on 21 February 1963.[72] His assassination that same year left the task to carry forward the proposal to his successor Lyndon Johnson. As the interim President stepped in to complete the Democrats' term in office, he made indigent citizens his top priority.[73] President Johnson wanted to tackle poverty at its core and gain the support of the population in view of the 1964 elections. His strategy proved to be successful as he was indeed elected with an overwhelming popular vote. The Democrats had also consolidated their position in the House of Representatives with a 2:1 majority. This convergence of political factors and the

---

[68] SA Law, *Blue Cross: What Went Wrong?* (New Haven, CT, Yale University Press, 1974) 12.

[69] See generally, TR Marmor, *The Politics of Medicare* (New York, Aldine de Gruyter, 2000).

[70] Annas, above (n 8) 30.

[71] Quadagno, *One Nation, Uninsured*, above (n 21) 67–69; Patel and Rushefsky, above (n 3) 57.

[72] See generally, SI David, *With Dignity: The Search for Medicare and Medicaid* (Westport, CT, Greenwood, 1985).

[73] Patel and Rushefsky, above (n 3) 57.

compromise reached with the for-profit sector (presented in the following section) enabled the enactment of the Amendments to the Social Security Act and thereby to the creation of Medicare and Medicaid.[74]

To this day, Medicare continues to be available to all Americans over 65, those who are disabled and those receiving social security cash benefits.[75] Its coverage extends to a large portion of the population and taxpayers are expected to contribute and benefit from this programme. Essentially it works as a national health insurance system for the elderly and eligible disabled.[76]

In contrast to Medicare, Medicaid emerged spontaneously as part of a compromise to secure the enactment of both amendments.[77] For the most part, the negotiations leading to the creation of the programme were kept under wraps, perhaps because most of Medicaid was an extension of the Kerr–Mills Act. Nonetheless, it offered a much more potent option.[78] Medicaid was also regarded as an afterthought to Medicare providing a safety-net programme to cover the deductibles and co-insurance costs of indigent Medicare patients.[79] The programme's primary objective was nevertheless first to provide poverty stricken Americans with financial assistance to meet their health care needs. This would be accomplished on the basis of a means test conducted by state governments.[80] To this day, the programme continues to delegate a great portion of the policy-making and day-to-day administrative responsibilities to states and local authorities, to maintain a 'unified system of health care'[81] for low-income individuals.[82]

Overall, notwithstanding certain anomalies, the federal entitlement programmes were a remarkable political success, as the nation's most vulnerable groups were finally granted equal access to health care services. The 1965 Social Security Amendments initiated the most important health care programmes of the twentieth century.[83] The elderly and the poor were given their own federally funded health care system. Even though it was incremental, quasi-universal health care had been established in the United States.

---

[74] See generally, K Davis and R Reynolds, *The Impact of Medicare and Medicaid on Access to Medical Care* (Washington DC, Brookings Institution, 1976).

[75] Patel and Rushefsky, above (n 3) 131.

[76] See generally, TR Reid, *The Healing of America: A Global Quest for Better, Cheaper, and Fairer Health Care* (New York, Penguin Press, 2009).

[77] Annas, above (n 8) 31.

[78] Moore and Smith, above (n 23) 48.

[79] See generally, RE Brown, 'Medicare and Medicaid: Band-Aid for the Old and Poor' in VW Sidel and R Sidel (eds), *Reforming Medicine: Lessons of the Last Quarter Century* (New York, Pantheon, 1983).

[80] Patel and Rushefsky, above (n 3) 86.

[81] See generally, SK Schneider, 'Intergovernmental Influences on Medicaid Program Expenditures' (1988) 48 *Public Administration Review* 756.

[82] Quadagno, *One Nation, Uninsured*, above (n 21) 75.

[83] Annas, above (n 8) 76.

## A. Propositions from Insurers, Employers and the Medical Profession

The final version of the 1965 Amendments to the Social Security Act creating the federally funded health care programmes for the elderly and the poor was the product of a compromise between propositions from President Johnson's Administration and the different approaches offered by the health care for-profit sector and the Republican Party. Indeed, Medicare took the form of a three-part programme that mirrored each proposal. Medicaid however was designed after a plan that the medical profession had put forward.

Medicare Part A was the Democratic Party and AFL–CIO's plan for a compulsory hospital insurance programme financed through payroll taxes and providing limited skilled-nursing and care homes. Medicare Part B reflected the Republican and Commercial insurers' proposal 'Bettercare',[84] which suggested a federally funded and voluntary private health insurance programme to take charge of physicians' services. The AMA, for its part, proposed 'Eldercare',[85] an altered version of the Kerr–Mills Act's MAA that was renamed 'Medicaid' under the legislation. This programme was to cater for the needs of the 'categorically' eligible 'deserving poor' through federal and state cash allowances, old-age assistance and aid to families with dependent children.[86] In the same way as an insurance policy, services would be paid for rather than managed by the government.[87]

Although insurers were not initially in favour of amendments to the Social Security Act, they quickly realised that the elderly population did not constitute an important source of profit and therefore became ready to leave this category of customers in the hands of the federal government. They had strategically planned for a 'worst-case scenario' (a publicly financed health care system) and sought to create for themselves a profitable role with 'Bettercare'. The AMA also formed a strong and organised lobbying group and despite their opposition to a federal programme for health care financing, they were willing to secure their interest with 'Eldercare'.[88] Thus, the compromise that was Medicare left a good number of health care services excluded from the programme and others only available with a co-payment. The elderly's misfortune became the private insurers' good fortune.

---

[84] Bettercare was written by Aetna lobbyists and sponsored by Representative John Byrnes, the ranking Republican on the Ways and Means Committee.

[85] 'Eldercare Branded Empty Propaganda' *AFL-CIO News* (20 February 1965) RG 233, Records of the House of Representatives, 89th Congress, Committee on Ways and Means, Legislative Files, Box 21, File: HR 6675-3 of 94.

[86] Quadagno, *One Nation, Uninsured*, above (n 21) 73–74.

[87] See generally, WA Jones, 'Medicaid 101: History, Challenges, and Opportunities' (2006) 16 *Ethnicity & Disease* 56.

[88] I Bernstein, *Guns or Butter: The Presidency of Lyndon Johnson* (Oxford, Oxford University Press, 1996) 171.

Relieved from the unpredictable costs associated with this high-risk population, insurers retained the supplemental market of 'Medigap' policies.[89] Also relieved of a burden, were the Blue insurers that saw their coverage rates lowered.[90]

Public support for a quasi-universal health care system was also unwearied. The idea of covering the uninsured had become acceptable as 68 per cent of Americans were already receiving some form of coverage through private health insurance.[91] Organised labour and the elderly found additional support in the White House and in Congress, ultimately forcing the for-profit sector to give in to the reform.[92]

The Amendments to the Social Security Act constituted a remarkable project bridging the traditionally divided domains of private medicine and public health.[93] Medicare and Medicaid had also created a precedent given that, up until that point, no other social security programme had made an equally significant commitment to its beneficiaries. The open-endedness of these programmes and their statutory entitlements were marks of a fixed political promise.[94] The government had committed to allocate virtually unlimited public funds to finance the care of the aged and the poor, and in essence would play the role of a third-party payer but without exercising direct control of the medical profession.[95]

In fact, the preamble to the original Medicare statute included an explicit prohibition against federal 'supervision or control over the practice of medicine or the manner in which medical services [were to be] provided … or the administration of any … institution, agency, or person [providing, medical services]'.[96] The governmental agenda was clear: give the elderly access to health care by buying into the existing institutions. The task division was simple: the government had to be in charge of the financing, whereas the for-profit sector would take charge of the execution. Thus, the private sector became responsible for the implementation of the programmes, which included managing quality assessments, day-to-day administrative duties and supervising fund disbursement.[97]

Congress had also worked to minimise the impact of these programmes on the medical profession. Medicaid and Medicare were, in reality, simple 'add-ons' paralleling the third-party payer system, even though the goal was to finance health care services for a new portion of the population and to ensure that all Americans received the same access to care. Interestingly, despite the important

---

[89] Quadagno, *One Nation, Uninsured*, above (n 21) 74.
[90] ibid, 75.
[91] ibid, 67–69.
[92] Almgren, above (n 16) 81–82.
[93] Annas, above (n 8) 30.
[94] ibid, 31.
[95] See generally, J Quadagno, 'Why the United States has no National Health Insurance: Stakeholder Mobilization Against the Welfare State, 1945–1996' (2004) (Extra Issue) *Journal of Health and Social Behavior* 25.
[96] Later amended and included in the act under Title XVIII Sections 1801 and 1803.
[97] Annas, above (n 8) 31–32.

push and pull during the negotiations, welfare egalitarian language emerged in the final version of the Act. Section 1901 under the title 'Grants to States for Medical Assistance Programs' stated:

> For the purpose of enabling each State, as far as practicable under the conditions in such State, to furnish (1) medical assistance on behalf of families with dependent children and of aged, blind, or permanently and totally disabled individuals, whose income and *resources are insufficient to meet the costs of necessary medical services*, and (2) rehabilitation and other services to help such families and individuals *attain or retain capability for independence or self-care*, there is hereby authorized to be appropriate fiscal year a sum sufficient to carry out the purpose of this title.[98]

The drafting conveyed the government's commitment to provide the necessary resources to level the playing field and grant all Americans the same access to health care services. 'Necessary medical services'[99] could be construed as a primary good in the welfare egalitarian sense as they enable the beneficiaries of the Act to 'retain [their] capability'.[100] Indeed, the amendments addressed the government's and the general population's concern for the most needy, and aimed to reach equality in capability more than equality of resources. The welfare of the aged was a focal point, and emphasis was placed on the capacity of the elderly to access health care services without barriers. The redistribution of resources under the Medicare Amendments could also be interpreted as equalising the health *functioning* of the 'categorically aged and deserving'[101] by giving them greater *capacity* to seek medical care.[102]

In theory, health policies committed to welfare egalitarianism should provide equal access to health care by granting individuals equal *capacity* to achieve good health. Welfare egalitarianism prefers equal *access* to available resources rather than committing to the unreachable goal of providing every patient with equal health care resources. Thus, the Amendments to the Social Security Act extended coverage to additional groups, thereby guaranteeing vulnerable Americans equal access to hospitals and medical care.

Welfare egalitarianism also emphasises equality of *real freedom* commensurate with equality of *condition*.[103] Medicare programmes therefore adopt a twofold approach. The national problem of adequate care for the aged had not been resolved with previous legislation, or at least to the extent anticipated. Limiting health care support for the aged to individuals falling below a set poverty threshold was deemed unacceptable by the federal government. Instead, it was more

---

[98] Staff of S Comm on Aging, 89th Cong Rep on Health Insurance and Related Provisions of Public Law 89–97 (Comm Print, 1965) Title XIX, Section 1901.
[99] ibid.
[100] ibid.
[101] ibid.
[102] ibid.
[103] See ch 2, section III.A.b.

adequate and feasible to increase health insurance protection under two separate but complementary programmes in order to make a significant contribution to economic security in old age.

These programmes also supplemented and, in some places, substituted private insurance to remove access barriers to care for the aged and the poor. Yet, contrary to Medicare, Medicaid's programme set no particular goals, nor did it define precise benefits. It had a safety-net function and was meant to provide services that were unaccounted for under Medicare. The programme had been gerrymandered to fit the contours of already existing federal welfare programmes.[104] Medicaid similarly embraced the resource egalitarian rhetoric that had been present in health care policy throughout the 1960s.[105] Resource allocation was again based on a means test; however, the category of the deserving poor (the aged, blind, disabled and families with dependent children) represented a larger vulnerable group compared with the medically aged alone. The resources mobilised were also far greater than under the predecessor MAA programme established under the Kerr–Mills Act.

## B. Ideas of Welfare Equality

It is the competing ideologies in American health care policy described at the beginning of this chapter that led to the compromised solution offered by Medicare and Medicaid. The tension between a need for a federally funded universal health care system and conversely the desire of the for-profit sector to limit the role of government in the financing and provision of health care services, had led to the advent of a hybrid and an incremental approach to health care coverage in the 1960s.[106] The three-part Executive Hearings before the Committee on Ways and Means of the House of Representatives[107] and the Hearings before the Committee on Finance of the United States Senate[108] reveal the clash and later middle ground reached between these two positions.

The for-profit stakeholders present at the hearings obviously voiced their objections to the project of a federally funded health care programme, and this, in explicit terms.[109] Among the most fervent interventions was the letter from

---

[104] Annas, above (n 8) 56.

[105] See section II.B. of this chapter.

[106] See generally, PB Ginsburg, 'Public Insurance Programs: Medicare and Medicaid' in HE Frech (ed), *Health Care in America: The Political Economy of Hospitals and Health Insurance* (San Francisco, CA, Pacific Research Institute for Public Policy, 1988).

[107] Executive Hearings Before the H Comm on Ways and Means, 89th Cong (1965) Part I; Executive Hearings Before the H Comm on Ways and Means, 89th Cong (1965) Part II; Executive Hearings Before the H Comm on Ways and Means, 89th Cong (1965) Part III.

[108] Social Security: Hearing on HR 6675 Before the S Comm on Finance, 89th Cong (1965).

[109] Executive Hearings Before the H Comm on Ways and Means, 89th Cong (1965) 77, 268, 327, 544, 607, 627, 645, 647, 696, 661; Social Security: Hearing on HR 6675, above (n 108) 48, 138, 446, 548, 634, 646, 647.

California doctor John Toth, which offered a plea in favour of a system promoting subsidiarity and that valued charitable care, rejecting outright a right to assistance. In line with the traditional libertarian ideology, Toth suggested limited state interference, minimal redistributive taxation and the provision of welfare services though charitable contributions. He wrote:

> The right of charity resides with the givers of charity, not with the receivers. If the recipients of charity have the right to receive it, then those providing the charity are obligated to give it to them, and it is no longer charity. So if the older folks' need for charity or for medical care becomes a right to charity or medical care, how did they get that right? And why just the older folks, etc? In our concern over being charitable to those that need it, let's not ignore the just concern of, those providing the charity.[110]

He was also critical of tax-based financing systems that, according to him, would lead to the violation of individual property rights:

> If he [(the aged)] earns the money, it is his by right (in justice); if he does not earn it, only two ways of obtaining it are possible – either by charity or by force – from someone else who has earned it. There are no other alternatives. Those who would say that they want to receive money, or benefits, or services which they have not earned but say they do not want charity, are actually saying that they want to receive these things from someone else by force (usually by governmental force; ie, taxation).[111]

Along with medical professionals, commercial insurers too were concerned with taxes being levied on the more fortunate but smaller portion of the population and redistribution of these incomes used to finance the needs of a greater number of vulnerable Americans.[112] Republican Congressman Broyhill made himself the spokesman of this faction summing up other fears and discontent:

> The membership of the House of Representatives, in acting on the Medicare political palliative should be cognizant of the meaningful fact that the two groups most knowledgeable of the medical and actuarial implications of the Medicare proposal oppose its enactment – these groups are the physicians and the health insurance industry. The concerns expressed by these groups are sustained by events throughout the world where government health programs have reached the critical juncture of unforeseen increases in, cost and declining quality of medical service. It is not by accident that the US citizens have available to them the highest standard of health care in the world under our free enterprise system. The enactment of Medicare will inescapably impair the quality and increase the cost of health care in this country similar to the deteriorating standards and increasing costs being experienced in such countries as Great Britain, France, and Italy.[113]

---

[110] Executive Hearings Before the H Comm on Ways and Means, 89th Cong, above (n 109) 646.

[111] Social Security: Hearing on HR 6675, above (n 108) 647.

[112] ibid 646, 647; Executive Hearings Before the H Comm on Ways and Means, 89th Cong, above (n 107) Part III, 77, 327, 544, 647, 696.

[113] Executive Hearings Before the H Comm on Ways and Means, 89th Cong, above (n 107) Part III, 268.

Conversely, ideas about liberal equality[114] emerged in almost 20 testimonies. Many of the discourses focused on equity, equality and fairness, but surprisingly none made an explicit mention of a need to equalise capabilities among Americans. A majority of arguments however did express concern for vulnerable groups[115] and pressed the state to provide indigent Americans with equal access[116] to health care services in order to ultimately provide them with equal opportunities.[117]

William Fitch, Director of the National Retired Teachers' Association and the American Association of Retired Persons, summed up the egalitarian perspective and explained that 'more comprehensive legislation would give a more just and equal treatment to a deserving group of older citizens who have struggled and who are struggling to maintain their independence and dignity during a period of rising living costs'.[118] Another representative of the elderly and retired group Mr Schottland made a similar point and emphasised that '[t]hese improvements would be in the direction of more adequate and comprehensive coverage; [providing] greater equity among different groups of recipients'.[119]

Interestingly, the egalitarian rhetoric was also used in later hearings by the for-profit sector to lobby in favour of the legislation as it became aware that federal programmes would alleviate pressure from their business. The Senior Vice President and Chief actuary at the Metropolitan Life Insurance Company contended that

> where the range of need among the aged is so great, it is especially important to make certain that any aid through Governments is utilized most effectively and in a manner that truly advances the health and welfare of all our citizens.[120]

Ultimately, the discussions during the Congressional and Senate hearings for the Amendment to the Social Security Act reflect the impasse reached by the American health care financing system after the failed attempt of the Kerr–Mills Act. The government had been given limited manoeuvring capacity and had to confine the project to the boundaries set by the for-profit sector. Nonetheless, to this day, Medicare and Medicaid continue to be the largest of public sector programmes (in terms of beneficiaries and proportion of the federal budget) and have endured

---

[114] Social Security: Hearing on HR 6675, above (n 108) 452, 532, 595, 644; Executive Hearings Before the H Comm on Ways and Means, 89th Cong, above (n 107) Part I, 125; ibid, Part II, 260, 365, 372; ibid, Part III, 319, 443, 549, 611, 612, 671, 672, 708.

[115] Social Security: Hearing on HR 6675, above (n 108) 168, 308, 319, 367, 705, 706; Executive Hearings Before the H Comm on Ways and Means, 89th Cong, above (n 107) Part I, 392; ibid, Part II, 11; ibid, Part III, 17, 75, 268, 379, 553, 727.

[116] Social Security: Hearing on HR 6675, above (n 108) 41, 129, 261; Executive Hearings Before the H Comm on Ways and Means, 89th Cong, above (n 107) Part I, 353, 464; ibid, Part III, 107, 109, 371.

[117] Social Security: Hearing on HR 6675, above (n 108) 317, 318, 321; Executive Hearings Before the H Comm on Ways and Means, 89th Cong, above (n 107) Part I, 353, 392.

[118] Social Security: Hearing on HR 6675, above (n 108) 308.

[119] ibid, 354, 318.

[120] Executive Hearings Before the H Comm on Ways and Means, 89th Cong, above (n 109) 454.

outstanding popularity in spite of the for-profit sector's lobbying and the critics' desire to curtail government spending.[121]

# IV. The Health Maintenance Organization and Resources Development Act (1973)

The decade following the implementation of the Amendments to the Social Security Act (1965) marked a shift in American health care policy. As health care expenditures were taking a more significant part of the federal budget, reflections on cost-management solutions started entering the political discourse.[122] Policies in the 1960s had aimed to increase the number of health care facilities, had encouraged biomedical research and investments in technology. All of it had to be reversed in the 1970s when the scale tipped in the opposite direction and the sector had to deal with a surplus in beds and physicians. Medicare's 'costplus' reimbursements scheme and its generous guidelines was giving an incentive to hospitals to provide superfluous tests and treatments to Medicare beneficiaries. The 'capital pass-through' provision of Medicare designed to improve patient care also encouraged hospitals to invest in technology and recover all their expenses with substantial cost-allowances.[123] Thus, in the 1970s access and quality of health care services had to be forsaken to prioritise cost reduction and tackle excessive spending.[124]

Paradoxically the growing dissatisfaction with the social security programmes also resurrected the idea of a national health insurance system during the presidential election campaign of 1968. The Democratic Party suggested 'Health Security', a plan under which the government was to be the single and only payer for all the American population's health care services.[125] Conversely, Republican candidate Richard Nixon was opposed to a compulsory federal project; however, for fear of being outdone, he offered his version of a nationalised health plan: the National Health Insurance Partnership Act.[126] Later, in office, he took another concrete step in favour of a regulatory approach to health care spending issues and proposed, in 1971, to enact a public–private partnership between the government and private insurers supported by an employer mandate.[127] The proposition included planning grants, loans and guarantees to introduce some new medical prepaid practice groups named HMOs.[128]

---

[121] Patel and Rushefsky, above (n 3) 129.
[122] ibid, 283.
[123] Almgren, above (n 16) 87–88.
[124] Patel and Rushefsky, above (n 3) 58.
[125] Quadagno, *One Nation, Uninsured*, above (n 21) 110.
[126] P Starr, *The Social Transformation of American Medicine* (New York, Basic Books, 1982) 393–405.
[127] Quadagno, *One Nation, Uninsured*, above (n 21) 115.
[128] Starr, *The Social Transformation of American Medicine*, above (n 126) 396.

Thus, on 29 December 1973, the HMO Act (1973) was passed through Congress and became part of Title XIII of the Public Health Service Act.[129] The government initially committed to a limited trial period to trigger consumers' and providers' interest and allow HMOs to develop.[130] Ultimately, the passage of the Act was a signal that the government had the desire to experiment with new forms of organisational schemes for the delivery of health care services.[131] The American health care system had been thus far comprised of medical entrepreneurs conducting small business ventures and controlling a majority of the system with no shared management or supervision.[132] Patients were often left without any clear response to their queries having to meet multiple providers for each instance of treatment.[133] The traditional model had eroded and triggered deficiencies ranging from a rise in the cost of medical services to an overall decrease in the quality of care.[134] The public's lack of information and the steep decline in the number of qualified primary care physicians had created significant access barriers.[135] Overall, health inequalities were mostly prominent in the poorer and rural parts of the population.[136] Thus, HMOs offered an alternative to this fee-for-service system. In exchange for a fixed monthly or annual prepaid instalment they provided a 'one-stop shop' with a comprehensive range of health services at the heart of each patient's community.[137]

The HMO Act operated another important shift in health care policy as it addressed issues surrounding methods of delivery of care and the structure of health care organisations. Previous reforms had solely focused on the financing and purchasing of health care services. Indeed, Medicare and Medicaid had created an allocation system that granted more Americans with access to care, but neither programme was taking charge of delivery of health care services.[138]

## A. A Cost Management Solution Supported by Insurers and Employers

Evangelical doctor Paul M Ellwood's idea of a health maintenance organisation represented a potent solution for the Nixon Administration to efficiently rationalise

---

[129] Health Maintenance Organization and Resources Development Act, 42 USC §300e (1973).

[130] M Smith Mueller, 'Health Maintenance Organization Act of 1973' *Bulletin* (March 1974) 35.

[131] JL Dorsey, 'The Health Maintenance Organization Act of 1973 (PL 93-222) and Prepaid Group Practice Plans' (1975) 13 *Medical Care* 1, 1.

[132] RT Holley and RJ Carlson, 'The Legal Context for the Development of Health Maintenance Organizations' (1971) 24 *Stanford Law Review* 644, 645.

[133] ibid, 645.

[134] HE Klarman, 'Approaches to Moderating the Increases in Medical Care Costs' (1969) 7 *Medical Care* 175, 175.

[135] Holley and Carlson, above (n 132) 647.

[136] ibid, 646.

[137] Smith Mueller, above (n 130) 35.

[138] Dorsey, above (n 131).

the open-endedness and excessive spending triggered by the federal health care programmes.[139] Inspired by individuals who were dissatisfied with the delivery of health care services, Ellwood had imagined a model closer and more responsive to the needs of the community. He realised that the fee-for-service system had been corrupted and was penalising efficient and competent doctors. According to Ellwood, the only way out of the crisis was to make primary care doctors the gate-keepers of the system. As first port of call to evaluate the patients' illnesses, primary care physicians had to be given the sole authority to refer patients to specialists within a closed network. Ellwood labelled his idea 'HMO' and promoted it to poli-cymakers as a pro-market solution.[140]

The proposition was ideally keeping the private sector in the loop and did not require the immediate expenditure of large sums of money.[141] Despite the AMA's unsurprising reluctance to approve the project, the idea gained the support of employers. Troubled by the rising cost of insurance, employers were more open to a new solution. The corporate sector successfully quelled the AMA's opposition and made the HMO legislation a triumph.[142] Nixon's supporters had understood that these organisations could significantly lower health expenditures by decreas-ing fee-for-service payments and that they could provide an alternative to the passage of a national health insurance plan. HMOs came to represent the promise that costs would be controlled and that, irrespective of one's health status, income, or place of residence, access to the system would be guaranteed.[143]

Concretely, HMOs would contract with providers and offer a relatively comprehensive range of services to their subscribers in exchange for a fixed and periodic instalment.[144] HMOs were to be non-profit organisations and re-inject any profits back into their structure to improve services and maximise the number of insured.[145] As for the employer mandate, corporations of 25 employees or more would have to include an HMO option to any benefit plans, regardless of a state law's prohibition to encourage the initiative.[146] The Act initially provided for a 30-day open-enrolment period every year. However, this provision created significant controversy. HMO managers were convinced that compliance would

---

[139] LD Brown, *Politics and Health Care Organization: HMOs as Federal Policy* (Washington DC, Brookings Institution Press, 1983) 206; see generally, JL Falkson, *HMOs and the Politics of Health Service Reform* (Chicago, IL, American Hospital Associations, 1980).

[140] D Bennahum, 'The Crisis Called Managed Care' in D Bennahum (ed), *Managed Care: Financial, Legal, and Ethical Issues* (Cleveland, OH, Pilgrim Press, 1999) 3; see generally, J Spidle, 'The Historical Roots of Managed Care' in *Managed Care: Financial, Legal and Ethical Issues* in D Bennahum (ed), *Managed Care: Financial, Legal, and Ethical Issues* (Cleveland, OH, Pilgrim Press, 1999) 16.

[141] Quadagno, *One Nation, Uninsured*, above (n 21) 115–16.

[142] ibid, 117.

[143] E Uyehara and M Thomas, 'Health Maintenance Organization and the HMO Act of 1973' (1975) Rand Corporation Paper Series 1.

[144] Dorsey, above (n 131).

[145] See eg, Bennahum, above (n 140); Spidle, above (n 140) 16.

[146] Annas, above (n 8) 780; Health Maintenance Organization and Resources Development Act, 42 USC §300e (1973) s 1310.

result in serious hardship because, in contrast to private insurance programmes, HMOs were not at liberty to turn down high-health-risk subscribers. Eventually this section of the Act was repealed.[147]

By far, preventive care was the most salient feature of these new structures; patients' responsibility was also put at the centre of the decision-making process. The maintenance and preventive care approach that characterised the policy gave it the potential to help control costs significantly. In the past, curative care had been emphasised and had relegated patients to a passive role. Under the new scheme, however, patients would be more likely to utilise primary care resources having paid for all services beforehand and incurring no additional cost upon consultation. Thanks to the prepayment scheme, the HMO system was granting patients some responsibility for their health. In addition, the organisation was providing access to empowering education; this would help patients take the first step in seeking medical assistance and, thereby, reduce costs associated with complications.[148] Specialist doctors nevertheless had reservations regarding the cost-effectiveness of preventive care. They believed that primary care medicine would always come at a high price because of the significant amount of resources that it required to have a minimal impact.[149]

The final version of the HMO Act of course also highlights the market logic behind the initiative.[150] The purpose of the Act was to have business tools to help reduce cost and maximise efficiency. HMOs were to utilise all the economic principles of vertical integration: a sole entity was to be responsible for the chain of command surrounding the treatment of patients and the continuity of care. Quality of care would also be increased thanks to continuous medical records[151] and referrals made within the same entity thereby improving the internal supervision of professionals and providers.[152] The initiative was providing important incentives to reduce costs and increase competition. Under the previous fee-for-service system, doctors had virtually no financial interest in keeping their patients in good health. In contrast, an HMO doctor's revenue would remain the same irrespective of his patients' health status. Thus, fixed and bundle payments were likely to encourage doctors to actively keep enrolees well and avoid unnecessary hospitalisation.[153]

Compared with other large-scale national programmes, the initiative more distinctly targeted the needs of local communities. HMOs created benefits at the

---

[147] Annas, above (n 8) 780–81.

[148] See generally, Uyehara and Thomas, above (n 143) 11.

[149] See generally, SO Schweitzer, 'The Economic of the Early Diagnosis of Disease' (Econometric Society, 1972).

[150] Health Maintenance Organization Act, 42 USC §300e (1973).

[151] See generally, RH Brook and RL Stevenson, 'Effectiveness of Patient Care in an Emergency Room' (1970) 283 *New England Journal of Medicine* 904.

[152] Holley and Carlson, above (n 132) 650.

[153] See generally, L Breslow and JR Hochstim, 'Sociocultural Aspects of Cervical Cytology in Alameda County, Calif' (1964) 79 *Public Health Reports* 107.

local level, fostered infrastructures to help individuals become more independent and flourish within the community. HMOs were not preoccupied with interpersonal relationships, nonetheless, the final version of the Act tackled some health care access barriers with solidarity. Indeed, HMOs were discouraged from skimming high-risk applicants or enrolling exclusively healthy consumers who were less likely to use their services.[154] Organisations were required, during a minimum period of 30 days every 12 months, to enrol a representative sample of consumers based on the population in their area of service. Age, income and other characteristics could not be taken into account to select these enrolees. If the organisation did not comply, its membership would automatically be denied or revoked on the basis of having an unrepresentative pool of consumers.[155]

Open enrolment was a cornerstone of HMO's potential contribution to competition in health care. The benefits of HMO membership had to be extended to the community in order to foster competition between HMOs and other insurance carriers.[156] These managed care entities were intended to palliate adverse selection problems. The Act established a new pooling mechanism that was no longer based on health risk but that mimicked the 1940s community-rated, employer-sponsored insurance schemes.[157] Section 1301(b)(1)(C) of the Act called for fixed payments under a community-rating system to reduce adverse selection, providing freer access and cheaper coverage.[158] Similar to an insurance scheme based on solidarity, the concept of community rating was introduced as a market tool to help reduce the cost of insurance and to provide services to a greater number of enrolees. The 'cost of providing care to the community [had to] be borne equally by all members of the community'.[159] Healthier groups producing more positive externalities would participate in the common good and subsidise the coverage of less healthy groups.[160] The open-enrolment provision prioritised the needs of the community over the welfare of individuals.

The Act also planned for a range of social services to be provided to communities.[161] Section 1307 sets out general guidelines for the administration of these programmes, prioritising HMOs located in medically underserved areas with a clear shortage of personal health services.[162] Control over group practices was also assumed to attract more medical professionals and resources to develop service delivery in those remote areas.[163] Congress surely intended for HMOs to improve the distribution of health care resources in underserved communities.

---

[154] Annas, above (n 8) 780.
[155] Uyehara and Thomas, above (n 143) 5.
[156] S Rep No 97-127 (1981) 60.
[157] ibid, 37–38.
[158] ibid, 35–36.
[159] ibid, 36.
[160] ibid.
[161] ibid, 6.
[162] ibid, 7.
[163] Holley and Carlson, above (n 132) 651.

With regard to the for-profit sector's role under the Act, the most crucial provision was certainly the 'mandatory dual choice',[164] under which employers were required to offer employees the choice of a prepaid practice group or of an individual practice system if available in the local community. Employers were nonetheless only required to match the amount offered by traditional health benefits. If the employee elected to enrol in a different plan, they would be responsible for the difference in the premium.[165] Even though mandatory dual choice provided each employee with greater autonomy,[166] corporate America still had the bigger end of the stick. The private system was untouched, and financial responsibilities unchanged, despite the enactment of the Act.

## B. Ideas of Libertarian and Communitarian Justice

Republican policymakers were pushing for more patient responsibility in health care. Interestingly they chose to borrow the idea of preventive medicine from communitarian systems in order to develop a cost-effective policy. In fact, the Act conveyed both libertarian and communitarian ideas. Both rhetoric also emerged during the five-part Congressional Hearings before the Subcommittee on Public Health and Environment for HMOs.[167] The negotiations also predominantly featured the medical profession and health care facilities managers even though the proposal was most strongly supported by American employers at the initial policy stages.

Indeed, doctors invited to the hearings shared their perspective on the role of hospitals in the community and their duties as physicians. More particularly, Dr Thomas F Frist, Vice President of the Hospital Corporation of America stressed the importance of subsidiarity and local autonomy in dispensing care. Speaking on behalf of his group, he stated:

> We are great in local control. We believe that every hospital in the community should be a community hospital with local autonomy, not taking directives from a central office, but taking aid in help and consultation from our central office. We are a great believer in not losing local autonomy.[168]

---

[164] Health Maintenance Organization Act, 42 USC §300e (1973) s 1301.

[165] Dorsey, above (n 131) 8.

[166] ibid, 7.

[167] Hearings Before the Subcomm on Public Health and Environment of the H Comm on Interstate and Foreign Commerce, Part I, 92nd Cong (1972); Hearings Before the Subcomm on Public Health and Environment of the H Comm on Interstate and Foreign Commerce, Part II, 92nd Cong (1972); Hearings Before the Subcomm on Public Health and Environment of the H Comm. on Interstate and Foreign Commerce, Part III, 92nd Cong (1972); Hearings Before the Subcomm on Public Health and Environment of the H Comm on Interstate and Foreign Commerce, Part IV, 92nd Cong (1972).

[168] Hearings Before the Subcomm on Public Health and Environment of the H Comm on Interstate and Foreign Commerce, Part IV, 92nd Cong (1972) 19.

Many of the for-profit stakeholders' testimonies also mentioned a need for transparency brought by market forces[169] and the importance of finding cost-containment solutions[170] through increased competitiveness[171] in health care evoking traditional ideas of libertarian justice appealing to the allocation of resources through an unsupervised exchange. Other instances[172] insisted on the importance of having 'the HMO compete in the open market with the insurance industry',[173] 'a market ... that allows the HMOs to grow and survive on the basis of their ability to attract physicians and consumers'.[174] Statements also emphasised 'the maximization of health services in providing effective health care, [and an attempt] to minimize the costs in operating the health system'.[175] These ideas assumed that in order to fulfil its 'promises' (efficiency and just allocation), the market had to create competition and enable the expression of individual choices.

A few other instances also stood out as they evoked ideas relating to communitarian justice. For instance, the President of the AHA, Stephen M Morris, made the case for a communitarian approach to health care in order to better represent the interests of society. This required engaging the community in the design of health care policies itself. He explained:

> Through some process, the community is brought in through representation in a meaningful capacity and have a direct input into the policymaking decision body of that organisation. They could be selected in a variety of ways, as long as you assure that there are spokesmen for not only different economic levels within the community, but also different ethnic groups, and so on, and minorities.[176]

Surprisingly, the AMA also supported the intervention adding that 'There [would] be many factors, economic, social, ethnic and racial, which [could] affect

---

[169] ibid, 70.

[170] ibid, 86, 310.

[171] ibid, 120; Hearings Before the Subcomm on Public Health and Environment of the H Comm on Interstate and Foreign Commerce, above (n 167) Part I, 314.

[172] At least 13 instances refer to the idea of health care markets, competition in provision and financing of services and referring to patients as consumers, see Hearings Before the Subcomm on Public Health and Environment of the H Comm. on Interstate and Foreign Commerce, 92nd Cong, above (n 167) Part I, 190, 314; Hearings Before the Subcomm on Public Health and Environment of the H Comm on Interstate and Foreign Commerce, 92nd Cong, above (n 167) Part II, 42, 66, 67, 146, 557; Hearings Before the Subcomm on Public Health and Environment of the H Comm on Interstate and Foreign Commerce, 92nd Cong, above (n 167) Part IV, 19, 70, 86, 120; Hearings Before the Subcomm on Public Health and Environment of the H Comm on Interstate and Foreign Commerce, 93nd Cong (1973) Part I, 83.

[173] Hearings Before the Subcomm on Public Health and Environment of the H Comm on Interstate and Foreign Commerce, 92nd Cong, above (n 167) Part I, 314.

[174] Hearings Before the Subcomm on Public Health and Environment of the H Comm on Interstate and Foreign Commerce, 92nd Cong, above (n 167) Part II, 66.

[175] Hearings Before the Subcomm on Public Health and Environment of the H Comm on Interstate and Foreign Commerce, 92nd Cong, above (n 167) Part IV, 86.

[176] Hearings Before the Subcomm on Public Health and Environment of the H Comm on Interstate and Foreign Commerce, 92nd Cong, above (n 167) Part II, 555.

participation in such program. Nevertheless, it is important to attempt to maintain an enrollment of a cross section of society'.[177]

Ultimately, the Nixon Administration was aiming at promoting individual liberty and allowing competitive forces to control the allocation of health care resources. HMOs were designed to help patient-consumers improve their circumstances through their own initiatives. Empowered thanks to information transparency and their capacity to engage with one centralised institution, patients would surely make responsible choices. Patients were meant to become market agents and active participants in the allocation process. Central government authority was not to interfere with the organisation's subsidiary power. Individuals would receive care at a lower and decentralised level to better address their needs and the issues at a community level. Thus, the final version of the HMO Act directly reflects the changes in the distribution of health care resources in the 1970s. The general perception was that central planning methods had to be set aside because they failed to reduce costs and did not account for individual choices in the same way that market mechanisms would.[178]

## V. The Affordable Care Act (2010)

During the 1990s, Democratic President Bill Clinton made another fruitless attempt at establishing a universal health care system in the United States.[179] Although his ambitious project foundered rapidly, it nonetheless produced an important legacy that inspired a major overhaul two decades later.[180] The Republican health care policies of President Nixon and President Bush during the 1970s and the 1980s also contributed ideas that became relevant during the shift towards a quasi-universal health care system in 2010.[181] The diverse prior initiatives only partly explain the unpredictable and piecemeal outcomes of 'Obamacare'. Interestingly, in 2009 the Democratic Party had achieved its biggest electoral victory since 1964 and it thought to be en route to another major victory with (newly elected) President Barack Obama's health care plan. The unpopularity and the burden of two wars in the Middle East had also helped the Party secure a majority

---

[177] ibid, 360.

[178] Holley and Carlson, above (n 132) 653.

[179] See generally, JS Hacker, *The Road to Nowhere: The Genesis of President Clinton's Plan for Health Security* (Princeton, NJ, Princeton University Press, 1997).

[180] President Bill Clinton encouraged states to apply for Medicaid waiver programmes, extended coverage for children and enacted the Health Insurance Portability and Accountability Act (1996) regulating insurance companies.

[181] The Republican Party sponsored HEART that brought about the Healthy American Act 2006 first proposing an individual mandate in health care. The idea was thereafter picked up by the Democratic Party. See J Quadagno, 'Right-Wing Conspiracy? Socialist Plot? The Origins of the Patient Protection and Affordable Care Act' (2014) 39 *Journal of Health Politics, Policy and Law* 35.

in the House of Representatives and the Senate.[182] Nevertheless, in spite of having complete control of all levels of government, the Democrats struggled to push the initial version of the ACA through Congress.[183]

In essence, the proposed health care reform was to 'provide affordable, quality health care for all Americans and reduce the growth in health care spending'.[184] First on the agenda was reducing the number of uninsured that had reached 50.7 million in 2009.[185] The insurance industry would be brought on board to guarantee that underwriters no longer refused applicants based on records of pre-existing conditions and that they limited increases in premiums. The dominant employer-based coverage would also have to be reformed to tackle the number of uninsured employees. The initial proposal also suggested a reform of Medicare's prescription drug coverage. Part D of the Social Security Program subsidised the costs of prescription drugs and prescription drug insurance premiums but had senior Americans pay substantial amounts out of pocket for medicines. Finally, the Obama Administration called for an extension of Medicaid's coverage for the 15 million Americans who did not meet the poverty threshold but who were nonetheless unable to afford the purchase of medical insurance.[186]

Initially underwriters were in support of the plan, a position that contrasted sharply with the hostility they had showed towards the Clinton health care reform in 1993. Certainly, insurers saw the universal requirement for coverage (the individual mandate) as a business opportunity that made up for the selective coverage prohibition imposed by the reform.[187] Similarly, the medical profession approved of the project.[188] What was remarkable, however, was the silence of major employers on the policy.[189]

Political forces, on the other hand, were categorically irreconcilable even though a bipartisan compromise had to be found in order for the proposed Bill to pass Congress' muster. On one side, conservatives worried about the repercussions of governmental interference in the realm of health care and the far Right Tea Party were creating a blockage. On the other, Democrats were pushing hard for the federally funded health care plan.[190] With a second term in office in sight,

---

[182] Patel and Rushefsky, above (n 3) 362.

[183] D Béland, P Rocco and A Waddan, 'Obamacare and the Politics of Universal Health Insurance Coverage in the United States' (2016) 50 *Social Policy & Administration* 428, 441.

[184] Patient Protection and Affordable Care Act, 42 USC § 18001 (2010).

[185] US Census Bureau, *Income, Poverty, and Health Insurance Coverage in the United States: 2010* (Washington DC, US Census Bureau, 2011), available at: www.census.gov/prod/2011pubs/p60-239.pdf.

[186] HS Berliner, 'Medicaid After the Supreme Court Decision' (2013) 8(1) *Health Economics, Policy and Law* 133, 134.

[187] Starr, *Remedy and Reaction*, above (n 13) 194–235.

[188] R Kirsch, 'The Politics of Obamacare: Health Care, Money, and Ideology' (2013) 81 *Fordham Law Review* 1737, 1740–44.

[189] See generally, ME Smyrl, 'Beyond Interests and Institutions: US Health Policy Reform and the Surprising Silence of Big Business' (2014) 39 *Journal of Health Politics, Policy and Law* 5.

[190] Starr, *Remedy and Reaction*, above (n 13) 214.

however, President Obama decided to move quickly and make the Bill into a law before the start of the presidential election campaign.

Thus, on 23 March 2010, after strenuous negotiations and a difficult reconciliation process, a compromised version was enacted. Unfortunately, the Obama Administration and Democratic Party enjoyed only a short-lived victory, as many states were starting to challenge the constitutionality of the health care law.[191] Adding to this looming judicial battle was eroding public support. The many stories of middle-income Americans affected by health care bankruptcy had initially helped gather the support of the population for a reform of the system but public opinion became deeply divided during the first stages of implementation.[192] The controversy reached its climax in the spring of 2012 when the Supreme Court heard an expedited case challenging both the individual mandate portion of the law and the Medicaid expansion of federal programmes portions of the ACA.[193]

## A.  Negotiating Universality Health Care with the For-Profit Sector

By and large, the intricacy of the ACA's final version stems from the many waves of negotiations that took place before reaching a compromise. The Act's complex nature also flows from its comprehensiveness. In fact, the reform was described as the most complete health care reform since the enactment of the Amendments to the Social Security Act (1965) that had set up Medicare and Medicaid. Indeed, only a handful of areas in health care were left untouched. Looking at the bigger picture, the Act made at least three notable contributions to American health care policy.

First, it established two mandates: one geared towards individuals and one geared towards employers. The individual mandate required all Americans to seek insurance coverage and failure to comply would result in a financial penalty. To help achieve this particular provision the insurance industry had to relax enrolment criteria and accept applicants regardless of pre-existing conditions.[194] Insurers were willing to compromise on these aspects considering that the individual mandate would bring in a new pool of young healthy applicants to spread actuarial risk and sponsor the cost of the riskier and older applicants.[195] Insurers also

---

[191] See generally, White, above (n 17).

[192] 'Kaiser Health Tracking Poll: The Public's Views on the Affordable Care Act' (Henry J Kaiser Family Foundation 2017), available at: www.kff.org/interactive/kaiser-health-tracking-poll-the-publics-views-on-the-aca/#?response=Favorable--Unfavorable&aRange=twoYear.

[193] *National Federation of Independent Business v Sebelius* 567 US 519 (2012).

[194] Patel and Rushefsky, above (n 3) 375.

[195] See generally, Luke Mitchell, 'Sick in the Head: Why America Won't Get the Health-Care System It Needs' [2009] *Harper's* 11.

became particularly supportive of the provision as they realised it would serve their political interests, quashing a public option to finance health care services in the United States. The industry had been lobbying extensively against a public system that would provide the insured with a more affordable and more attractive option than their commercial plans.[196]

The Act also established an employer mandate that required employers to provide their employees with an affordable insurance option. Failure to comply would result in financial penalties.[197] Large and small employers, as well as workers' unions, had a lot at stake in the negotiation. The government had the desire to re-examine employer-based insurance and enhance workplace wellness programmes.[198] Essentially, the future of this system was put in the hands of the health care policymakers, as employers were not substantially contributing to the conversation.[199]

A second important contribution made by the ACA, also in an effort to reduce health care costs and expand coverage, was the creation of health care insurance exchanges.[200] The law called for states to create virtual market places for the benefit of applicants seeking coverage from non-group insurance. However, in the event that a state would refuse or fail to set up the exchange, the federal government would step in, create and run the virtual platform.[201] More than simply offering an opportunity to purchase insurance, the exchanges would have the ability to assist any applicant with choosing the most appropriate insurance plan and to help them determine whether they were eligible for public programmes.[202] In principle, the competition generated by the managed market places was to drive down insurance prices and provide applicants with more purchasing autonomy.[203] The provision was based on the theoretical assumption that insurance exchanges were more likely to achieve satisfactory results as they have capacity to create stable insurance pools with virtually no adverse selection. The insurance exchange programmes would extend these advantages to small employers and individuals to produce many positive externalities, such as lower transaction costs, increased

---

[196] Jonathan Martin, 'SEIU Takes Pragmatic Stance' *Politico* (24 September 2009), available at: www. politico.com/news/stories/0909/27502.html; Tom Hamburger and Kim Geiger, 'Healthcare Insurers Get Upper Hand' *Los Angeles Times* (24 August 2009).

[197] US Chamber of Commerce, *Employer Mandate* (2015).

[198] See generally, AE Moran, 'Wellness Programs After the Affordable Care Act' (2013) 39 *Employee Relations Law Journal* 75.

[199] See generally, J Quadagno, 'The Role of Specific Political Factors: Interest-Group Influence on the Patient Protection and Affordability Act of 2010: Winners and Losers in the Health Care Reform Debate' (2011) 36 *Journal of Health Politics, Policy and Law* 449.

[200] See generally, Stephen Zuckerman and John Holahan, 'Despite Criticism, the Affordable Care Act Does Much to Contain Health Care Costs' (2012) (October) *The Urban Institute Policy Center* 1.

[201] Patel and Rushefsky, above (n 3) 376.

[202] See generally, B Fernandez and AL Mach, *Health Insurance Exchanges Under the Patient Protection and Affordable Care Act* (Washington DC, Congressional Research Service, 2013); Patel and Rushefsky, above (n 3) 376.

[203] Patel and Rushefsky, above (n 3) 379.

competition, and multiple options for coverage.[204] As of April 2018, 16 states and the District of Columbia had set up state-run insurance markets and 34 states were fully or partially operated by the federal government.[205]

The third pivotal contribution made by reform was the expansion of the Social Security programmes (Medicaid and Medicare). The law would require states to expand the Medicaid eligibility for individuals up to 138 per cent of the federal poverty line in order to eradicate the 'Medicaid gap' that had left four million adults uninsured because their income exceeded the threshold but remained too low to qualify for coverage through state exchanges.[206] Medicare part D relating to the coverage of the cost of prescription drugs was also to be expanded to gradually tackle another loophole in the system.[207]

The goal of the ACA was to ultimately ensure that insurance markets would no longer be structured on risk assessments but focused on improving health care delivery and efficiency. The Act thereby took a unique and radical approach that fundamentally modified the role of the for-profit sector in the American health care system.[208]

## B. Libertarian Ideas of Justice Versus Ideas of Liberal Equality

The hearings surrounding the ACA were lengthy and animated. They addressed decisive issues that led a new approach to health care financing in the United States. An analysis of discourses of justice in the four-part Hearing before the Committee on Ways and Means of the House of Representatives[209] and the two-part Hearing of the Committee on Health, Education, Labor, and Pensions of the Senate, reveal arguments in favour and against the proposed reform. Strikingly, ideas of justice are present in nearly all the 1,093 pages of hearings. These discussions also evoked

---

[204] Timothy S Jost, 'Health Insurance Exchanges and the Affordable Care Act: Eight Difficult Issues' (The Commonwealth Fund, 2010), available at: www.commonwealthfund.org/publications/fund-reports/2010/sep/health-insurance-exchanges-and-the-affordable-care-act.

[205] 'State Health Insurance Marketplace Types' (Henry J Kaiser Family Foundation, 2018), available at: www.kff.org/health-reform/slide/state-decisions-for-creating-health-insurance-exchanges.

[206] See generally, BD Sommers, 'Health Care Reform's Unfinished Work: Remaining Barriers to Coverage and Access' (2015) 373 *New England Journal of Medicine* 2395.

[207] Patel and Rushefsky, above (n 3) 378.

[208] A Monahan and D Schwarcz, 'Will Employers Undermine Health Care Reform by Dumping Sick Employees?' (2011) 97 *Virginia Law Review* 125, 147.

[209] Health Reform in the 21st Century: Hearings Before the H Comm on Ways and Means, 111th Cong (2009) Part I; Health Reform in the 21st Century: Hearings Before the H Comm on Ways and Means, 111th Cong (2009) Part II; Health Reform in the 21st Century: Hearings Before the H Comm on Ways and Means, 111th Cong (2009) Part III; Health Reform in the 21st Century: Hearings Before the H Comm on Ways and Means, 111th Cong (2009) Part IV; Hearings Before the S Comm on Health, Education, Labor, and Pensions, 111th Cong (2009) Part I; Hearings Before the S Comm on Health, Education, Labor, and Pensions, 111th Cong. (2009) Part II.

the divisive health care policy in debate in the United States, as both camps used the rhetoric of justice to defend their positions.

On one side, the moderate and ultra conservative witnesses made numerous references to classic libertarian ideas to advocate a more competitive and cost-effective[210] market[211] for health care. For instance, Dr Gratzer, a Senior Fellow at the conservative think tank, the Manhattan Institute for Policy Research, claimed that:

> Market competition can contain the high cost of insurance – if Congress and the States would only allow it to take place. Efforts at creating equity and fairness in the health insurance market – done with the best intentions – have created dramatic differences in price across the country … The Federal Government can promote regulatory strategies that will increase interstate insurance competition.[212]

Conservative witnesses also reiterated other fundamental precepts of the libertarian theory, namely, a just allocation free of state intervention. They thereby argued in favour of the status quo as they were particularly critical of the idea of having a federally organised system that could disrupt the private insurance market and negatively impact America's competitiveness.[213]

Conversely, liberals and Democrats in favour of the initiative upheld their views on affordable coverage options[214] and universal health care for vulnerable groups[215] by relaying ideas in support of welfare equality.[216] They argued that the proposed reform had to equalise the capacity of needy and vulnerable individuals to access health care rather than provide them with equal health care resources. In fact, more than 14 instances condemned private insurers' treatment of high-risk applicants and demanded that the law abolish discrimination based on

---

[210] Health Reform in the 21st Century: Hearings Before the H Comm on Ways and Means, 111th Cong, above (n 209) Part I, 213.

[211] Health Reform in the 21st Century: Hearings Before the H Comm on Ways and Means, 111th Cong, above (n 209) Part I, 10, 49, 268; ibid, Part II, 13; ibid, Part III, 13, 25, 29, 35, 79; Hearings Before the S Comm on Health, Education, Labor, and Pensions, 111th Cong, above (n 209) Part I, 33, 68, 72.

[212] Health Reform in the 21st Century: Hearings Before the H Comm on Ways and Means, 111th Cong, above (n 209) Part I, 49.

[213] Health Reform in the 21st Century: Hearings Before the H Comm on Ways and Means, 111th Cong, above (n 209) Part III, 41; Hearings Before the S Comm on Health, Education, Labor, and Pensions, 111th Cong, above (n 210) Part I, 43, 57.

[214] Health Reform in the 21st Century: Hearings Before the H Comm on Ways and Means, 111th Cong, above (n 209) Part I, 201, 130, 131, 133, 235; ibid, Part II, 27; ibid, Part III, 121; ibid, Part IV, 44; Hearings Before the S Comm on Health, Education, Labor, and Pensions, 111th Cong, above (n 209) Part II, 36, 37.

[215] Health Reform in the 21st Century: Hearings Before the H Comm on Ways and Means, 111th Cong, above (n 209) Part I, 119, 143, 149, 217, 324, 333, 336, 339, 343, 347, 399; ibid, Part III, 30, 60, 112, 114; Health Reform in the 21st Century: Hearings Before the H Comm on Ways and Means, 111th Cong, above (n 209) Part IV, 15, 16, 18, 35; Hearings Before the S Comm on Health, Education, Labor, and Pensions, 111th Cong, above (n 209) Part I, 55; ibid, Part II, 13, 15, 18, 36, 43, 44.

[216] Health Reform in the 21st Century: Hearings Before the H Comm on Ways and Means, 111th Cong, above (n 209) Part I, 99, 115, 123, 168, 324, 337, 343, 389, 384, 399; ibid, Part IV; Hearings Before the S Comm on Health, Education, Labor, and Pensions, 111th Cong, above (n 209) Part II, 11, 38.

pre-existing conditions.[217] The Department of Health and Human Services Secretary Kathleen Sebelius, herself a staunch advocate of the reform, restated the importance of 'getting rid of some of the pre-existing medical condition barriers that allow a skewed market'.[218]

At expected, the proponents of the welfare egalitarian approach were critical of the libertarian discourse and the allocation of health care resources through an unregulated market.[219] Some witnesses also reflected on the uniqueness of health care and its 'social good' attributes.[220] Dr Flowers, Co-Chair of Physicians for a National Health Program, pointed out that 'the price we are paying for the profit-driven healthcare market is the squandering of our economic, mental and physical health as a Nation. The market is the wrong model. Healthcare is not a commodity. It is a human right'.[221] Esteemed Professor of Political Economy, Uwe Reinhardt, also asserted that 'Americans, too believe that our health system ought to be operated on the *Principle of Social Solidarity*, that is, that health care should be viewed as a social good'.[222]

All the negotiations raised pragmatic concerns regarding the financing and delivery of health care. An underlying social discussion also brought to the surface considerations of justice that polarised the debate. Although a faction of the for-profit sector was keen on protecting its interests, many other for-profit stakeholders saw the project as an opportunity to rectify the trajectory that had been crippling the American health care system.

## C.  An Unprecedented Judicial Battle

Following the brief period of conciliation that led to the enactment of the ACA, there began a tumultuous phase of implementation. Although comprehensive, the Act had left the system in a fragmented state. Employer-based insurance was still the most important form of private coverage and Medicare and Medicaid remained responsible for the majority of America's health care needs.[223] The reform also

---

[217] Health Reform in the 21st Century: Hearings Before the H Comm on Ways and Means, 111th Cong, above (n 209) Part I, 121, 136, 324, 344; ibid, Part II, 13, 16; ibid, Part III, 6, 115; ibid, Part IV, 17, 85, 144; Hearings Before the S Comm on Health, Education, Labor, and Pensions, 111th Cong, above (n 209) Part I, 35, 36; ibid, Part II, 36.

[218] Health Reform in the 21st Century: Hearings Before the H Comm on Ways and Means, 111th Cong, above (n 209) Part II, 13.

[219] Health Reform in the 21st Century: Hearings Before the H Comm on Ways and Means, 111th Cong, above (n 209) Part III, 28; ibid, Part IV, 17.

[220] Health Reform in the 21st Century: Hearings Before the H Comm on Ways and Means, 111th Cong, above (n 209) Part II, 75; ibid, Part IV, 14, 15, 16, 17, 22, 23, 98.

[221] Hearings Before the S Comm on Health, Education, Labor, and Pensions, 111th Cong, above (n 209) Part I).

[222] Health Reform in the 21st Century: Hearings Before the H Comm on Ways and Means, 111th Cong, above (n 209) Part IV, 15.

[223] Patel and Rushefsky, above (n 3) 395.

demanded a lot of heavy lifting and resources from individual states, be it for the creation of health care exchanges or the expansion of Medicaid.[224] Rapidly the discontent stateside grew into a firm opposition leading state attorneys general to file over 27 lawsuits.[225] Most challenges attacked the constitutionality of the individual health insurance mandate on the basis that the provision substantially infringed individual freedom and that Congress and federal government had no prerogative to interfere with individual property rights by imposing the purchase of goods.[226] The cases were eventually combined into the *National Federation of Independent Businesses, et al v Sebelius*[227] recourse presented before the Supreme Court of the United States in the spring of 2012.[228]

On 28 June 2012 the Court handed its decision in the twofold case. The first part of the judgment explored the reasons for upholding the ACA's individual mandate. With a majority of 5:4 the Justices had ruled that the provision constituted an invitation rather than an order to purchase insurance. The mandate was therefore a constitutional act of Congress authorised through its power to tax and spend for the welfare of its citizens and the penalty associated with non-compliance was to be interpreted as a tax and not a fine. Chief Justice Roberts' opinion supporting the decision provided what commentators interpreted as a high-minded approach that intended to bridge the Court's ideological divide and restore its reputation. Others found, to the contrary, that his opinion was merely an impoverished reading of the Commerce Clause jurisprudence, which would further narrow the powers of the federal government in coming decades.[229]

Remarkably, no references were made to equality, fairness or ideas of justice even though the challenge created an opportunity for high-level constitutional lawyers to raise resource-allocation issues before the Supreme Court. In fact, the decision did not constitute an out-of-the-box judgment. No core issues of distributive justice were addressed or argued before the Court. Issues were resolved with a conventional reading of the Constitution and nuanced with some political considerations. The Court also failed to recognise that, because of their importance in American society, health care resources had to be distributed according to principles of justice. Controversially, Justice Scalia offered a plea in favour of repealing

---

[224] RF Rich, E Cheung and R Lurvey, 'The Patient Protection and Affordable Care Act of 2010: Implementation Challenges in the Context of Federalism' (2013) 16 *Journal of Health Care Law & Policy* 77, 85; Sirpal, above (n 14) 327.

[225] Paige Winfield Cunningham, 'Rebellion by States Could be Hazardous to Health Care Overhaul' *The Washington Times* (25 August 2011), available at: www.washingtontimes.com/news/2011/aug/25/rebellion-by-states-could-be-hazardous-to-health-c; Brandon Stewart, 'List of 27 States Suing Over Obamacare' *The Daily Signal* (17 January 2011), available at: www.dailysignal.com/2011/01/17/list-of-states-suing-over-obamacare.

[226] See generally, M Buettgens, B Garrett and J Holahan, 'Why the Individual Mandate Matters' (The Urban Institute, 2010).

[227] *National Federation of Independent Business v Sebelius* 567 US 519 (2012).

[228] Patel and Rushefsky, above (n 3) 15.

[229] See generally, C Fried, 'The June Surprises: Balls, Strikes, and the Fog of War' (2013) 38 *Journal of Health Politics, Policy and Law* 225.

the individual mandate and even compared the purchase of health care insurance to the purchase of a crown of broccoli.[230] Justice Ginsburg nonetheless rebutted the analogy and explained that health care resources were unique as all members of society may require health care during their lifetime and the same could not be said of any other consumer good.[231]

Ultimately, the individual mandate was intended to achieve a quasi-universal health care system in the United States. In certain aspects the provision relays elements of welfare equality. It proposes that a portion of an individual's income be dedicated to increase health *functionings*. Improving the prospect of coverage for uninsured and under-insured Americans equalises access to health care services and increases the overall population's capacity to achieve a higher level of welfare. Nonetheless, the Court's decision was not grounded in a discussion of universality of care, nor did it address any other broader legal issues such as the absence of a right to health care in the United States.

However, the decision did address a second issue relating to the validity of Medicaid's expansion under the ACA.[232] Initially the power of the federal government to compel action through funding was not brought into question, but shortly after the implementation states realised that it was not possible to opt out of the requirement without losing federal funds that were available under the original Medicaid programme and that the penalty for non-compliance with the provision was too severe. The programme's expansion was initially projected to insure 32 million Americans, with almost half being childless adults.[233] Essentially, the ACA was to create a new mandatory coverage requirement for this population, but if a state chose not to cover the new group, it would lose all its Medicaid funding. Thus, the 26 states that led the challenge argued that the provision was coercive. Since they could not afford to lose Medicaid funding they felt compelled to expand the coverage.[234]

Seven to two Justices ruled that the expansion was indeed impermissible and concluded that even though Congress may attach conditions to federal funds, tying new money and existing Medicaid payments to participation in the expansion violated the Tenth Amendment of the Constitution.[235] Chief Justice Roberts also explained that the expansion was 'no longer a program to meet the health care needs of the neediest among us but an element of a national plan to provide universal health insurance coverage' and that states had not agreed nor could

---

[230] *National Federation of Independent Business v Sebelius* 567 US 519 (2012) I C.

[231] 'Unlike the market for almost any other product [(including broccoli)] or service, the market for medical care is one in which all individuals inevitably participate. Virtually every person residing in the United States, sooner or later, will visit a doctor or other health care professional'. In *National Federation of Independent Business v Sebelius* 567 US 519 (2012) II D a.

[232] Berliner, above (n 186) 133.

[233] ibid, 134.

[234] ibid 135.

[235] ibid.

have anticipated such a drastic change in the Medicaid programme.[236] The federal government could therefore spend for the general welfare; however, its ability to address rationing issues and to impose a programme that could benefit the most vulnerable part of the population was significantly curtailed by the decision.

On the whole, the Supreme Court judgment in *National Federation of Independent Businesses, et al v Sebelius* should be read in the light of the American constitutional tradition that refuses to recognise a category of positive rights to health care. The decision illustrates the Court's inability to directly address distributive justice issues without leaning on the Constitution. Throughout it avoided a discussion on rationing in health care. The Court also failed to recognise the importance of contextualisation required by the reform. As the federal government attempted to achieve in an unparalleled manner universal health care in the United States, the Court should have adapted its interpretation to reflect the tumultuous history of American health care policy. Essentially, the Court's judgment should have accounted for the issues that have affected health care policy in the United States that led up to the enactment of the ACA instead of reverting to a sterile interpretation of the Constitution.[237]

To date, Republicans and conservative politicians are still steadfastly opposed to the ACA and have made 60 attempts to dismantle and repeal the law.[238] Among which, are two other failed Supreme Court challenges in the cases of *King v Burwell* (2015)[239] and *Zubik v Burwell* (2016).[240]

# VI. Conclusion

Health care reforms in the United States reflect health care policy's constant oscillation between the project of a federal health care system and the opposite ambition of having health care resources allocated through a free market.

With a favourable social and political climate in the 1960s, the federal government envisaged the expansion of social security to provide coverage for the elderly. The failed attempt that constituted the Kerr–Mills Act (1960) offered a crucial

---

[236] See generally, RM Landers, 'The Dénouement of the Supreme Court's ACA Drama' (2012) 367 *New England Journal of Medicine* 198.

[237] S Germain, 'Taking "Health" as a Socio-Economic Right Seriously: Is the South African Constitutional Dialogue a Remedy for the American Healthcare System?' (2013) 21 *African Journal of International and Comparative Law* 145, 163–69.

[238] Richard Cowan and Susan Cornwell, 'House Votes to Being Repealing Obamacare' *Reuters* (Washington DC, 13 January 2017), available at: www.reuters.com/article/us-usa-obamacare/house-votes-to-begin-repealing-obamacare-idUSKBN14X1SK.

[239] In *King v Burwell* 576 US (2015), the Supreme Court provided an interpretation of the provisions pertaining to tax credits and insurance exchanges of the ACA.

[240] *Zubik v Burwell* 578 US (2016), challenged to the contraceptive mandate of the ACA.

stepping stone towards a bolder policy that would redefine health care financing in the twentieth century. The enactment of the Amendments to the Social Security Act (1965) leading to the creation of Medicare and Medicaid brought quasi-universal coverage to the American population. Visibly both programmes were the result of a compromise struck with medical professionals and insurers. Similar to debates around the Kerr–Mills Act, negotiations of the amendments relayed many elements of liberal equality.

In the 1970s for-profit actors continued to shape the American health care system as the Republicans came into power and attempted to reduce the out-of-control health care spending. American employers' considerable input and influence on institutions of power helped shape President Nixon's HMO initiative. Presented as a market policy, HMO offered a new mode of delivery rooted in the idea of community input and local access to care. Naturally, ideas of libertarian justice and communitarianism were brought forward during Congressional hearings on the HMO Act (1973).

The end of the century saw yet another attempt to organise a federal health care system. However, President Clinton's plan never came to fruition. Two decades later President Obama successfully reconciled the traditionally opposing views on health care to offer one of the most comprehensive and controversial reforms in history. Once more, old and new ideas of justice entered the debate. Opponents of the Act preferred libertarian rhetoric and supporters argued in favour of equal access to health care.

By and large, despite consistent efforts to curb expenses and remove access barriers, throughout history for-profit stakeholders have successfully opposed the socialisation of medicine and consolidated an incremental system to finance and deliver health care.[241] The history and analysis of laws implementing major health care reforms further expose path dependency in American health care policy, something that has precluded the achievement of universal health care in the United States. Essentially, the powerful trifecta of doctors, insurers and employers has used rhetoric and ideas of justice to set modes of distribution that secured their vested interests.[242]

---

[241] See generally, E Elhauge, *The Fragmentation of US Health Care: Causes and Solutions* (Oxford, Oxford University Press, 2010); During the course of the 20th century, seven major legislative attempts were made to attain some form of universal health care system in the United States. See TJ Litman and LS Robins, *Health Politics and Policy*, 2nd edn (New York, Delmar, 1991) 4.

[242] Patel and Rushefsky, above (n 3) 56.

# 5

## For-Profit Stakeholders in British Health Care Policy

'There is only one thing worse than fighting with allies, and that is fighting without them'.[1]

Winston S Churchill

## I. Introduction

The relationship of for-profit actors with each of the governments in power in the United Kingdom has defined the stakeholders' role in the British health care system. At the inception of the NHS, policy was built on a democratic consensus that encouraged doctors to participate in the elaboration of strategies that directly impacted the delivery of health care services. Commitment on the part of the medical profession had to be secured in order to provide health care services throughout the country and universally.[2] The NHS was then structured along bureaucratic lines, where the government would command the policy agreed away from public scrutiny and control outcomes with its monopoly on the allocation of health care resources.[3] Essentially, the 'compact' that the profession had negotiated with the post-war government had created a relationship of co-dependency between the doctors and Whitehall. The system needed the profession to deliver and organise health care services, and the profession needed the system to survive.[4]

However, during the course of the 1970s scarcity of resources had led the NHS to stagnate. Discretionary decisions at the clinical level were also blamed for the lack of efficiency affecting health care services.[5] Thus, in the 1980s, 'command and control' was replaced with the Thatcher government's market approach in

---

[1] Winston Churchill, Chequers (1 April 1945).
[2] D King and E Mossialos, 'The Determinants of Private Medical Insurance Prevalence in England, 1997–2000' (2005) 40(1) *Health Services Research* 195, 195–96.
[3] A Cawson, *Corporatism and Welfare: Social Policy and State Intervention in Britain* (London, Heinemann Educational Publishers, 1982) 89.
[4] I Crinson, *Health Policy: A Critical Perspective* (London, Sage Publications, 2009) 111.
[5] ibid.

health care.[6] The government no longer needed the medical profession's stamp of approval to legitimise reforms and doctors had lost their hegemony over health care policy.[7] The Conservative government had embarked on a redesign of the organisation and introduced the purchaser–provider divide in health care. As the Labour Party came into power in the late 1990s, the commercialisation of medicine was also undertaken.[8] This time the change more directly affected the status of the medical profession as GP and consultant contracts were renegotiated.[9]

New Labour also encouraged the participation of the private sector in health care financing with the pursuit of private financing initiatives.[10] The consumerist turn that had been initiated in the 1990s was eventually completed by the Coalition government in the 2000s. The radical reform in fact went beyond New Labour's policies. The Health and Social Care Act (2012) placed the patient at the heart of the system and gave medical professionals a support role. Health care had become a market; the private sector was now encouraged to compete with the profession to provide the best and most cost-efficient services to patients. These changes also shaped the place given to the independent sector (private and corporate entities) in the financing and provision of health care services in the twenty-first century.

Thus, over the past 70 years 'the compact' between the government and the medical profession has transformed from a 'command-control' model into a system focusing on choice and flexibility in the provision of health care services to embrace a patient-focused and consumerist model.[11] Obviously, as the profession reacted and adapted to policy shifts each of these approaches has had a considerable impact on the autonomy and the role of doctors. This chapter therefore proposes to examine in greater detail each phase of the relationship to determine the degree of influence the medical profession may have had on British health care reforms. The first part fleshes out elements of a broader social context and looks at the medical profession's role in the health care system in time, as well as its reaction to these pivotal moments. This analysis will help explain how the profession's response has shaped its role in health care policy. The remainder of the chapter examines more broadly the role of the private sector in health care looking beyond the role of the medical profession. In the last part of the chapter, attention is given to the different private initiatives in health care focusing on the PFI and

---

[6] J Allsop, *Health Policy and the NHS Towards 2000* (London, Longman, 1995) xii.

[7] R Klein, 'Carolyn Hughes Tuohy, Accidental Logics: The Dynamics of Change in the Health Care Arena in the United States, Britain and Canada' Book Review (2000) 20 *Journal of Public Policy* 105, 106.

[8] C Newdick, 'Promoting Access and Equity in Health: Assessing the National Health Service in England' in CM Flood and A Gross (eds), *The Right to Health at the Public/Private Divide: A Global Comparative Study* (Cambridge, Cambridge University Press, 2014).

[9] PL Bradshaw and G Bradshaw, *Health Policy for Health Care Professionals* (London, Sage Publications, 2004) 14.

[10] Newdick, above (n 8) 109.

[11] Allsop, above (n 6) 9.

LIFT schemes of the 1990s, the parallel market of private medical insurance and the growing role of the independent sector in satisfying consumerist health care policy.

# II.  The Medical Profession: A Defensive and Dissident Force

The conflicted relationship between doctors and the British state has shaped numerous aspects of major health care reforms in the United Kingdom. Right at the inception the medical profession was able to gain significant leverage because of its opposition to Aneurin Bevan the Minister for Health's project of a universal health care system. Through tough negotiations, it secured its independence and a 'tacit' concordat that gave it the power to exert strong influence over health care policy at the systemic level. For the following three decades, the medical profession was therefore consistently involved in decisions affecting clinical care as well as decisions impacting the organisation of the health care system.[12] The profession had successfully established a 'monopoly of legitimacy' because of its expertise and influence.[13] The British Medical Association (BMA) (the medical profession's trade union) along with the prestigious institutions of the Royal Colleges of Medicine helped the profession gain some traction in health care policy.[14] However, during the course of the 1980s the government began to limit the role of the medical profession in policymaking to more unilaterally impose cost-containing measures. From that point forward the medical profession had to adapt to major changes in the NHS in order to preserve its role and the core values upholding the universal health care system.

Through a historical narrative, the following section aims to explain the role of the medical profession in the NHS during these key reformative periods to better understand the changing nature of its engagement in health care policy. The analysis also sheds light on the part played by representatives of the medical profession, the BMA and Royal Colleges of Medicine in health care policy shaping.

## A.  Establishing the Terms of the Concordat (1950s–70s)

During the late nineteenth century, as trade unions propelled the debate on public assistance to the national level, foundations were laid for welfare, education and health care reforms. Following suit, the Liberal government introduced the

---

[12] CH Tuohy, 'Dynamics of a Changing Health Sphere: The United States, Britain, and Canada' (1999) 18(3) *Health Affairs* 114, 118.

[13] R Klein, *The New Politics of the NHS: From Creation to Reinvention*, 7th edn (London, Radcliffe Publishing, 2013) 51–52.

[14] R Baggott, *Understanding Health Policy* (Bristol, Policy Press, 2015) 118.

National Insurance Act (1911) at the beginning of the twentieth century to help workers secure health coverage. This entailed a contribution on the part of the employee and the employer, as well as a small state subsidy. Although dependants remained uninsurable and hospital care was left outside the scope of the scheme, GP services, prescriptions and treatment for tuberculosis were made available free of charge under these policies.[15]

Because of their inability to secure any form of coverage, the poorer and unemployed parts of the population struggled to gain access to the private voluntary hospitals. Most often, these patients were redirected towards the Poor Law System of public health care facilities. In some places, conditions were so dreadful that vulnerable women were forced to give birth on the street.[16] The piecemeal and incremental method of health care delivery was affecting the nation and a systemic approach had yet to be established. The needs of different social groups were met incidentally by a patchwork of coverage and provision, and dramatically lacked coordination. Thus, in 1926 a Royal Commission proposed to finance health care services through general taxation in order to guarantee access to health care services for the entire population.[17] Even though the changes represented minor advances for medical services, they provided an important new perspective that triggered a change in the public's attitude towards hospital care.[18]

Doctors, for their part, remained a highly autonomous and self-regulating profession, with a lack of accountability and representation towards the population. Social historian Arthur Marwick went so far as describing the state of pre-war health care in the United Kingdom as 'a primitively unstable mixture of class prejudice, commercial self-interest, professional altruism, vested interest, and demarcation disputes'.[19] The medical profession was protective of the clinical autonomy it had secured with its expertise and social status.[20] During the Second World War, however, with the advent of the Emergency Medical Service,[21] politicians were forced to generate solutions and discuss issues with members of the profession.[22]

The Coalition government also tasked Sir William Beveridge with drafting a report that aimed to take stock and reflect on the general state of the welfare system.[23] The conclusions of the *Social Insurance and Allied Services*[24] review,

---

[15] S Boyle, 'United Kingdom (England): Health System Review' (WHO Regional Office of Europe, 2011) 25; A Wall and B Owen, *Health Policy*, 2nd edn (London, Routledge, 2002) 5.

[16] Crinson, above (n 4) 59; S Ainsworth, 'The Birth of the NHS' (2008) 36(1) *Practice Nurse* 38, 38.

[17] N Vetter, *The Public Health and the NHS: Your Questions Answered* (Oxon, Radcliffe Medical Press, 1998) 22–24.

[18] ibid, 24.

[19] T Delamothe, 'NHS at 60: Founding Principles' (2008) 336 *British Medical Journal* 1216, 1218.

[20] Crinson, above (n 4) 110.

[21] R Titmuss, *History of the Second World War: Problems of Social Policy* (London, HM Stationery Office, 1950) 54–73.

[22] Wall and Owen, above (n 15) 5.

[23] Vetter, above (n 17) 26.

[24] WH Beveridge, *Social Insurance and Allied Services* (London, HM Stationery Office, 1942).

published in 1942, were particularly alarming about health care services. Poverty, unemployment and poor education were affecting the health of the nation and demonstrated an important lack of access to resources.[25] The population neverthe-less greeted the sweeping report with enthusiasm as it outlined the basic principles for the creation of a centralised health care system.[26] The reaction of the BMA, to the contrary, was rather negative leading the government to rein in its ambi-tions. Finally, two years later, the White Paper *A National Health Service*[27] issued a policy proposal inspired by Beveridge's work.[28] It was those promises of a 'new' welfare state potentially leading to significant changes in social policy that helped the Labour Party get elected after the war.[29]

In 1945, the medical profession did not echo the outpour of support from the population and continued to oppose the proposition. Doctors were particularly unsupportive of the newly appointed Minister for Health, Aneurin Bevan, describ-ing him as 'a dictator and autocrat – strongly suggestive of the Hitlerite regime'.[30] The broad consensus around the need for reform that had emerged during the war did not translate into agreement on the methods to achieve a comprehensive health care system.[31] Doctors were resisting Bevan's proposition of a public system of nationalised hospitals, convinced that it threatened their autonomy and clinical freedom.[32]

Negotiations therefore continued beyond the enactment of the National Health Service Act (1946) that provided the legal basis for the creation of the NHS.[33] Doctors simply would not accept being turned into state servants.[34] The Royal Colleges of Medicine led by medical consultants and specialists were adamant that they would not concede a loss in autonomy. Nevertheless, they, unlike the GPs, welcomed the nationalisation of voluntary hospitals as many of these facilities were in a precarious financial condition after the war. Medical consultants could therefore benefit from the state stepping in and creating a steadier flow of finance.[35] The high level of remuneration that was promised and the compensation offered for the loss of private income due to their full-time commitment to the national service also eased some of the concerns of the secondary care providers.[36] An even greater concession on the part of the government was to eventually allow medical consultants and specialists to pursue the private practice of medicine alongside

---

[25] Vetter, above (n 17) 26.
[26] ibid, 27.
[27] Ministry of Health, *A National Health Service* (Cmd 6502, 1944).
[28] Wall and Owen, above (n 15) 7.
[29] Vetter, above (n 17) 21.
[30] Ainsworth, above (n 16) 38.
[31] Baggott, above (n 14) 23.
[32] Vetter, above (n 17) 23.
[33] Allsop, above (n 6) 27.
[34] Ainsworth, above (n 16) 38.
[35] Allsop, above (n 6) 26–27.
[36] Vetter, above (n 17) 28.

the work they would perform for the NHS. Consultants and specialists would also retain control over their employment conditions, namely the appointment of new staff, internal promotions and merit awards.[37]

Things were dramatically different for primary care doctors. GPs, as a group, had a lot of animosity towards the government and the Royal Colleges of Medicine. They felt betrayed by their colleagues and thought of themselves as second-class citizens in comparison to medical consultants and specialists who had been offered optimal work conditions.[38] It was initially suggested that GPs would become salaried and their practices would be re-grouped into health centres run by local authorities.[39] Bevan quickly understood that again he had to compromise, but this time to the BMA, and so he did. GPs were to remain independent contractors with a great degree of autonomy and payment for their services would continue to take the form of a capitation fee for each patient.[40] This led a number of GPs to sign on to the NHS, leaving no other option to the BMA but to concede and accept Bevan's offer.[41]

It was only eight weeks prior to the launch of the NHS the medical profession finally came on board. Medical consultants and GPs had secured their autonomy, their status, work conditions and most importantly some influence over decisions impacting resource allocation. Doctors were given important spending powers and indirectly held the reigns of the NHS's equitable distribution.[42] Beyond their discretionary power in clinical care, they had been made the 'gatekeepers' of the system. They could assess health care needs and reallocate resources.[43] Health care policy had thereby become an agreement between the central government in charge of the budget and doctors controlling how these monies were to be distributed.[44]

Thus, on 5 July 1948 the NHS was finally up and running. A comprehensive system, free of charge, promoting good health and offering access to services based on need rather than ability to pay, had been created.[45] There would be no difference in the treatment between affluent and indigent patients or between healthier and unhealthier parts of the population. Contributions to the system however would be proportional to levels of income.[46] Unfortunately, as early as 1949, the government realised the high and unsustainable cost associated with this ambitious project. Bevan had also underestimated the burden the NHS would put on the greater economy. He was then forced to revise his health care budget estimate of

---

[37] Allsop, above (n 6) 26; Vetter, ibid, 31–32.
[38] Vetter, ibid, 33.
[39] ibid 29.
[40] Allsop, above (n 6) 27.
[41] Wall and Owen, above (n 15) 7.
[42] Crinson, above (n 4) 61.
[43] ibid, 110.
[44] Klein, *The New Politics of the NHS*, above (n 13) 61.
[45] Vetter, above (n 17) 29–30.
[46] ibid, 30.

£170 million a year to £225 million.[47] Inflation and the cost of additional services that were initially unaccounted for also led the government to levy prescription charges and to impose fees on dental and ophthalmic services.[48]

By the NHS' tenth anniversary the country as a whole was facing a severe period of austerity. The level of resources available for health services had become stagnant as the expansion of social security spending on education services was becoming more important.[49] Although the management structure was unchanged, the next decade would be a period of consolidation during which additional resources would be freed to expand and update hospital care.[50] Strategic planning of primary care services was also initiated during the course of the 1960s.[51]

GPs as a group had organised and distanced themselves from the BMA by creating the Royal College of General Practitioners that oversaw the profession and helped develop training opportunities.[52] The profession needed to re-group to gain more leverage as many areas of the country were underserved and in need of more primary care doctors. The government had therefore decided to provide financial incentives to GPs to relocate. It had also been decided that GPs would pay collectively for additional staff thereby financially penalising good practices.[53] The pressure was rising; many primary care doctors felt constrained and left the profession. Others were more eager to negotiate higher capitation fees.[54] Kenneth Robinson, Health Minister and himself the son of a GP, responded to these grievances with the Family Doctor's Charter (1966).[55] The Charter allowed higher capitation fees and the reimbursement of 70 per cent of the cost of ancillary staff and new buildings to GPs.[56] This renewed compromise reflected the limited potential for change in health care policy and the influence of clinical practice in the health care consensus politics of the 1960s.[57]

As health care costs were ramping up and more health care facilities were needed, Edward Heath's Conservative government outlined a plan to proceed with major administrative and structural changes in health care services. The government had called in consultants to advise on the complexities of the NHS in the first of many efforts to reduce costs.[58] The 1972 White Paper *National Health Service Reorganisation* relayed the advice and proposed to unify all three branches of the

---

[47] ibid, 47.
[48] ibid.
[49] S Harrison and R McDonald, *The Politics of Healthcare in Britain* (London, Sage Publications, 2008) 10.
[50] C Webster, *The National Health Service: A Political History* (Oxford, Oxford University Press, 2002) 1–65; Klein, *The New Politics of the NHS*, above (n 13) 64–65.
[51] C Ham, *Health Policy in Britain*, 2nd edn (Basingstoke, Macmillan, 1992) 20.
[52] Vetter, above (n 17) 41.
[53] Crinson, above (n 4) 62.
[54] Vetter, above (n 17) 41.
[55] *The Family Doctor Charter* (London, HM Stationery Office, 1966).
[56] Wall and Owen, above (n 15) 44.
[57] Klein, *The New Politics of the NHS*, above (n 13) 65.
[58] Vetter, above (n 17) 50.

NHS (family practitioner services, hospital services and personal health services) under one system of administration.[59] Less than a year later the National Health Service Reorganisation Act (1973) had translated into law the bureaucratic transformation. The NHS was to be unified to guarantee strong strategic planning and execute the government's priorities in health care.[60]

More concretely, hospital building and strategic financial planning would be devolved to new entities, in total 14 Regional Health Authorities that were to govern 90 Area Health Authorities, themselves overseeing Family Practitioner Committees. These committees were tasked to administer GP, pharmacist, dentist and optician contracts. District Management Teams would also help with the lower level of management and Community Councils acting as consultative bodies would be introduced to represent patients in health care.[61] GPs nevertheless remain largely independent from the structure and preserved their autonomy.[62]

The reorganisation was based on the idea that 'economies of scale' were most efficient and power had to be re-grouped into central entities.[63] Unfortunately, the effects were disappointing and yielded much criticism. The political consensus on health care policy thereby unravelled.[64] In the mid-1970s animosity also arose around the hospital paid beds controversy. Medical consultants, with the Royal College of Surgeons and the Royal College of Physicians, had to defend the hard-fought permission they had acquired in 1946 to engage in private practice medicine while working for the NHS. Even though it had been established that patients had the choice to pay separately to receive specialist treatment, the Labour Party was actively attempting to phase pay beds out of NHS hospitals.[65] Tensions in the doctor–government 'public–private' relationship were raising more profound questions of equality, optimum use of resources and value for money in health care.[66]

When secondary care providers finally threatened to take industrial action, Barbara Castle, Labour Secretary of State for Health and Social Services, reassured medical consultants and specialists and confirmed that she had no intention of outlawing the treatment of private patients. However, plans were still made to

[59] Department of Health and Social Security, *National Health Service Reorganisation: England* (Cmnd 5055, 1972).

[60] Allsop, above (n 6) 48.

[61] PK Ahmed and L Cadenhead, 'Charting the Developments in the NHS' (1998) 24 *Health Manpower Management* 222, 223.

[62] Allsop, above (n 6) 54.

[63] Vetter, above (n 17) 52.

[64] Wall and Owen, above (n 15) 18; Vetter, ibid, 54.

[65] B Edwards, J Linton and C Potter, *The National Health Service: A Manager's Tale 1946–1992* (London, Nuffield Provincial Hospitals Trust, 1993) 27; C Williamson, 'The Quiet Time? Pay-beds and Private Practice in the National Health Service: 1948–1970' (2015) 28 *Social History of Medicine* 576, 577.

[66] G MacLauchlan and A Maynard, *The Public Private–Mix for Health* (Oxford, Nuffield Provincial Hospitals Trust, 1982) 1–2.

reduce pay beds in NHS hospitals; the policy would be short lived and reversed by the incoming Conservative government.[67] Castle did not want to ruffle any more of the medical professionals' feathers since GPs had also threatened to hand in mass resignations. These disputes were an important turning point in the doctor–government relationship, since for the first time medical professionals had made no ethical objections to taking industrial action.[68]

## B.  Redefining the Roles (1980s–90s)

Unfortunately, the hostility survived the change in government. In 1979, in spite of its campaign commitment to increase spending in health care, the newly elected Conservative government was clashing with doctors on several issues, namely overspending in health care, the reorganisation of health care services and GP contracts.[69] Financial turmoil brought about by the first oil crisis had also caused important inflation. The government was determined to control and cut public spending as well as reduce taxes. Social entitlements were therefore significantly decreased, and NHS funding became steadily tighter.[70] More radically, the utilities and telecommunication sectors were privatised in the hope that deregulation would increase efficiency.[71] Prime Minister Margaret Thatcher also encouraged the private practice of medicine with some tax incentives, but this had only a minor impact on the NHS. The population's support for the publicly financed health care system was unwavering and was putting a damper on the government's libertarian and neoliberal ambitions.[72]

Secretary of State for Health and Social Security, Norman Fowler, nevertheless ordered a review of the system. Roy Griffiths, deputy chairman and managing director of Sainsbury's supermarkets was put in charge and produced a damning report. Griffiths concluded that the NHS suffered from great inefficiencies due to a lack of leadership[73] and infamously stated that, 'if Florence Nightingale were carrying her lamp through the corridors of the NHS today she would almost certainly be searching for the people in charge'.[74] The NHS therefore needed to be restructured to become more efficient, businesslike and do away with the traditional management by consensus.[75] According to the Griffiths Report (1983),[76]

---

[67] Baggott, above (n 14) 26.
[68] Edwards, Linton and Potter, above (n 65) 28.
[69] Baggott, above (n 14) 118.
[70] Vetter, above (n 17) 63.
[71] J Le Grand, N Mays and J Mulligan, *Learning from the NHS Internal Market* (London, King's Fund Publishing, 1998) 2.
[72] Baggott, above (n 14) 23–27.
[73] Bradshaw and Bradshaw, above (n 9) 12.
[74] R Griffiths, *NHS Management Inquiry: Report to the Secretary of State for Social Services* (Department of Health and Social Security, 1983) 24.
[75] Bradshaw and Bradshaw, above (n 9) 12.
[76] Griffiths, above (n 74).

cost-containment measures, performance indicators and competition stimuli had to be placed at the top of the agenda.[77] Discussions about bringing in managers from the private sector to provide the NHS with a hard-hitting approach also emerged from the review;[78] but the NHS had never been managed like a company, it was administered as an organisation, an essential public good that belonged to the taxpayers.[79]

Thus, for fear of a public uproar, the government decide to only tighten up the money without taking any formal action. Problems of increasing waiting lists, wards closures and shortage of human resources however continued to affect the quality of care and had brought the hospital sector close to collapse. Therefore, when the Royal Colleges of Medicine publicly rang the alarm with a formal declaration, Thatcher was left with no other option than to take action.[80] In January 1988, shortly after her third electoral victory, she ordered a ministerial committee to look into potential solutions that would not require an increase in public spending.[81] Initial discussions took place behind closed doors away from the public and the medical community's scrutiny. They dealt with health care financing issues and more particularly the possibility of enhancing the private sector's involvement or adopting an insurance-based system; but both solutions were rejected.[82] The NHS remained financed through general taxation.

The White Paper *Working For Patients*[83] that summed up the conclusions of the review nevertheless made a bold policy proposal. The government had decided to restructure the NHS into an internal market. The sale and purchase of health care services would occur within the health care system to trigger a 'dictated competition'. 'Purchasers', health authorities and groups of GPs, would seek to get the best, most affordable and responsive services from the health care 'providers', made up of GPs and NHS trusts (groups of two or more hospitals).[84] The transactions would take the form of yearly block contracts stating the quantity, quality and price of the purchased health care services.[85] Implicitly, NHS managers and doctors would take on new leadership roles similar to that of businesspersons in the private sector.[86] The proposed changes to the structure of the NHS were also meant to tilt the scale back in favour of the government and purchasing entities since, thus far, providers had had a considerable amount of influence in the allocation of health care resources.[87]

---

[77] Boyle, above (n 15) 27.
[78] Vetter, above (n 17) 63.
[79] Bradshaw and Bradshaw, above (n 9) 13.
[80] Le Grand, Mays and Mulligan, above (n 71) 3–4.
[81] Vetter, above (n 17) 73.
[82] ibid.
[83] Department of Health, *Working for Patients* (Cm 555, 1989).
[84] C Ham, *Management and Competition in the NHS* (Abingdon, Radcliffe Medical Press, 1997) 16–22.
[85] Boyle, above (n 15) 110.
[86] AM Pollock, *NHS plc: The Privatisation of Our Health Care* (London, Verso, 2004) 43.
[87] Tuohy, 'Dynamics of a Changing Health Sphere', above (n 12) 121–22.

The government, backed by the media, was accusing doctors of engaging in outdated and inefficient practices because of their self-serving interests.[88] However, doctors no longer wanted to be perceived as money hungry professionals. Thus, in the midst of this radical change the medical profession and the BMA had to revamp their image. The union was now presenting itself as the strongest supporter of the NHS. What was good for the NHS was good for the doctors.[89] The doctor–patient relationship had also evolved, and a change of perspective had arisen at the clinical level. Patients were invited to take an active role in their treatment and the management of their health. It was important for them to take responsibility for their lives and to challenge the medical professional's paternalistic approach. Doctors also had to be more responsive to their patients' needs.[90] Thus, the announced reform relayed this new vision and aimed to have 'money follow the patient',[91] be it in the NHS or in the private sector. The medical profession had no choice but to adapt and fight to sustain the universal system and its status.

Interestingly, a substantial portion of the White Paper specifically focused on primary care services. The government was convinced that GPs could play a central role in the implementation of cost-cutting policies. Primary care providers occupied a place at the heart of the system as a point of call for patients and gatekeepers for hospital care. They had significant knowledge of local services available to the population and could interact personally with consultants in hospitals instead of the more detached health authorities.[92] Most importantly, primary care doctors had acquired a large degree of autonomy by managing their budget outside the control of the Department of Health.[93] GPs therefore had to be made accountable for their choices at the clinical level and their impact on the allocation of health care resources at a systemic level.[94] In order to do so, the government had suggested in a previous Green Paper imposing performance-related pay.[95] A proposal that, expectedly, the doctors had firmly resisted. But under the new reforms, GP practices with a list size of at least 5,000 patients would be given the self-serving status of fundholding and the freedom to manage their own budgets in order to purchase secondary care for their patients and cover prescription costs.[96]

GPs would be incentivised to strictly hold to their budgets. At the end of each year, they would be entitled to any residual money to purchase additional

---

[88] Le Grand, Mays and Mulligan, above (n 71) 2.

[89] Vetter, above (n 17) 69.

[90] I Kennedy, *The Unmasking of Medicine* (London, Allen & Unwin, 1981) 123; I Illich, *Limits to Medicine: Medical Nemesis – The Expropriation of Health* (London, Penguin Books, 1977) 21–47.

[91] *Working for Patients*, above (n 83) 729.

[92] Le Grand, Mays and Mulligan, above (n 71) 6.

[93] Pollock, *NHS plc*, above (n 86) 141.

[94] ibid.

[95] Department of Health and Social Security, *Primary Health Care: An Agenda for Discussion* (Cmnd 9771, 1986).

[96] Vetter, above (n 17) 82; Baggott, above (n 14) 27.

equipment or to employ new staff for their practice. Conversely, if the costs of patient care exceeded the budget, the burden would also be borne by the practice. GPs were therefore indirectly given a motivation to undertreat patients and to decline higher-risk patients who would become high users of services. Treatment plans were to be based on financial incentives rather than clinical judgements.[97] For these reasons GPs fiercely opposed the proposition made by the White Paper. Primary care doctors felt a sense of belonging to the NHS and valued its principles and philosophy of equality in treatment. Thereby, with the help of the BMA, they took it upon themselves to publicly campaign against the proposed reforms, but despite the demonstrations and the petitions sent by London GP surgeries to Downing Street, Health Minister, Kenneth Clarke, pushed the reform Bill through Parliament.[98] The National Health Service Community Care Act became the law on 29 June 1990.

The government went ahead with the reforms but the internal market ideal never fully materialised and GP fundholding did not spark great enthusiasm. The first wave of fundholders had enjoyed leverage over their colleagues in secondary care services, feeling empowered by their ability to move resources to meet their patients' health care needs.[99] However, they quickly discovered that they could only spread risk across the narrow pool of patients within their surgeries and that they had to carry the burden of the high transaction costs associated with secondary care contract negotiations. Taken together, GP fundholding was unsustainable.[100]

Despite the incremental visible changes, over the course of a decade medical professionals had seen their role dramatically redefined. Primary care doctors were thought of as purchasers, medical consultants and specialists were thought of as providers and the profession no longer had leeway in the negotiations of systemic health care policy. Thatcher had not privatised the NHS, but she had set the term for a new relationship between the government and the medical profession.[101] Even though the basic principles of the institution were at a 'fixed point', the reforms had significantly redesigned the structure of health care services.[102]

After Thatcher's resignation in November 1990, Prime Minister John Major followed in the footsteps of the previous government. The structure of the internal market remained in place and participation of the private sectors in health care was accelerated with the Private Finance Initiative (PFI) (as presented in the next part of this chapter). Unfortunately, the radical reform did not achieve the projected efficiencies and services were not improving. One-third of hospital trusts were

---

[97] Pollock, *NHS plc*, above (n 86) 143–44.
[98] ibid, 142.
[99] ibid, 144–45.
[100] ibid, 143–44.
[101] Le Grand, Mays and Mulligan, above (n 71) 2.
[102] Baggott, above (n 14) 27.

failing to meet some of their financial targets, and waiting times in non-emergency services were on the rise.[103] Health care facilities could not truly compete with one another because the government would not allow inefficient hospitals to shut down, as this would leave some districts without health care facilities.[104]

The Major government wanted to mend fences with the BMA and the medical profession to re-establish the traditional approach of mutual accommodation.[105] The government also had to address human resources issues and particularly the retention of GPs in the NHS; it therefore worked towards the introduction of a national GP contract. Thus, the Primary Care Act (1997) introduced the Personal Medical Services with which GPs could maintain their patient lists and keep their status as independent contractors. They, however, also elected to become salaried employees of the NHS.[106] Finally, the Act also proposed that nurses and health visitors help with the primary care workload by treating patients with minor injuries and by running some prevention clinics.[107]

During this period the Labour Party had capitalised on the lingering inefficiencies in health care and written a manifesto that was geared towards the NHS for the 1997 general elections. Tony Blair had famously declared: 'the very simple choice that people have in the next 24 hours is this. It is 24 hours to save our National Health Service'.[108] Certainly it was partly because of its proposed health care policies and its new market-friendly banner that Labour came into power with a landslide victory. New Labour was rejecting the internal market rhetoric but quickly understood it had to keep its core characteristic, the purchaser–provider divide.[109] Minister of Health, Frank Dobson, had rushed to announce the end of the 'internal market' during the early days of Tony Blair's government; however, the bureaucracy behind the purchaser–provider split and NHS trusts could not be abolished.[110] Regardless, the newly elected government had other plans to modernise the NHS.

The White Paper *The New NHS: Modern, Dependable*[111] was published in December 1997, only a few months after the general election. The publication outlined an approach to regulate the overutilisation of health care resources and to make the system more 'efficient' and 'equitable'.[112] One of the main propositions was to abolish GP fundholding and replace it with local primary care

---

[103] Pollock, *NHS plc*, above (n 86) 44–45.
[104] ibid, 44.
[105] Baggott, above (n 14) 22.
[106] Pollock, *NHS plc*, above (n 86) 146.
[107] ibid, 147.
[108] Tony Blair, MP (Speech at the Trimdon Labour Club, Trimdon, 30 April 1997).
[109] R Robinson and A Dixon, *Health Care Systems in Transition: The United Kingdom* (Copenhagen, European Observatory on Health Care Systems, 1999) 27–28.
[110] Pollock, *NHS plc*, above (n 86) 53; Tuohy, 'Dynamics of a Changing Health Sphere', above (n 12) 124.
[111] Department of Health, *The New NHS: Modern, Dependable* (Cm 3807, 1997).
[112] Crinson, above (n 4) 67.

commissioning groups.[113] Primary Care Groups (PCGs) would be constituted of an executive committee made up of GPs, nurses, pharmacists and members of the community. This deciding body would be given a defined mandate to provide strategic advice on clinical care and commission hospital and community services.[114] The goal was to provide greater accountability for administrators and clinicians under a 'clinical governance' structure.[115] Thus, after the publication of the White Paper and a piloting period, the Health Act (1999) formally abolished GP fund-holding and made a provision for the Secretary of State to establish the renamed Primary Care Trusts (PCTs). These entities would to undertake the commissioning functions of health authorities and PCGs.

Innovative regulatory instruments envisioned to help set national health care standards and to improve the allocation of health care resources were also rolled out during the same period.[116] The National Institute for Clinical Excellence (NICE) (now the National Institute for Health and Care Excellence) started operating in 1999. NICE, as a special health authority, was to offer advice and guidelines on the management of clinical conditions based on its appraisal of clinical evidence and the cost-efficiency of drugs, treatments and medical equipment. NICE guidelines would be used to determine the appropriate intervention as well as the need for a referral to a specialist.[117] The goal was to standardise the rationing process and make the allocation of health care resources more explicit and transparent.[118] Also established in 1999, the Commission for Health Improvement (CHI) was meant to report directly to the Secretary of State for Health to provide an extra layer of accountability in clinical care. The CHI would monitor the quality of health care services provided to the population and the implementation of national guidance.[119]

## C. Adapting to the Dynamics of Consumerism in Health Care (2000s–the Present)

Another flagship of the Blair government was the 'Third Way' philosophy that emerged more strongly during the second mandate of the Labour government.[120]

---

[113] Baggott, above (n 14) 30.

[114] CH Tuohy, 'Reform and the Politics of Hybridization in Mature Health Care States' (2012) 37 *Journal of Health Politics, Policy and Law* 611, 620.

[115] Tuohy, 'Dynamics of a Changing Health Sphere', above (n 12) 124.

[116] Boyle, above (n 15) 28.

[117] See generally, M Rawlins, 'In Pursuit of Quality: The National Institute for Clinical Excellence' (1999) 353 *The Lancet* 1079.

[118] E Jackson, *Medical Law: Text, Cases, and Materials*, 4th edn (Oxford, Oxford University Press, 2013) 65.

[119] See generally, K Walshe, 'Improvement through Inspection? The Development of the New Commission for Health Improvement in England and Wales' (1999) 8 *Quality in Health Care* 191.

[120] See generally, S Driver and L Martell, *Blair's Britain* (Cambridge, Polity Press, 2002).

The 'Blairite' doctrine incorporated traditional socialist principles of equality in health care with a neoliberal ideology promoting partnerships with the private sector and decision-making processes focused on patients' choice.[121] The White Paper, *The NHS Plan: A Plan for Investment, A Plan for Reform* (2000),[122] drafted by the newly appointed Health Minister Alan Milburn, embodied this philosophy.[123] Some critics even saw the publication as a plan to usher in the privatisation of the health care system.[124]

Indeed, policy propositions for an increased participation of the private sector in the delivery and financing of health care services to modernise the NHS and to more adequately cater for the public's needs were put forward.[125] The reform was to bring an end to excessive waiting times and generate economic incentives to improve efficiency in health care services.[126] The PFI scheme established under the Major government was to be expanded as well as a similar project for primary care services.[127] The private sector would be invited to take part in the provision of critical and elective surgeries but treatment would still be commissioned and paid for by the NHS.[128] Essentially, the proposed reform envisioned another relationship in health care, this time between the private independent sector and the government.

The White Paper nevertheless gave a special place to the medical profession. 'Doctors, nurses and managers' were to be the 'key architects' of the reform.[129] In fact, Milburn had deeply involved the presidents of the Royal Colleges and the Chairman of the BMA Council in the policy exercise. The purpose was to establish consensus and mobilise support for a potential reform before proceeding with any radical changes.[130] Obviously, human resources were central to the success of the initiative. More money had to be invested in technology and more doctors and nurses needed to receive training to improve access to care and to redesign the NHS to fit patients' expectations.[131]

From a structural standpoint, The *NHS Plan* (2000) also suggested that the PCG should become the PCT by 2004. However, the date was brought forward in 2002. The government announced in the White Paper *Shifting the Balance of Power*[132] that it would proceed with the last phase of the conversion and would

---

[121] N Mays, A Dixon and L Jones, *Understanding New Labour's Market Reforms of the English NHS* (London, King's Fund, 2011) 6–7.
[122] Department of Health, *The NHS Plan: A Plan for Investment, A Plan for Reform* (Cm 4818-I, 2000).
[123] Klein, *The New Politics of the NHS*, above (n 13) 213.
[124] AM Pollock, 'NHS No More?' (2016) 89(12) *Community Practitioner* 28, 28.
[125] Baggott, above (n 14) 29.
[126] R Cookson et al, 'Effects of the Blair/Brown NHS Reforms on Socioeconomic Equity in Health Care' (2012) 17 *Journal of Health Services Research & Policy* 55, 55.
[127] Baggott, above (n 14) 31.
[128] Pollock, *NHS plc*, above (n 86) 70.
[129] Department of Health Press Release, 'A National Plan for a National Health Service: Five Teams to Focus on NHS Challenges' (23 March 2000).
[130] Klein, *The New Politics of the NHS*, above (n 13) 213–14.
[131] ibid.
[132] Department of Health, *Shifting the Balance of Power within the NHS* (2001).

replace the 95 health authorities with 30 strategic health authorities to oversee all PCTs.[133] As part of these important restructuring efforts, the Blair government also established Foundation Trusts under the Health and Social Care (Community Health and Standards) Act (2003). These new entities, under the supervision of a new regulator, Monitor, were meant to better respond to market forces and patients' choice by having a greater degree of autonomy from the Secretary of State for Health with regard to human resources and investment in health care.[134]

This wave of modernisation of course had a significant impact on medical professionals' status and clinical autonomy. The health care policy discourse had also evolved, and patients were more independent, informed, empowered and had to be involved in their treatment. They had preferences and needed to be given choices. Metrics and targets measuring performance and quality of services were discussed.[135] The Labour government had decided to introduce a system of 'payment by result' (PBR) to replace the fundholding block contracts. From then on, consultants and specialists would be paid based on the work they had performed. Health care providers would get reimbursed for individual treatments based on a 'tariff' (price for a bundle of procedures). Patients would be offered the choice among health care services suppliers making them compete for the work. Suppliers of health care services would therefore have to be more competitive with their offers.[136] Even though PBR was intended to bring greater efficiency to the system and reduce costs, it also provided an incentive for doctors to overtreat patients in hospital settings to maximise their level of reimbursement.[137]

The medical profession had, however, not felt the need to contest any of New Labour's health care policies, and had even collaborated with the government on the *NHS Plan* (2000). This cooperative attitude was due in part to the doctors' experience with policy making during the Thatcher era. The Conservative government in the 1980s had purposely silenced the medical profession. Doctors had however come to realise that Thatcher's radical projects did not yield significant changes to their working conditions and therefore there may have been no need to fiercely oppose reformative efforts. Also, change under the Labour government had come more progressively and therefore did not allow for major confrontation between the medical profession and Whitehall.[138] Nevertheless, the added pressure to perform had led the BMA to attempt a renegotiation of GP and consultant contracts.[139] Overall, the discussions on the primary care providers' agreement ran rather seamlessly, despite the initial antagonistic attitude of the BMA.[140]

---

[133] Pollock, *NHS plc*, above (n 86) 145.

[134] AM Pollock, D Price and P Brhlikova, 'Classification Problems and the Dividing Line Between Government and the Market: An Examination of NHS Foundation Trust Classification in the UK' (2011) 82 *Annals of Public and Cooperative Economics* 455, 463.

[135] J Newman and E Vilder, 'Discriminating Customers, Responsible Patients, Empowered Users: Consumerism and the Modernisation of Health Care' (2006) 35 *Journal of Social Policy* 193, 199–200.

[136] Baggott, above (n 14) 167.

[137] ibid, 168.

[138] Klein, *The New Politics of the NHS*, above (n 13) 235–36.

[139] ibid, 236.

[140] ibid.

GPs had negotiated their independent contractor status in exchange for the provision of medical coverage to all their registered patients 24 hours a day and 365 days a year in 1948 at the creation of the NHS. Over the span of five decades, their responsibilities had, however, grown significantly. Their role encompassed primary care services but also the management of chronic conditions, prevention activities, the treatment and support of those suffering from a mental health condition and even minor surgeries. Having already had to organise 'out of hours coverage' to fulfil their commitments, GPs were now demanding that their role be confined to a set of core services.[141] As requested, the new contract enclosed precise definitions for various levels of clinical care. Services provided to patients in need of terminal care or in need of a consultation for a potential illness would fall under the category of 'essential' medical services. For these instances and for 'additional services', namely contraceptive, maternity and cervical screening services, as well as 'out of hours' care, GP practices would be paid a lump sum. However, in cases where practices would opt out of the provision of 'additional services' a fixed amount for each of the services not provided would be deducted from the global sum. These amounts would thereafter be open to tenders from other providers. Finally, 'enhanced services' were to include (but would not be limited to) the treatment of women during labour, the monitoring of patients on anticoagulants or patients at risk of a stroke. These services would be commissioned locally at a national tariff.[142]

Under the new contracts the national terms and conditions of service for GPs would also be abolished, so practices would therefore no longer have to provide a 24-hour comprehensive service. This radical break from the past reflected the changing demographics of the profession. A career in primary care services had attracted more women than in the past and younger GPs were also craving the security of salaried employment and more flexible working hours. Under the new contract, GPs would only be required to provide a 'minimum package of health care'. The PCT would become responsible for 'additional' and 'enhanced' services not covered by primary care professionals. The PCT would have the opportunity to outsource services and allow market forces to penetrate the primary care sector. GPs had thereby forfeited their monopoly on the provision of primary care services and spoiled the holistic nature of family medicine by giving up on continuity of care.[143] From 2004 onwards, PCTs would also negotiate contracts directly with general practices instead of the Secretary of State contracting with individual GPs through the BMA. The PCT would essentially have to ensure the equitable allocation of GPs and primary care resources within their area.[144]

Consultants also entered into a renegotiation process with the government. Conversation did not run as smoothly for the secondary providers as they did for

[141] Pollock, *NHS plc*, above (n 86) 147.
[142] ibid, 149.
[143] ibid, 148–50.
[144] ibid, 150.

GPs. The Department of Health had two firm objectives: it needed to reinforce its managerial control over consultant doctors and aimed to limit the private practice of medicine. The government therefore proposed that secondary care providers be given a defined set of responsibilities and that newly appointed consultants be required to provide seven years of exclusive and full-time service to the NHS. Attempts had also been made to purchase the right to the private practice of medicine, but this costly proposition, along with the two other proposals, were rejected outright by medical consultants. Instead, Whitehall and medical consultants agreed, rather vaguely, that under the new contract managers and doctors would jointly work out what needed to be done in exchange for a 27 per cent increase in pay.[145]

GPs and consultants were also successful in obtaining better training. These new arrangements had made NHS doctors some of the best paid medical professionals in Europe.[146] GPs had once again secured their autonomy. The contract was adapted to the needs of a new generation of primary care professionals providing women and younger GPs with more flexibility. Consultants, for their part, had resisted the state's managerial control and made remarkable financial gains.[147] Ultimately, peaceful and cordial relations with the BMA had come at a great cost for the Department of Health. The government nevertheless claimed that it had negotiated a contract that encouraged health care services of a greater quality and a new partnership with private providers.[148]

Unsurprisingly, during the general election campaign of 2005 the topic of health care reform continued to be at the forefront. Significant deficiencies still needed to be addressed, notably, hygiene in hospitals, the burdensome bureaucracy of the NHS, the growing role of the private sector in health care and the distorting effect of government targets.[149] Ultimately, the Labour Party was undefeated and brought Gordon Brown into power in 2008 to form a third consecutive Labour government. Although Brown did not intend to revert to the 'Old' Labour ideology, he valued the foundational principles of the NHS (comprehensive and free at the point of use) and wanted to mend fences with the medical profession. Indeed, he did not want to reverse the work done by his leadership rival Tony Blair but was critical of some of his policies.[150]

Brown therefore appointed a senior clinician as Health Minister and tasked him to conduct a review of the system based on a wide consultation. Lord Darzi decided to work closely with members of the medical community.[151] The *High*

---

[145] Klein, *The New Politics of the NHS*, above (n 13) 237.
[146] ibid.
[147] ibid.
[148] ibid, 236–37.
[149] Baggott, above (n 14) 23.
[150] ibid, 32.
[151] ibid, 119.

*Quality Care for All: NHS Next Stage Review* (Darzi Review),[152] published in June 2008, made some recommendations that focused on increasing the quality, safety and effectiveness of health care services, all of which mandated the collaboration of doctors. Medical professionals and the private and voluntary sectors were called on to work more closely together to integrate services.[153] Patient involvement was also a key feature of the publication. The review suggested that patients should be given the right to make choices and hold budgets for health care to access more personalised services.[154]

Soon enough, another general election was right around the corner. However this time, health care policy had been left in the background and the NHS barely featured in the 2010 campaign.[155] The Conservative Party Manifesto discreetly mentioned that, if elected, a Conservative government would 'increase health spending in real terms every year'[156] and 'strengthen the powers of GPs as patients' expert guides through the health care system ... putting them in charge of commissioning local services'[157] and that it would 'scrap politically motivated targets'.[158] The document was strategically silent on the topic of a reform in health care.[159] The Liberal Democrats, equally parsimonious on the topic, stated in their programme that, once in power, they would 'cut the size of the Department of Health by half'[160] and 'scrap Strategic Health Authorities'.[161] Lastly, the Labour Party that was already embracing a largely conservative ideology in health care proposed policies revolving around patient choice, competition and the expansion of the role of private providers in health care.[162] Overall, there were no live controversies on the topic, and there were some interesting overlaps between the parties' platforms.[163]

Ultimately the Conservative Party failed to secure a majority in Parliament and was forced to form a coalition. Thus, Conservative leader David Cameron had to persuade Liberal Democrat leader Nick Clegg that some of their visions were aligned, particularly with regard to health care policy.[164] Both parties agreed

---

[152] Department of Health and Social Care, *High Quality Care for All: NHS Next Stage Review Final Report* (Cm 7432, 2008).

[153] Baggott, above (n 14) 32.

[154] ibid, 33.

[155] N Timmins, *Never Again? The Story of the Health and Social Care Act 2012* (Institute for Government and the King's Fund, 2012), available at: www.kingsfund.org.uk/publications/never-again 50–78.

[156] Conservative Party, *Invitation to Join the Government of Britain: The Conservative Manifesto 2010* (London, Conservative Research Department, 2010) 45.

[157] ibid, 46.

[158] ibid.

[159] H Glennerster, 'The Coalition and Society (III): Health and Long-Term Care' in A Seldon and M Finn (eds), *The Coalition Effect, 2010–2015* (Cambridge, Cambridge University Press, 2015) 294.

[160] Liberal Democrats, *Change That Works for You: Liberal Democrat Manifesto 2010* (London, Liberal Democrat Publications, 2010) 40–41.

[161] ibid, 41.

[162] Baggott, above (n 14) 23.

[163] Glennerster, above (n 159) 291.

[164] A Adonis, *5 Days in May: The Coalition and Beyond* (London, Biteback Publishing, 2013) 137–57.

that more choice was needed and that commissioning bodies could benefit from more freedom.[165] NHS finances also needed to be 'protected' to do more with the resources already available.[166] Furthermore, the Conservatives were keen on pursuing the New Labour policies of increased competition among providers and PBR.[167] The Liberal Democrats, however, had agreed to an alliance on the basis of incremental changes and bar on a reorganisation of the system. Finally, the reduction of public spending became the common objective of the Coalition government.[168] The Conservatives were convinced that during the Labour era the state had grown out of proportion to the private sector and created an imbalance that had to be rectified.[169]

Obviously, the proposal of new health care reform came as a clash of thunder even though it had been years in the making in the mind of Andrew Lansley, former Shadow Secretary of State for Health, and current Secretary of State for Health under the Coalition. While in opposition Lansley had prepared his plan for far-reaching legislation that he hoped would be 'irreversible for a political generation'.[170] He had also tested the water with medical consultants during the electoral campaign proposing that central targets be removed to let secondary care providers focus on their clinical care. He told GPs, on the other hand, that they would be allowed to return to a fundholding-type of management.[171]

In fact, Lansley's forward thinking and planning can account for the speed at which the White Paper *Equity and Excellence: Liberating the NHS* (2010)[172] was published after the Coalition came into power. The speedy proposal for a groundbreaking reorganisation of the NHS stemmed directly from his proposals.[173] The reaction, however, was unexpectedly negative. The medical profession, media and even the Liberal Democrats opposed this major overhaul and made their voices heard.[174] In the midst of the controversy and ferocious responses from the general public and health care stakeholders, Cameron called for a 'pause' in the legislative process followed by a period of consultation. 'The Future Forum' would then collect different perspectives on the proposed reform.[175]

Following the consultation process, an unusually large number of amendments were made to the proposal. The Bill also re-entered Parliament in January 2012 and finally received royal assent to become law in March 2012.[176] The final

---

[165] Baggott, above (n 14) 39.

[166] Glennerster, above (n 159) 292.

[167] Baggott, above (n 14) 35.

[168] M Mullard and R Swaray, 'New Labour Legacy: Comparing the Labour Governments of Blair and Brown to Labour Governments since 1945' (2010) 81 *The Political Quarterly* 511, 511.

[169] ibid.

[170] Glennerster, above (n 159) 292–93.

[171] ibid, 293.

[172] Department of Health and Social Care, *Equity and Excellence: Liberating the NHS* (Cm 7881, 2010).

[173] Baggott, above (n 14) 40.

[174] Glennerster, above (n 159) 297; for a more detailed account of the legislative battle that led to the enactment of the Health and Social Care Act (2012): see section IV of ch 6.

[175] Glennerster, above (n 159) 297–98.

[176] Baggott, above (n 14) 119.

Act mostly addressed structural changes to the NHS. It abolished strategic Health Authorities and PCTs and replaced them with Clinical Commissioning Groups (CCGs).[177] These entities were to be responsible for allocating the majority of health care resources. Boards composed of hospital representatives and GPs would commission primary care and hospital services to local communities.[178] NHS trusts, having acquired the status of Foundation Trusts, would have more autonomy and the opportunity to administer resources according to the needs of their communities.[179] Patients would also be empowered and given the choice between 'qualified providers' to receive care.[180] Most certainly, competition and choice constituted the heart of the reform. The consumerist wave had taken over the NHS. Increased choice also meant that the private sector was on an equal footing with NHS providers. The decision-making process was decentralised and brought down to the local level with the CCGs. Health care had become a market and the policy-making arena had expanded to include commercial stake-holders and patients.[181] Nonetheless, health care services remain free at the point of use and financed through general taxation.[182]

The reactions to the final version of the Act and subsequent reform were mixed. Some saw the redesign as a wasted opportunity considering that the NHS was facing more pressing problems because of an ageing population and limited resources in England. The structure created by the Act had also made changes in the sectors of long-term and social care more difficult to implement.[183] Others, more pessimistic, described the Health and Social Care Act as the prelude to the NHS' demise. They believed that health care had been stripped of its public service attributes and had been commoditised. Indeed, a higher share of contracts was to be awarded to corporations. This could mean that the altruistic motivations behind the NHS could be severely eroded. Finally, at the opposite end of the spectrum, supporters of the Act welcomed the possibility of an increase in productivity in the sector, which could be triggered by competition brought about by the presence of private providers.[184]

## III. Private Initiatives in Health Care

Values of equity, democracy, accountability and hierarchical management characterised public administration in post-war Europe. Naturally, these features were

---

[177] 'The Structure of the New NHS' (British Medical Association, May 2017), available at: www.bma.org.uk/collective-voice/policy-and-research/nhs-structure-and-delivery/nhs-structure-new.
[178] 'Commissioning' (The British Medical Association), available at: www.bma.org.uk/advice/employment/commissioning.
[179] Webster, *The National Health Service: A Political History*, above (n 50) 2.
[180] Glennerster, above (n 159) 296.
[181] Baggott, above (n 14) 120.
[182] Glennerster, above (n 159) 300.
[183] ibid, 303.
[184] ibid, 303–04.

also embedded in the NHS at its creation in 1948.[185] Unfortunately, less than a decade later, the honourable goal of equality in health care had become the system's greatest challenge. In order to meet this standard and patients' growing expectations, the medical profession had to considerably adapt. Over the course of the 1990s, the government even started to call on the private sector to finance infrastructures and, at the beginning of the millennium, to supplement and diversify the supply of health care services.[186] By contrast, private medical insurers and the independent sector have never explicitly entered into a partnership with the public sector, but have grown in parallel with the system and continue to play a niche and peripheral role in the provision and the financing of wealthier patients' health care needs.[187]

This section of the chapter proposes to focus on all three aspects of these private initiatives to understand how these dynamics have impacted the publicly financed NHS over the past 70 years. The analysis starts with the wave of PFI in the 1990s and explores the new millennium Local Improvement Finance Trust (LIFT); two schemes that had ignited a trend of public–private partnerships in health care. Next, the place that private medical insurance (PMI) has carved itself outside of NHS universal coverage is discussed. Finally, the recent growth and development of the independent sector and commercial industry in health care is explained to put into perspective the new landscape of health care services delivery in the UK.

## A. Private Finance Initiatives: PFI and LIFT

Prior to the centralisation of health care services and the nationalisation of hospital infrastructures under the NHS, health care facilities fell under the purview of local government making for an inequitable distribution of resources.[188] Regrettably, Aneurin Bevan had also miscalculated the burden and demands for the renewal of national hospitals and the maintenance of decrepit NHS estates. Within the first years of the creation of the NHS he was already proposing to turn to the market to make up for the lack of funding and to allow hospital boards to borrow (with interest) from the private sector.[189] But this constituted a politically costly alternative that was too difficult to pursue. The construction and upkeep of hospital buildings, therefore, continued to be financed through general taxation, national insurance

---

[185] Pollock, Price and Brhlikova, above (n 134) 467; see generally, A Dunshire, 'Then and Now Public Administration, 1953–1999' (1999) 47 *Political Studies* 360.

[186] Newdick, above (n 8) 115.

[187] I Kennedy and A Grubb, *Medical Law* Oxford, Oxford University Press, 2000) 131.

[188] C Webster, *The Health Services Since the War: Problems of Health Care*, vol 2 (London, HM Stationery Office, 1990) 261–62.

[189] D Gaffney et al, 'The Private Finance Initiative: NHS Capital Expenditure and the Private Finance Initiative – Expansion or Contraction?' (1999) 319 *BMJ* 48, 48–51.

contributions and grants.[190] In the 1960s, an attempt to revamp hospital investment planning was again unsuccessful with more than two-thirds of the scheme failing to be completed.[191] Within the next 10 years, the government had reached a point of no return with severe declines in investment during the economic crisis. As government borrowing was insufficient, alternative sources of financing had to be permitted. Regional health authorities, therefore, used proceeds from the sale of land to generate some capital, something that gradually became common practice in order to raise capital.[192]

The Thatcher era brought a new political discourse of competition and efficiency to health care policy. The introduction of the internal market with the National Health Service Community Care Act (1990) also altered the funding of health care facilities and the financing of investment.[193] Hospitals were reconfigured as trusts that were essentially public corporations in charge of the provision of health care services. This implied that the cost of capital and depreciation had to be accounted for and charged out to purchasers. Hospitals were asked to take on the responsibility of capital repayment, as well as infrastructure maintenance and improvement costs.[194] Until then, new equipment and buildings had been covered at 'no cost' by the government.[195] However, with funding dramatically declining, the model became unsustainable. The Secretary of State opted to loan out buildings and equipment to trusts in exchange for repayment.[196] The government had embraced the idea because it firmly believed that it would give trust managers a greater sense of responsibility and encourage them to use resources more efficiently.[197] Most importantly, the capital charging system was setting precedent for the forthcoming PFI.[198]

As Thatcher stepped down as Prime Minister in the autumn of 1990 John Major took over the leadership of the Conservative government. Also having his mind set on curbing public spending, he adopted a similar approach as his

---

[190] D Gaffney et al, 'The Private Finance Initiative: The Politics of the Private Finance Initiative and the New NHS' (1999) 319 *BMJ* 249, 251.

[191] Gaffney et al, 'The Private Finance Initiative: NHS Capital Expenditure and the Private Finance Initiative', above (n 189) 48.

[192] ibid, 48–49.

[193] J Shaoul, A Stafford and P Stapleton, 'NHS Capital Investment and PFI: From Central Responsibility to Local Affordability' (2011) 27 *Financial Accountability & Management* 1, 3.

[194] J Shaoul, 'Charging for Capital in the NHS Trusts: To Improve Efficiency?' (1998) 9(1) *Management Accounting Research* 95, 95.

[195] AM Pollock, J Shaoul and N Vickers, 'Private Finance and "Value for Money" in NHS Hospitals: A Policy in Search of a Rationale?' (2002) 324 *BMJ* 1205, 1205–06.

[196] Gaffney et al, 'The Private Finance Initiative: NHS Capital Expenditure and the Private Finance, above (n 189) 51.

[197] See generally, J Froud et al, 'Persuasion Without Numbers? Public Policy and the Justification of Capital Charging in NHS Trust Hospitals' (1998) 11 *Accounting, Auditing and Accountability Journal* 99.

[198] Gaffney et al, 'The Private Finance Initiative: NHS Capital Expenditure and the Private Finance Initiative', above (n 189) 49.

predecessor to health care policy.[199] Significant numbers of hospital closures were being recorded and health care facilities management was in crisis. Thus, notwithstanding great controversy, in 1992, the government introduced the PFI, 'the largest new building programme in the history of the NHS'.[200] It was meant to be an alternative to raising taxes and to increasing the government's borrowing requirements for capital investment. During that period, a recession was also severely affecting the construction industry with some of its stakeholders lobbying Whitehall for support.[201] Therefore, to respond to the demand of the industry, the proposition was rolled out across many sectors, namely, defence, transport, education, social housing and waste management.[202]

In health care, the idea was to have banks, construction companies and management firms coming together to finance, design, build and operate hospitals.[203] Health care trusts would commission the construction of a facility to these consortiums and the PFI group would finance the works to build the hospital, provide specific activities and maintain the premises for a period of 30 to 60 years in exchange for an annual fee.[204] Essentially, the government was to defer its spending until the repayment date and acquire ownership of the hospital through lease back.[205] Therefore, just like under the capital charge system of the 1980s, financial responsibility would lie with the trust, but under PFI, trust managers would no longer have control over facilities financing.[206]

Offering substantial returns and potentially boosting the activity of the building industry, the government was convinced that the private sector would be keen to participate in the scheme. Nevertheless, it took some time to reach an agreement with the private sector on some of the technicalities involved in the policy.[207] At its beginning the scheme also cautiously gained in popularity, but a few years later, with most large-scale public projects adopting PFI procurements, it dominated as a financing technique.[208] During that decade, the New Labour government secured a majority in Parliament and Blair decided to take over the project by pushing the 'left over' Conservative Bill through Parliament. Thus, in 1997 the NHS Private Finance Act was enacted. The legislation further clarified

---

[199] AM Pollock, D Gaffney and M Dunnigan, 'Public Health and the Private Finance Initiative' (1998) 20 *Journal of Public Health Medicine* 1, 1–2.

[200] Shaoul, Stafford and Stapleton, above (n 193) 1.

[201] Pollock, *NHS plc*, above (n 86) 56.

[202] Robinson and Dixon, above (n 109) 22.

[203] A Talbot-Smith and AM Pollock, *The New NHS: A Guide* (New York, Routledge, 2006) 7.

[204] Pollock, *NHS plc*, above (n 86) 56.

[205] Gaffney et al, 'The Private Finance Initiative: NHS Capital Expenditure and the Private Finance Initiative', above (n 189) 48.

[206] Shaoul, Stafford and Stapleton, above (n 193) 4.

[207] Pollock, *NHS plc*, above (n 86) 56.

[208] See eg, AM Pollock, D Price and M Liebe, 'Private Finance Initiatives During NHS Austerity' (2011) 342 *BMJ* 324, 417; D Gaffney et al, 'The Private Finance Initiative: PFI in the NHS – Is There an Economic Case?' (1999) 319 *BMJ* 116, 116–17.

and cemented the government's partnership with the private sector.[209] At the turn of the new millennium, New Labour also issued a response to the proposals made under *The NHS Plan* (2000)[210] with a follow up White Paper, *Delivering the NHS Plan – Next Steps on Investment, Next Steps on Reform* (2002).[211] The new policy confirmed that 55 major hospital schemes would be carried out with PFI, in addition to the 34 projects already using the procurement method.[212] Furthermore, private sector consortiums would have the opportunity and the commercial freedom to develop non-NHS services in PFI operated facilities.[213]

In the absence of new capital and the possibility of selling assets to produce some cash flow, health care trusts were left with no other option but to turn to PFI to remain competitive and invest in their facilities.[214] Entrepreneurs in the United States in the 1990s had also understood these difficulties; the construction and maintenance of hospitals therefore had become a high-growth industry.[215] At that time, potential collaborations between British hospitals and their American counterparts were discussed. The public–private partnership was then expected to produce trillions of dollars in managed care business.[216]

To this day, PFI are still used to raise capital for NHS England health care facilities. In 2017, 127 contracts totalling £13 billion were agreed for the NHS and social care.[217] This financing method has endured because governments continue to believe they may benefit from potential gains in management and in the transfer of financial risk to the private sector.[218] It has also been argued that PFI is better 'value for money' than traditional financing techniques since the private sector always looks for ways to maximise its benefits and decrease costs when building and maintaining facilities.[219] Essentially, the government seeks to have the private sector bear most of the risk during the construction of the project.[220]

---

[209] R Klein, 'The Twenty-Year War Over England's National Health Service: A Report from the Battlefield' (2013) 38 *Journal of Health Politics, Policy and Law* 849, 851.

[210] Department of Health, *The NHS Plan: A Plan for Investment, A Plan for Reform*, above (n 122).

[211] Department of Health, *Delivering the NHS Plan – Next Steps on Investment, Next Steps on Reform* (Cm 5503, 2002).

[212] Pollock, *NHS plc*, above (n 86) 56–57.

[213] Gaffney et al, 'The Private Finance Initiative: The Politics of the Private Finance Initiative and the New NHS', above (n 190) 252.

[214] Gaffney et al, 'The Private Finance Initiative: NHS Capital Expenditure and the Private Finance, above (n 189) 51.

[215] Gaffney et al, 'The Private Finance Initiative: The Politics of the Private Finance Initiative', above (n 190) 252; see generally, R Kuttner, 'Columbia/HCA and the Resurgence of the For-Profit Hospital Business' (1996) 335 *New England Journal of Medicine* 362.

[216] Gaffney et al, ibid.

[217] J Appleby, 'Making Sense of PFI' (Nuffield Trust, 2017), available at: www.nuffieldtrust.org.uk/resource/making-sense-of-pfi.

[218] See generally, European Investment Bank, 'The EIB and Public–Private Partnerships' (1998) 2 *EIB Information* 97.

[219] Pollock, Shaoul and Vickers, above (n 195) 1205.

[220] Pollock, Price and Liebe, above (n 208) 418.

However, even though PFI provides an alternative to financing through taxation and may help avoid an instantaneous increase in public debt, in reality, benefits do not always match the government's expectations.[221] The scheme places most of the responsibility onto the local health care economy. It also has a substantial impact on public authorities' budgets and thereby the money allocated to clinical care.[222] Indeed, the budget to finance health care resources voted by Parliament each year and allocated to every region reveals the trusts' capacity to spend on capital during that set period.[223] Certainly, PFI has displaced the financial burden from the government to NHS trusts, forcing a transfer in responsibility and costs management that prevent the articulation of a coherent national strategy to finance hospitals.[224]

On the other hand, PFI schemes continue to be attractive to the private sector because of the high returns on the capital employed.[225] As lending to government continues to be considered a low-risk activity, the financial markets have responded positively to the initiative by charging low interest rates for PFI loans,[226] but the high profit incentives that drive the private sector to engage in PFI have also been a source of concern.[227] Some academics have suggested that the scheme is an attempt made by the government to drive 'privatisation by the back door'. Indeed, in spite of constant reassurances that the initiative is not meant to impact the delivery of services, PFI has not yielded significant benefits and, in some respects, has threatened the core values of the NHS.[228] In a sense, public funds have been diverted for the private sector to grow, construct and acquire some NHS assets. Resources are no longer allocated based on projected needs, rather, trust plans are based on corporate 'mission statements' and 'vision'.[229] It is possible that this shift is part of a wider agenda that would involve the private sector more directly in the provision of health care services.[230]

The scheme has also generated a significant affordability gap for health care trusts.[231] Claims of value for money have been, for the most part, inaccurate considering trusts' inability to plan for care with limited resources and a portion

---

[221] Gaffney et al, 'The Private Finance Initiative: The Politics of the Private Finance Initiative and the New NHS', above (n 190) 251.

[222] Pollock, Price and Liebe, above (n 208) 418.

[223] Gaffney et al, 'The Private Finance Initiative: NHS Capital Expenditure and the Private Finance Initiative', above (n 189) 50.

[224] Pollock, Shaoul and Vickers, above (n 195) 1205.

[225] Gaffney et al, 'The Private Finance Initiative: The Politics of the Private Finance Initiative and the New NHS', above (n 190) 252.

[226] Pollock, Price and Liebe, above (n 208) 417.

[227] Baggott, above (n 14) 193.

[228] Pollock, Gaffney and Dunnigan, above (n 199) 2.

[229] Pollock, *NHS plc*, above (n 86) 58.

[230] Gaffney et al, 'The Private Finance Initiative: The Politics of the Private Finance Initiative and the New NHS', above (n 190) 249–51.

[231] Pollock, Shaoul and Vickers, above (n 195) 1205.

of their budgets reassigned to capital payments.[232] In fact, the banking crisis that had led to an increase in interest rates at the beginning of the millennium greatly affected the PFI market.[233] The transfer of risk from the taxpayer to the private sector did not compensate for the higher costs associated with the financing scheme.[234] Regardless, the private sector continues to be interested in growing its profit margins and decreasing the fees associated with setting up the contracts (legal and financial advisers) even though these transactional costs are increasingly high, much higher than they would have been for a publicly financed project.[235]

It has also been suggested that PFI is a regressive instrument that tends to create greater inequalities in health care.[236] The gap between what the trust and health care purchasers can spend on financing and the charges demanded by the private sector have led regions to cut essential aspects of health care delivery.[237] Human resources have been affected and services have been reduced. In some hospitals, programmes have even had to be terminated.[238] The increased costs associated with PFI also have consequences at the national level.[239] The government has had to step in to provide subsidies and divert resources away from clinical care to help trusts pay PFI costs.[240]

Over the course of a year, PFI management fees also vary greatly across NHS trusts facilities.[241] Audits in the 1990s suggested that these discrepancies were contributing to the widening affordability gap.[242] However, it is most likely that construction and maintenance costs in a publicly financed system would not have affected the local health care system in such a dramatic manner.[243] On the whole, critics of the initiative have claimed that PFI brings no significant benefits to the NHS and that it does not significantly improve the level of service since it brings no new money to the government; in fact, that the initiative has proven to be more expensive than public financing.[244]

---

[232] Gaffney et al, 'The Private Finance Initiative: NHS Capital Expenditure and the Private Finance, above (n 189) 51.

[233] Pollock, Price and Liebe, above (n 208) 418; M Hellowell, 'Unhealthy Option?' *Public Finance* (30 October 2008), available at: www.publicfinance.co.uk/2008/10/unhealthy-option-mark-hellowell.

[234] See eg, Pollock, Price and Liebe, ibid; M Hellowell and AM Pollock, 'The Private Financing of NHS Hospitals: Politics, Policy and Practice' (2009) 29(1) *Economic Affairs* 13, 14–15; AM Pollock and D Price, 'Has the NAO Audited Risk Transfer in Operational Private Finance Initiative Schemes?' (2008) 28 *Public Money & Management* 173, 175–76.

[235] Shaoul, Stafford and Stapleton, above (n 193) 4.

[236] Gaffney et al, 'The Private Finance Initiative: The Politics of the Private Finance Initiative and the New NHS', above (n 190) 249.

[237] Gaffney et al, 'The Private Finance Initiative: NHS Capital Expenditure and the Private Finance Initiative', above (n 189) 51.

[238] ibid, 48.

[239] ibid.

[240] ibid, 51.

[241] Pollock, Price and Liebe, above (n 208) 418.

[242] ibid, 419; National Audit Office, *The Performance and Management of Hospital PFI Contracts* (London, HM Stationery Office, 2010).

[243] Shaoul, Stafford and Stapleton, above (n 193) 6.

[244] M Pollock, Shaoul and Vickers, above (n 195) 1205; Pollock, *NHS plc*, above (n 86) 57.

Interestingly, in spite of the criticism, the New Labour government undertook a similar scheme for the primary care sector in 2001 introducing the LIFT programme. The primary sector initiative took the form of investment 'vehicles' that could facilitate joint ventures with the private sector to finance the construction and refurbishment of GP premises or to help set up 'one-stop' health centres where patients could access primary care doctors, pharmacists, physiotherapists and podiatrists.[245] Public and private stakeholders were to be re-grouped under a partnership, 'LIFTCo', to take ownership of premises and land, or to refurbish facilities. The premises would then be leased to GPs with the possibility of adding some support services, such as cleaning and maintenance, as part of the rental agreement.[246]

The presence of these consortiums in the primary care sector grew gradually as GPs increasingly had to turn to private corporations to upgrade their facilities.[247] LIFT became an attractive option to GPs practising in underserved areas, as primary care providers no longer had to bear the risk and commitment associated with property ownership to secure premises.[248] Although leading the NHS to channel a portion of its revenues into the private sector, the impact the scheme has had on primary care services is uncertain.[249]

## B. Private Medical Insurance

Over 80 per cent of health care services are publicly funded in the United Kingdom.[250] Similar to other European welfare states, PMI accounts only for a small and declining percentage of health care financing.[251] The private insurance market comprises of company paid plans for which employers subsidise a portion of their employees' health care policy cost, and individual 'out of pocket' insurance policies that are sought and paid for by the insured.[252] However, during the 1970s, PMI had undergone some growth.[253] In the 1980s the Conservative government, in search of the means of reducing public spending, and hoping to share some of the financial burden of the NHS, was also pushing for further expansion of the

---

[245] Pollock, ibid, 156.

[246] Talbot-Smith and Pollock, above (n 203) 94.

[247] Pollock, *NHS plc*, above (n 86) 151.

[248] ibid, 157.

[249] ibid, 159.

[250] Office for National Statistics, 'Expenditure on Healthcare in the UK: 2013' (Office for National Statistics, 2015), available at: www.ons.gov.uk/peoplepopulationandcommunity/healthandsocialcare/healthcaresystem/articles/expenditureonhealthcareintheuk/2015-03-26 6.

[251] AJ Taylor and DR Ward, 'Consumer Attributes and the UK Market for Private Medical Insurance' (2006) 24(7) *International Journal of Bank Marketing* 444, 445–46.

[252] ibid, 446.

[253] Commission on the Future of Health and Social Care in England, *The UK Private Health Market* (The King's Fund, 2014) 2.

PMI market. Thatcher had proposed, with limited success, a tax relief for individuals over 60 seeking private health care insurance.[254] In the 1990s and 2000s the costs of health care services were on the rise and PMI saw its market shrink because of an affordability crisis. Insurers trying to absorb and cope with the swelling costs had to considerably increase premiums.[255]

Data and research on the role played by private medical insurance is therefore limited; however, literature does shed some light on the motivations that lead individuals to the purchase of private insurance.[256] Most often, individuals seek to improve their experience of health care services, or to complement the universal coverage offered by the NHS with voluntary insurance.[257] The desire to avoid waiting lists or to have a broader choice of specialists also motivate certain individuals to enrol in company paid or out of pocket plans. Finally, individuals seeking customised care to match their demands for greater comfort and privacy have more prominently turned to PMI to finance their health care needs.[258]

PMI can either be substitutive, complementary or supplementary. With substitutive private insurance schemes, employers or individuals purchase coverage for interventions that are not provided for under public programmes, usually treatment for curable short-term illness or injury.[259] Complementary insurance products assist with the cost of services that are partly covered by the NHS.[260] Supplementary insurance, for its part, offers individuals a greater choice of providers and faster access to health care services with the private policy.[261] The latter remains the most dominant form of PMI in England.[262]

Patients therefore have the choice to seek medical care under the NHS or turn to a private provider for treatment. The choice is influenced by the severity of illness, the cost of care and the treatment waiting time.[263] All these factors have a direct bearing on the purchase of PMI.[264] There is no unique profile of an individual seeking private health care coverage. However, PMI users seem to share certain features. Individuals that are in a committed relationship living with a spouse or a partner are typically more likely to seek PMI coverage.[265] On the contrary, families

---

[254] Taylor and Ward, above (n 251) 445.
[255] Pollock, *NHS plc*, above (n 86) 68.
[256] See eg, C Propper, 'The Demand for Private Health Care in the UK' (2000) 19 *Journal of Health Economics* 855, 857; Taylor and Ward, above (n 251) 445.
[257] Propper, ibid, 874.
[258] Webster, *The National Health Service: A Political History*, above (n 50) 11.
[259] King and Mossialos, above (n 2) 196.
[260] ibid.
[261] T Besley, J Hall and I Preston, 'Social Security and Health Care Consumption: A Comparison of Alternative Systems Private and Public Health Insurance in the UK' (1998) 42 *European Economic Review* 491, 492.
[262] Boyle, above (n 15) 88.
[263] Propper, above (n 256) 859.
[264] King and Mossialos, above (n 2) 209.
[265] Taylor and Ward, above (n 251) 450.

with multiple children are less likely to turn to private insurance to finance their health care needs. This may be because the cost of multiple dependants under one policy is too high for the advantages that it may bring to the household.[266] Some studies also indicate that there is an inversely proportional tendency to seek private coverage than to seek treatment with the NHS.[267] The demand for PMI is subject to individual levels of income and professional status.[268] Self-employed individuals are also more likely to seek PMI in order to receive care as promptly as possible to counter potential loss of income during a period of illness.[269] Employees covered under company paid plans, for their part, are typically young and well-educated individuals with a higher socio-economic status and supporters of centre-Right politics.[270]

Overall, although demand for private insurance has been relatively flat and minimal for the past decade, PMI may erode the foundations of universality of care with individuals opting out of the NHS for particular treatments and interventions.[271] Indeed, an increase in private coverage could discourage taxpayers funding the NHS to subsidise a system they are making no use of. This could potentially translate into the NHS becoming the 'poor service for the poor'.[272]

## C. The Independent Sector Responding to Consumerism in Health Care

From the foundation of the NHS up until the creation of the internal market, health care services delivery was monolithic and engaged only a limited number of identifiable stakeholders. GPs, NHS medical consultants, specialists, nurses and professionals in hospital settings held a monopoly over health care provisions. Patients were given virtually no choice of treatment and no opportunity to feed back their clinical care experience to the provider. Essentially, clinical care followed a paternalistic model where patients were passively told the treatment they required and guided towards the appropriate provider.[273]

At the beginning of the 1980s, however, the Conservative government had decided to commission ancillary and support services to the private sector, thereby initiating a cultural shift in public services. The 1989 White Paper *Working for*

---

[266] ibid.

[267] ibid 449.

[268] See eg, C Emmerson, C Frayne and A Goodman, 'Should Private Medical Insurance Be Subsidised?' (The King's Fund, 2001) 49, 56; King and Mossialos, above (n 2) 209.

[269] Taylor and Ward, above (n 251) 449.

[270] King and Mossialos, above (n 2) 195.

[271] Besley, Hall and Preston, above (n 261) 496.

[272] Propper, above (n 256) 856.

[273] Alan Milburn, Secretary of State for Health (Speech at the Annual Social Services Conference, Cardiff, 16 October 2002).

*Patients*[274] echoed this trend and introduced a consumer-centred approach in health care.[275] The NHS was then encouraged to purchase care from private providers to alleviate capacity and waiting list issues. It became possible for health care purchasers to directly commission services from private providers without an intermediary. At that time, some health care trusts also started building new wings to their facilities to treat private patients. The market had been formally opened up to private providers even though the independent sector still did not constitute a substantial part of health care delivery.[276]

In the late 1990s, after two decades of Conservative leadership, the newly elected Labour government was equally welcoming of the independent sector's active participation in health care. It had the ambition to reduce costs and increase patients' choice and autonomy.[277] Blair's health care policy mainly focused on a consumerist approach to the delivery of care. It aimed at introducing new market mechanisms to trigger more competition in delivery of services and at promoting the independent sector's involvement to increase patients' choice of secondary care providers.[278] Propositions to this effect were formulated in the *NHS Plan* (2000).[279] During that period, the Independent Healthcare Association also committed to take part in a collaborative framework with the government. PCTs were encouraged to make use of the independent sector to deliver NHS services and health authorities were given permission to include private providers in their planning of operations.[280] As part of the concordat, the government also mandated that a choice of at least one private sector provider be offered to all NHS patients in need of elective care.[281] This agreement was coupled with the establishment of a programme of independent treatment centres that also involved overseas providers in the delivery of a large number of interventions on behalf of the NHS.[282]

Whitehall operated other structural and organisational changes that indirectly supported the new consumerist approach. For instance, in the primary care sector, the enactment of the new GP contract with the provision laid out for 'out of hours' primary care services also called for the independent sector's involvement.

---

[274] *Working for Patients*, above (n 83).

[275] Newman and Vilder, above (n 135) 193.

[276] Baggott, above (n 14) 193.

[277] ibid.

[278] S Peckham and M Sanderson, 'Patient Choice: A Contemporary Policy Story' in M Exworthy (ed), *Shaping Health Policy: Case Study Methods and Analysis* (Bristol, The Policy Press, 2012) 220.

[279] I Greener et al, 'How Did Consumerism Get into the NHS? An Empirical Examination of Choice and Responsiveness in NHS Policy Documents' (2006) 29 *Cultures of Consumption Paper Series* 1, 10–16.

[280] Department of Health, *For the Benefit of Patients: A Concordat with the Private and Voluntary Health Care Provider Sector* (2000).

[281] Boyle, above (n 15) 114.

[282] T Foubister et al, *Private Medical Insurance in the United Kingdom* (Copenhagen, European Observatory on Health Systems and Policies, 2006) vii, 7; see generally, Health Committee, *Independent Sector Treatment Centres*, 4th Report (2005–06, HC 934-I).

Companies, such as Serco and Virgin, felt compelled to compensate for the hours GP practices would no longer cover.[283] With regard to secondary care, the newly available status of Foundation Trusts was giving providers greater autonomy and a budget to engage with the independent sector.[284] By and large, New Labour was on a quest for more efficiency that focused on health care providers but that also aimed to redefine the place of patients in the NHS. Academics were nevertheless critical of these policies and argued that the NHS was no longer a social enterprise acting for the benefit of the population; it had become a holding company franchising out services to public and private providers.[285]

Gradually, the paternalistic approach that had characterised the doctor–patient relationship during the first 40 years of the universal system was replaced by an individualised approach to care. Similar to private sector companies, the NHS had to adapt to the more diverse needs of its customers rather than to have patients adapt to health care providers' processes.[286] Advances in technology had also given rise to a new set of expectations. The change in culture initiated at the beginning of the 1980s had climaxed in the 1990s. The medical profession was no longer dominating the health care policy arena nor was it imposing its knowledge in clinical care. Treatment had become a collaborative effort and health care policy had to reflect the rise in patient autonomy.[287] With more choice patients would be empowered and become more responsible. With more providers, including some from the private sector, competition would peak and prices would be lowered.[288]

Thus, even after the end of the Blair era, the millennium brought other policies that facilitated the independent sector's participation in health care. For instance, up until 2009, patients had to opt out of NHS services if they wished to receive private care on the basis that the partial provision of private services could dilute equality of access to care in the system.[289] However, the *NHS Patients who wish to Pay for Additional Care*[290] policy modified the exception to allow concurrent use of NHS services and private health care:

> Patients may pay for additional private healthcare while continuing to receive care from the NHS. However, in order to ensure that there is no risk of the NHS subsidising private care: It should always be clear whether an individual procedure or treatment is privately funded or NHS funded. Private and NHS care should be kept as clearly separate as possible. Private care should be carried out at a different time to the NHS care

---

[283] National Audit Office, *Memorandum on the Provision of the Out-of-Hours GP Services in Cornwall* (HC 2012–13, 1016).

[284] Baggott, above (n 14) 193.

[285] Talbot-Smith and Pollock, above (n 203) 7.

[286] Newman and Vilder, above (n 135) 196.

[287] See eg, Crinson, above (n 4) 119; Pollock, *NHS plc*, above (n 86) 69.

[288] Baggott, above (n 14) 200–01.

[289] Department of Health, *A Code of Conduct for Private Practice* (2004), available at: www.nhsemployers.org/~/media/Employers/Documents/Pay%20and%20reward/DH_085195.pdf.

[290] Department of Health, *Guidance on NHS Patients Who Wish to Pay for Additional Private Care* (2009) www.gov.uk/government/uploads/system/uploads/attachment_data/file/404423/patients-add-priv-care.pdf

that a patient is receiving. Private care should be carried out in a different place to NHS care, as separate from other NHS patients as possible. A different place would include the facilities of a private healthcare provider, or part of an NHS organisation which has been permanently or temporarily designated for private care, such a private wing, amenity beds or a private room. Trusts may also want to consider using the services of a home healthcare provider where this is clinically appropriate. Putting in place arrangements for separation does not necessarily mean running a separate clinic or ward. As is the case now, specialist equipment such as scanners may be temporarily designated for private use as long as there is no detrimental effect to NHS patients.[291]

Even though this marked a substantial change in attitude, the foundational core of the NHS still had to be preserved. Since it was unimaginable to have patients with equal health care entitlements treated differently in the same ward, private care delivery would remain separate from the delivery of NHS treatments.[292] Notwithstanding this technicality, the policy recognised the complementary and non-substitutive role of the independent sector in the twenty-first century health care system.[293]

Finally, in 2012, the Coalition government took another step in the direction of the private sector with its groundbreaking reform. The Health and Social Care Act (2012) introduced new methods of commissioning health care services with the CCGs taking over the PCTs' purchasing role.[294] CCGs were given the mandate to purchase the best available care including services delivered by the independent sector. Consequently, in past years a greater number of contracts have been awarded to the private sector in health care.[295]

Although only limited data is available on the impact of the independent sector's stakeholders on health care policy, a noticeable revolving door between the sector and the executive branch certainly exists. The private health care industry has had a tendency to maintain close links with the government and legislators, by at times, offering consultancy or more explicitly lobbying in favour of certain policies.[296] On the flip side, the independent sector has a tendency to recruit former government staff members for its industry.[297] This may explain the population's scepticism towards the private sector.[298] A portion of the public is still convinced that for-profit companies, while maximising their gains, will hurt the NHS by overcharging for services and compromise the equal provision entitlement.[299]

---

[291] ibid.

[292] Newdick, above (n 8) 116.

[293] Pollock, *NHS plc*, above (n 86) 73.

[294] Baggott, above (n 14) 194–95.

[295] See generally, G Iacobucci, 'A Third of NHS Contracts Awarded Since Health Act Have Gone to Private Sector' (2014) 349 *BMJ* 1.

[296] Pollock, *NHS plc*, above (n 86) 80.

[297] Baggott, above (n 14) 125.

[298] M Fotaki et al, *Patient Choice and the Organisation and Delivery of Health Services: Scoping Review* (Manchester, NCCSDO, 2005).

[299] Baggott, above (n 14) 195.

# IV. Conclusion

The creation of the NHS in 1948 constituted an outstanding social achievement but it also gave a new and more prominent role to the medical profession. As doctors became central figures in health care policy, medical expertise was no longer limited to clinical input. The foundational concordat between the medical profession and the government indirectly positioned the 'for-profit' sector at the heart of the universal health care system and at the heart of any decision relating to the NHS. Indeed, for the next 40 years, the government would have to have doctors at the negotiating table to secure their engagement and collaboration.[300] Although the relationship between the medical profession and the government continued to be consensual and mutually beneficial, in 1974 the financial strains affecting the NHS called for some reorganisation.[301] As Thatcher came into power at the end of the 1970s, efficiency problems were seriously threatening the future of the system. The Prime Minister, therefore, proceeded with a radical and unilateral reform without the input of the medical profession. With this, the terms of the relationship were redefined, and the system deeply restructured.

Before its implementation, the National Health Service and Community Care Act (1990), establishing the purchaser–provider divide in health care, brought about considerable animosity.[302] Mainly, the medical profession felt threatened by the market rhetoric, although in reality the reform did not encroach on doctors' autonomy nor did it change health care financing methods. GPs would continue to be independent contractors and would be allowed to generate profits, and medical consultants would continue to be directly employed by the NHS and be allowed to engage in the private practice of medicine.[303] Furthermore, the government remained in control of health care financing and the commissioning of health care services thereby protecting the core values of the NHS.[304]

Thus, as New Labour came into power it rapidly abandoned its project to abolish the systemic division in health care. Even though health care delivery would be more focused on the patients rather than providers, the purchasing and provision of services would remain separate. The market ideology also brought a consumerist approach to health care. Whitehall was now promoting partnerships with the independent for-profit sector to finance NHS infrastructures (with PFI) and supply some of its treatments (with a formal concordat).[305] The idea was that with the independent sector formally invited to participate in the NHS enterprise,

---

[300] Crinson, above (n 4) 57.
[301] Wall and Owen, above (n 15) 81.
[302] Boyle, above (n 15) 27.
[303] Tuohy, 'Dynamics of a Changing Health Sphere', above (n 12) 124.
[304] 'About the National Health Service (NHS) in England' *NHS Choices* (13 April 2016), available at: www.nhs.uk/NHSEngland/thenhs/about/Pages/overview.aspx.
[305] Pollock, *NHS plc*, above (n 86) 70.

patients could benefit from more choice in health care.[306] During this period, the medical insurance industry also developed in parallel to the public system but reached stagnation at the beginning of the new millennium.

In the twenty-first century, the NHS continued to face numerous challenges, namely an ageing population and growing public expectations. Major issues affecting the delivery of health care services also led the Coalition government to propose a groundbreaking reform, building in part on its predecessor's private initiatives. The idea was to emulate the private sector to create greater competition and make the most of available resources.[307] The success of the NHS could no longer be measured only by its ability to provide first-class health care services, for it had to do it in a cost-efficient manner.[308] Unsurprisingly, the medical profession was not welcoming of any of these drastic changes and vigorously resisted the Coalition reformative efforts. Nonetheless, the Health and Social Care Act became law in March 2012. The independent sector was set to penetrate the public sphere more deeply to improve patients' experience and resolve lingering scarcity issues.

---

[306] Crinson, above (n 4) 57.
[307] Wall and Owen, above (n 15) 81.
[308] ibid, 74.

# 6

# Locating Ideas of Justice in British Health Care Reforms

'Illness is neither an indulgence for which people have to pay, nor an offence for which they should be penalised, but a misfortune, the cost of which should be shared by the community'.[1]

Aneurin Bevan

## I. Introduction

Minister for Health Aneurin Bevan had the desire to 'generalise the best health advice and treatment'[2] with a national system of care 'available to the whole population freely'.[3] His project was founded on the misconception that a finite amount of ill health was present on the territory, and that it could be tackled with efficient health care services that would eliminate all future health care costs.[4] In a sense, he created the NHS 'in a place of fear'.[5] Fear that death and diseases would decimate the work force, and fear that health care costs would drive the population to poverty.[6] This apprehension also instilled the four core principles of the NHS. First, Bevan believed that only *collectivism* and the centralisation of health care services could guarantee equal and equitable access to the entire population. There was a necessity to respond to fear with a collective action led by the state.[7] Second, Bevan had the ambition to provide a *comprehensive* system to crush the effect of ill health on the population. Health care services had to be available 'from the cradle to the grave'[8] and had to take into account individuals' health care needs.

---

[1] Aneurin Bevan, Minister for Health 1945–51.

[2] National Health Service HC Bill (1946) 45–49.

[3] ibid.

[4] DJ Hunter, *Desperately Seeking Solutions: Rationing Health Care* (London, Longman, 1997) 20.

[5] Aneurin Bevan wrote in 1952 a monograph entitled 'In Place of Fear', relating the period of the creation of the NHS: A Bevan, *In Place of Fear* (New York, Simon and Shuster, 1952).

[6] N Vetter, *The Public Health and the NHS: Your Questions Answered* (Oxon, Radcliffe Medical Press, 1998) 1–7.

[7] J Allsop, *Health Policy and the NHS Towards 2000* (London, Longman, 1995) 28; A Talbot-Smith and AM Pollock, *The New NHS: A Guide* (New York, Routledge, 2006) 2.

[8] See generally, G Rivet, *From Cradle to Grave: The History of the NHS 1988 Onwards Second Part* (London, Blurb, 2017).

Third, health care services had to be *universally* available, financed through general taxation and free at the point of use. Finally, the enterprise would also require the collaboration of the medical profession because of its expertise, its ability to effectively relieve sickness and its capacity to organise health care services. Although its implementation initially challenged Bevan, *professional autonomy* was also central to the project.[9]

By and large, the foundation of the NHS rested on ideas of solidarity, fairness and equality in health care, and the understanding that resources had to be shared in order for the rich and the poor to have the same access to services.[10] Over the years, governments in power have had their own interpretation of this commitment. To various extents, the foundational principles were preserved during the successive health care reforms, even though means to achieve these goals have had to be reinvented. In this respect, *collectivism, universality of care* and *professional autonomy* exhibit a particular form of path dependency in British health care policy.[11] These core values have also led the medical profession to vest itself with a protective role. The government, on the other hand, because of diminishing resources and growing health care needs, has had to ration resources to finance and provide health care services to the entire British population.[12]

These different approaches relay aspects of moral political philosophy and the organising principles.[13] Indeed, the foundational values of the NHS upheld by the medical profession reflect a vision of liberal equality and solidarity in health care, whereas the efforts of various governments to manage health care costs echo utilitarian, libertarian and at times, neoliberal theories. Nonetheless, these observations do not provide sufficient tangible evidence that ideas of justice have made their way into the NHS reforms.

The health care policy-making process in the UK is complex and evolving because it has had to adapt to society and the changing nature of the relationship between for-profit actors and the state. This chapter therefore proposes to shed light on these aspects to understand the place of justice in British health care reforms. The analysis focuses on for-profit stakeholders' relationship with government during these reformative periods and the historical context that gave rise to three major health care reforms: the NHS Act (1946), the NHS and Community Care Act (1990) and the Health and Social Care Act (2012). The White Papers initiating these efforts are also presented in order to unpack how the founding principles have instilled path dependency in health care policy. Finally, discourses used by Members of Parliament (MPs) during the Second Reading of each health

---

[9] Allsop, above (n 7) 28–29; AM Pollock, 'NHS No More?' (2016) 89(12) *Community Practitioner* 28, 28.

[10] C Newdick, 'Promoting Access and Equity in Health: Assessing the National Health Service in England' in CM Flood and A Gross (eds), *The Right to Health at the Public/Private Divide: A Global Comparative Study* (Cambridge, Cambridge University Press, 2014) 107.

[11] Pollock, 'NHS No More?', above (n 9) 28.

[12] DJ Hunter, *The Health Debate* (Bristol, Policy Press, 2016) 44.

[13] See generally ch 2.

care Bill are analysed to determine whether discourses of justice have informed the initial stages of the law-making process and the final version of each Act.[14]

The chapter starts with the inception period; a period during which the post-war government had formulated the project of creating a unified system of care in spite of the medical profession's fierce opposition. As a result, the NHS Act (1946), creating the NHS, also implicitly formalised a tacit concordat between the state and the medical profession. The Act tied in the fate of the institution to that of its providers. The NHS and Community Care Act (1990) presented in the second part of the chapter, however, marks an important shift in the relationship between the medical profession and the state. Margaret Thatcher's decision to separate the financing from the provision of health care planted the seed of competition in the NHS and a new managerial trend. The reform also signalled the government's ability to operate change without the approval of the medical profession. The Act was a defining moment introducing the internal market in health care and using a libertarian approach to allocate resources. The system nonetheless continued to pursue equality in health care. The last part of the chapter discusses the most recent and controversial health care reform of the NHS, the NHS Health and Social Care Act (2012). The Coalition government had taken on the most extensive overhaul of the NHS since its creation and faced significant push back on the part of the medical profession and the British public. The analysis demonstrates how the egalitarian foundations of the NHS have been eroded with a consumerist rhetoric focused on patients' choice and the introduction of formal partnership with private and independent providers in health care.

This chapter concludes that British health care reforms and the legislation enacted to implement these policies draw from elements of justice that fostered path dependency in the NHS. The system built on three core values has in many aspects been the victim of its own success as health care needs and demands have grown, and resources have become scarcer. The medical profession opposed to the privatisation of the system has also had to compromise and accept the growing participation of the private and independent sector.

## II.  The National Health Service Act (1946)

The provision of health care services in the United Kingdom at the beginning of the twentieth century largely depended on the Poor Law hospital system and private voluntary health care facilities.[15] Local government ran most hospitals and

---

[14] See appendix for the detail of textual occurrences analysed in the primary sources.

[15] JS Hacker, 'The Historical Logic of National Health Insurance: Structure and Sequence in the Development of British, Canadian, and US Medical Policy' (1998) 12 *Studies in American Political Development* 57, 65.

community doctors helped with the decentralised and uneven ambulatory services to the best of their abilities. Public health and sanitation were under the purview of multiple decision-making bodies, and publicly funded mental health services were provided through a system of county asylums. The disparate organisation of services and the lack of coordination among institutions of care contributed to the poor allocation of resources in the country. Health care financing was also piecemeal. Health insurance was mostly the privilege of the upper class, even though, under the National Insurance Act (1911) and Lloyd George's insurance scheme, workers could benefit from free GP care.[16] Charities, nonetheless, had to help a majority of Britons cope with their rising health care costs. Scientific knowledge was also outpacing existing institutions and the modernisation and expansion of technical scientific knowledge called for the improvement of health care services.

In comparison to its then Dominions (Canada, Australia and New Zealand) the United Kingdom was falling behind because of a lack of resources and the absence of coordination among entities dispensing care.[17] Yet, in contrary to its American counterpart, the British health care system had, at that stage, achieved more with limited means. It had some voluntary hospitals and a small network of publicly funded institutions.[18] Efforts to centralise health care services had already begun in the late nineteenth and early twentieth centuries.[19] Thus, prior to the creation of the NHS, the idea of a national health care system had been in the making for many decades. Nevertheless, it took a constellation of factors to achieve the most 'outstanding example of socialised medicine in the western world'.[20]

The Coalition government had laid the groundwork for the creation of a national health service during the Second World War with the creation of the national Emergency Medical Service (1939) and the report on Social Insurance and Allied Services (Beveridge report, 1942).[21] Both initiatives had helped gain the public's approval.[22] The rising socialist ideology and the impression left by two world conflicts also helped initiate reflection on the values that would later become pillars of the health care institution. Essentially, the enactment of the NHS Act (1946) was the by-product of a particular social and historical context, 50 years of enquiry and intense negotiations between the state and the medical profession.[23]

---

[16] See generally, AS Pringle, *The National Insurance Act, 1911* (Edinburgh, William Green & Sons, 1912).

[17] C Webster, *The National Health Service: A Political History* (Oxford, Oxford University Press, 2002) 23.

[18] C Webster, *The Health Services Since the War: Problems of Health Care*, vol 1 (London, HM Stationery Office, 1988) 23.

[19] I Crinson, *Health Policy: A Critical Perspective* (London, Sage Publications, 2009) 61.

[20] Webster, *The National Health Service: A Political History*, above (n 17) 23.

[21] R Klein, *The New Politics of the NHS: From Creation to Reinvention*, 7th edn (London, Radcliffe Publishing, 2013) 17–18.

[22] D Black, 'Change in the NHS' (1992) 13 *Public Health Policy* 156, 157.

[23] I Kennedy and A Grubb, *Medical Law* (Oxford, Oxford University Press, 2000) 131.

Thus, on 5 July 1948 Britain became the first country to offer free entitlement to medical care to its entire population with the creation of the NHS.[24]

## A. The Beveridge Report

The war had driven the United Kingdom into an economic depression, placing greater emphasis on issues of social security and igniting a spirit of solidarity that helped introduce new discussions at a national level.[25] The enemy had also humiliated the country because of the poor state of its social system. In the span of only a few months of occupation, Germany's Luftwaffe had been successful in coordinating all hospitals under the civil defence regional association. This was a greater achievement than British politicians and planners had accomplished over the previous two decades.[26]

Thus, Walter Elliot, Minister of Health during the war, promised to establish a comprehensive hospital service.[27] However, to take action he first had to take stock. Preliminary work was initiated during the summer of 1941 with the creation of the Committee on Social Insurance and Allied Service. The goal of the working group was to identify and provide solutions to the issues brought about by the haphazard and piecemeal growth of the social security system. Economist Sir William Beveridge immediately took charge of the committee and decided to broaden its original scope. The political elite and population's dissatisfaction with social security system had shaped his convictions and gave him greater ambitions.[28]

He chose to reconstruct the social security system in its entirety, seriously undermining the initial intent to limit the review to hospital services. With regard to health care services, he also called for a radical overhaul.[29] Rather than limiting his task to an enquiry into the insurance system, the exercise encompassed many other policy areas such as medical treatment, prevention of unemployment and family provisions.[30] To him, the war had set the stage for 'a revolutionary moment ... a time for revolutions, not for patching'.[31] He took the analysis as an opportunity to prompt the government's commitment to a post-war social reform. He therefore proceeded with the review and compiled his recommendations in a report published on 20 November 1942.[32]

---

[24] Klein, *The New Politics of the NHS*, above (n 21) 1; S Boyle, 'United Kingdom (England): Health System Review' (WHO Regional Office of Europe, 2011) 26.

[25] Webster, *The National Health Service: A Political History*, above (n 17) 8.

[26] ibid, 6.

[27] ibid, 7.

[28] J Harris, *William Beveridge: A Biography* (Oxford, Clarendon Press, 1997) 378–79.

[29] Webster, above (n 17) 7.

[30] Harris, above (n 28) 387.

[31] WH Beveridge, *Social Insurance and Allied Services* (London, HM Stationery Office, 1942) 1.

[32] See generally, HE Sigerist, 'From Bismarck to Beveridge: Developments and Trends in Social Security Legislation' (1943) 13 *Bulletin of the History of Medicine* 365.

Problems affecting England during the war years were indeed 'giants on the road to reconstruction [:] disease, ignorance, squalor and idleness'.[33] The memories of the Poor Law hospital system's incapacity to deal with the victims of the 1940 bombings had to be replaced with a concrete solution.[34] According to the committee, the only way to fight the 'want'[35] was to put together a solidary national system.[36] The system had to be equal, universal and based on 'needs' rather than 'means'.[37] Emphasis was put on the notion of 'subsistence' to argue that social security should account for inequalities rather than focus on one's financial capacity.[38]

More concretely, the report suggested that 'medical treatment covering all [required care should] be provided for all citizens by a national health service' and proposed to finance the system through central taxation.[39] The project relayed a Durkheimian notion of solidarity, in which the state imposes social obligations for the benefit of all its citizens. The report mentions that

> [a]fter trial of a different principle, it has been found to accord best with the sentiments of the British people that an insurance organised by the community by use of compulsory power, each individual should stand in on the same terms; none should claim to pay less because he is healthier or has more regular employment. In accord with that view, the proposals of the Report mark another step forward to the development of State insurance as a new type of human institution, differing both from the former methods of preventing or alleviating distress and from voluntary insurance. The term 'social insurance' to describe this institution implies both that it is compulsory and that men stand together with their fellows. The term implies a pooling of risks except so far as separation of risks serves a social purpose.[40]

For Beveridge, it was the responsibility of 'the State to offer security for service and contribution. [To] organis[e] security ... not [to] stifle incentive, opportunity, responsibility; in establishing a minimum',[41] making for a fundamentally egalitarian system. By meeting the needs of its citizens, the state could provide sufficient health care entitlements to enable the pursuit of opportunities. Health care, like police protection or the maintenance of the roads, had to be free at the point of use and available to all, to grant each individual the same protection and opportunities.[42]

Without explicitly referencing the doctrine of liberal equality, the report nevertheless established health care as a primary good. In order to guarantee equal

---

[33] Beveridge, above (n 31) 1.
[34] Harris, above (n 28) 378.
[35] Beveridge, above (n 31) 1.
[36] Harris, above (n 28) 409–10.
[37] See generally, Beveridge, above (n 31).
[38] Harris, above (n 28) 386.
[39] Beveridge, above (n 31) 7.
[40] ibid, 6–7.
[41] ibid, 1.
[42] B Edwards, J Linton and C Potter, *The National Health Service: A Manager's Tale 1946–1992* (London, Nuffield Provincial Hospitals Trust, 1993) 3.

access to services, the allocation of resources had to be put in the hands of the public power. An unequal distribution would be tolerable to provide the entire population with the same opportunities and level the playing field. The most needy and the least advantaged would ultimately be favoured by the system. Although minimal, the Beveridge plan aimed at providing protection against poverty and aid based on needs. Wartime politicians would also have to take a stance on the content of a 'social minimum'.[43]

Although acclaimed by the general population, the results of the inquiry created controversy among interest groups. Voluntary hospital lobbying groups along with the BMA had launched a virulent attack against the planners and had been successful in blocking the initiative. Disagreement stalled the reform and precluded the achievement of consensus over a new system.[44] Beveridge's ideas however, helped initiate a debate that led to the publication of the Coalition government's White Paper *A National Health Service* in February 1944. The policy document proposed a comprehensive health care service organised and delivered through a centralised system. Themes of equality in health care and the urgency to address the population's health care needs formed the basis of the document.[45]

## B. The Foundations of the First Universal Health Care System

Labour Prime Minister Clement Attlee appointed Aneurin Bevan to the Ministry of Health as he came into power after the war. Attlee was convinced that Bevan had sufficient strength to reinitiate discussions and lead the negotiations on the creation of a centralised health care system.[46] Bevan believed in a bold, civilised and forward-thinking health care service for the United Kingdom. He was ambitious and demonstrated an ability to take decisive and constructive action.[47] In fact, a show of strength was likely to be necessary now that the BMA had eroded the government's ability to produce a coherent health care policy with its relentless negotiations during the war.

In spite of the tension, Bevan had decided to re-establish the Ministry's supremacy.[48] He strategically began by gaining the trust of the health service planning operation staff hoping to diffuse the pessimistic atmosphere that years of quarrelling over the future of health care services had embedded. He also

---

[43] EK Den Bakker and GW De Wit, 'Social Security in a European Perspective' (1983) 8 *Geneva Papers on Risk and Insurance* 248, 255.

[44] Webster, *The National Health Service: A Political History*, above (n 17) 8.

[45] Ministry of Health, *A National Health Service* (Cmd 6502, 1944).

[46] Webster, *The Health Services Since the War*, above (n 18) 76.

[47] Webster, *The National Health Service: A Political History*, above (n 17) 13.

[48] ibid, 14.

aimed to manage the discontent of senior officials and the medical profession to produce health care policy more effectively.[49] Bevan's plans, however, constituted a dramatic break from the past, as he took little to no input from outside interests.[50] He proposed a tripartite system that would reorganise the functioning of hospitals, teams of GPs and health centres. Health care services were also expected to function 'subject to local influence' although they would primarily remain under central control. Finally, the system would be financed through general taxation and founded on solidarity. More affluent Britons would pay proportionally more for the same level of service received than indigent Britons. The poorer part of the population would have its health care needs 'subsidised' by the wealthier class.[51] The government had objected to confining the provision of health care services to the least affluent individuals as it implied a means-based approach. Bevan could not bring himself to assess the wealth of patients as a condition to provide health care services.[52]

Alas, Bevan not only faced opposition from the medical profession. He also had to deal with issues in the political arena. The Conservatives were objecting to the proposal. They saw his plan to nationalise voluntary hospitals as an attack on charitable institutions. They were also convinced that the regulation of doctors' salaries would result in a full-time salaried service. As the proposed Bill made its way through the legislative process, they unconventionally opposed the proposition during the Third Reading in the House of Commons. Even though he had the support of the majority in the Commons, Bevan also faced criticism within his own camp.[53] A faction of the Labour Party, conversely to the Conservatives, thought that the system should offer a full-time salaried service. They also strongly opposed the idea of having paid beds in state hospitals. Finally, both camps agreed that the limited involvement of local government in the allocation and provision of health care services could be problematic.[54]

Bevan successfully brushed off the opposition in Parliament with some minor amendments to the Bill. The NHS Act was thereby enacted on 6 November 1946.[55] Lord Beveridge saluted Bevan's success, as for the first time a 'true Ministry of Health' was given the authority and duties to finally stamp out ill health.[56] Outside Parliament, the victory was not so swift. Voluntary hospital administrators worried that free health care services and the suppression of access barriers would dampen public interest and charitable contributions, which, most certainly, would harm the system. The government responded to their concerns but would

---

[49] ibid.
[50] Minister of Health, *Memorandum on the Future of the Hospital Services* (Ministry of Health, 13 December 1945) 20, 22.
[51] Webster, *The Health Services Since the War*, above (n 18) 97–98.
[52] Vetter, above (n 6) 30.
[53] M Foot, *Aneurin Bevan: A Biography Vol 2, 1945–60* (London, Paladin, 1975) 104, 155–56.
[54] Webster, *The Health Services Since the War*, above (n 18) 97–98.
[55] Webster, *The National Health Service: A Political History*, above (n 17) 15.
[56] Webster, *The Health Services Since the War*, above (n 18) 100.

not concede. It could no longer rely on fear to stimulate charity. The argument ultimately silenced the voluntary hospitals and local authority representatives.[57]

The medical profession made a better case for its members.[58] The patchwork quilt of services delivered before 1948 was based on private agreements between doctors and patients. Now, the BMA had to take a firm stand in negotiating the role of doctors under a new public system. Doctors had initially voted 'no' to the Act and refused to join the ranks of the NHS.[59] They did not want to settle for a secondary role in health care.

Although equally fundamental, issues brought forward by medical consultants and GPs were different. Medical consultants were pushing for regionalised health care services, although they were not averse to the idea of a nationalised system. They were more preoccupied with the remuneration they would receive under the new system. Bevan strategically negotiated and offered a compromise. Medical consultants would still be allowed to practise medicine privately in NHS hospitals even though they would be employed under a full-time or part-time NHS contract. They would also be given distinctions in the form of capitation fees to reward excellence and to compensate for any loss of private earnings. Bevan had lobbied the medical consultants and, as he later claimed, had 'stuffed their mount with gold'[60] and for the government these concessions were worth making. Bevan had finally secured the cooperation of medical consultants.[61]

GPs also entered negotiations with distrust and unwillingness to compromise. They were dissatisfied with what the government had proposed and were particularly disgruntled with Bevan.[62] They wanted to preserve their right to sell the goodwill value associated with their medical practices and wanted their remuneration to be based on a capitation fee free of government control.[63] Although they initially also refused to join the NHS, with the medical consultants on board, they found themselves in a more precarious position. Eventually, the anxiety and the fear of losing patients to other practitioners made some GPs cave in and sign NHS contracts.[64] The rest were able to reach a reasonable compromise with the government.[65] They remained independent contractors on the condition that they would cooperate with the NHS enterprise. Although they were barred from charging fees to patients, they had the monopoly over primary care services and were permitted to engage in the private practice of medicine.[66]

---

[57] T Delamothe, 'NHS at 60: Founding Principles' (2008) 336 *British Medical Journal* 1216, 1218.

[58] Webster, *The National Health Service: A Political History*, above (n 17) 26.

[59] See generally, Edwards, Linton and Potter, above (n 42).

[60] S Ainsworth, 'The Birth of the NHS' (2008) 36(1) *Practice Nurse* 38, 38.

[61] Webster, *The National Health Service: A Political History*, above (n 17) 26.

[62] Ainsworth, above (n 60) 38.

[63] Webster, *The National Health Service: A Political History*, above (n 17) 27.

[64] Ainsworth, above (n 60) 38.

[65] Webster, *The National Health Service: A Political History*, above (n 17) 28; National Health Service Act 1946, Part IV 33–36.

[66] AM Pollock, *NHS plc: The Privatisation of Our Health Care* (London, Verso, 2004) 153.

Overall, the negotiations marked a turning point for the medical profession. The for-profit sector's activism had made strides during the negotiation process and help medical professionals secure their independence and a unique status under the new system.[67] Clinical decisions, but also the planning and management of health care services, would have to involve medical consultants and GPs.[68] For-profit stakeholders had tacitly agreed to protect and safeguard the NHS' core egalitarian principles in exchange for their autonomy. Ultimately, the British population and the medical profession had entered into a social contract that laid the foundations of the new health services.[69]

## C. Ideas of Liberal Equality

The three-day debates for the Second Reading of the National Health Service Bill[70] that led to the enactment of the NHS Act (1946) were characteristic of peacetime adversarial politics, but also relayed deeper concerns and ideas of liberal equality at the core of the NHS.[71] Bevan began the discussion with some introductory remarks and for the most part dominated the debate. Throughout his intervention he stressed the importance of equality and universality of care and argued that subsidiarity was an unhelpful method to organise the provision of health care services. He even contended that 'it [was] repugnant to a civilized community for hospitals to have to rely upon charity ...'.[72] He further explained that centralisation was necessary and that 'it [was] quite impossible ... to hand over the voluntary hospitals to the local authorities'.[73] In order to achieve universality of care subsidiarity had to be discarded. He talked about a social contract as the basis of the system, and asked:

> If it be our contract with the British people, if it be our intention that we should universalise the best, that we shall promise every citizen in this country the same standard of service, how can that be articulated through a rate-borne institution which means that the poor authority will not be able to carry out the same thing at all?[74]

Other MPs mentioned the stigma associated with charity, thereby supporting Bevan's argument. For instance, Labour MP Harold Boardman stated that 'working men and working women ... [did] not want charity whether the source [was] good or bad. Charity at its best humiliates'.[75] Many other interventions were critical of

---

[67] Klein, *The New Politics of the NHS*, above (n 21) 19–20.
[68] Allsop, above (n 7) 30.
[69] H Eckstein, 'Pressure Group Politics' (1960) 35 *Academic Medicine* 1069, 1069.
[70] HC Second Reading 30 April 1946, vol 422, cols 43–142; HC Second Reading 1 May 1946, vol 422, cols 59–313; HC Second Reading 2 May 1946, vol 422, cols 323–417.
[71] R Baggott, *Understanding Health Policy* (Bristol, Policy Press, 2015) 25.
[72] HC Second Reading 30 April 1946, vol 422, cols 43–142, 47.
[73] ibid, 49.
[74] ibid.
[75] HC Second Reading 1 May 1946 vol 422, cols 59–313, 284.

the principle of subsidiarity and also attacked libertarian rhetoric in health care.[76] Participants in both hearings called for more solidarity within the community to share health care risks, financial burdens and called for a universal system of health care benefits.[77]

Parliamentary Secretary to the Ministry of Health, Charles Key, even targeted the for-profit stakeholders in his remarks to explain how their interests may not be aligned with the needs of the community. He argued that 'the interests of the community demand [a] distribution of medical services ... organised with the claims and needs of patients and not the whims and fancies of practitioners as the guiding factor'. His reflection brought forward the foundational principles of equality in resources and access to health care at the core of the NHS. He explained how it was necessary to build a system based on solidarity and that

> the fundamental relationship between doctor and patient [would] remain what it [was]. The great difference [would] be that we shall not pay fees for attention. We shall pool our resources as a community and pay doctors for our general care, irrespective of our individual needs.[78]

Ideas of liberal equality emerged in most of the discussions; in particular, the importance of providing equal access to health care to enable the realisation of life plans was a theme of many interventions.[79] Labour MP Frederic Messer described the new Bill as an initiative that needs 'to bring within the reach of every working man the opportunity of treatment without having to put his hand in his pocket and pay for it at the time he was ill'.[80] Health care services were to encourage mutual support among members of British society to foster a sense of responsibility and to provide more resources for Britons to improve their opportunities to achieve life plans. Parliamentary Secretary to the Ministry of Health, Charles Key, further evoked the idea asking:

> Why should these local citizens, with greater means at their disposal, and greater opportunities for development, do less than their predecessors have done? I am convinced that they will do more. With the growing sense of social responsibility which is so evident in our people today, greater interest, greater initiative and greater participation in the development of our social service will become more potent than ever before.[81]

The medical community, for its part, was left outside the walls of Parliament. The BMA and its interests were therefore mostly underrepresented. Addressing the role of the medical profession in the new system, the Lord Privy Seal, Arthur

---

[76] HC Second Reading 30 April 1946, vol 422, cols 43–142, 47, 73; HC Second Reading 1 May 1946 vol 422, cols 59–313, 213, 247, 283.

[77] HC Second Reading 30 April 1946, vol 422, cols 43–142, 71; HC Second Reading 1 May 1946 vol 422, cols 59–313, 213, 220, 312.

[78] HC Second Reading 1 May 1946, vol 422, cols 59–313, 214.

[79] HC Second Reading 30 April 1946, vol 422, cols 43–142, 82, 137; HC Second Reading 1 May 1946, vol 422, cols 59–313, 275.

[80] HC Second Reading 30 April 1946, vol 422, cols 43–142, 137.

[81] HC Second Reading 1 May 1946, vol 422, cols 59–313, 208.

Greenwood, voiced his disapproval of a market approach in medicine. He also contended that medical professionals were misperceived and that, with enough professional autonomy, they could be invaluable partners to foster a comprehensive health care system in Britain. In response to the Conservative Party that was supporting the profession he stated that:

> What [members of the Opposition] say, in effect, is that, unless doctors are allowed to buy and sell practices like hucksters in the market place, and unless they can retain their private enterprise, they are not going to be good public servants. I deny that. In the public hospitals of this country today there are full-time salaried men who never earn a guinea in fees. Is anybody going to suggest that they are bad doctors because there is not the motive of personal gain? I do not believe it, and I say that the younger doctors, who do not want to scramble and save money with which to buy practices and many of whom have served in the Forces, are public-spirited men who are prepared to serve the public without the incentive of being able to buy or sell practices or go running round with a good bedside manner to collect more and more patients. I do not believe what hon Members have suggested of the medical profession.[82]

Similarly, Bevan thought financial incentives could potentially compromise the integrity of the health care system. He was firmly opposed to the merchandising of health care and therefore gave no concrete sign of a compromise to the medical community during the discussions. Indeed, the concordat between the state and the medical profession was achieved only after the legislative process was completed. Nevertheless, despite grievances and protest, doctors struck an advantageous deal with the government and gained important leverage. Thus, the NHS was launched in July 1948 with the medical profession finally on board. Bevan had 'universalize[d] the best' health care services, divorced the ability to pay for health care from the provision of quality treatments,[83] and 'provide[d] the people of Great Britain, no matter where they [were], with the same level of service'[84] free of charge at any point of use.[85] His ambitions to improve and maximise the British population's good health had materialised through the advent of an egalitarian system. He hoped that the national health system could serve its intended purpose: exhaust ill health in the territory, improve and reduce the costs of medical treatment and provide better care to workers to consolidate a more productive workforce.

## III. The National Health Service and Community Care Act (1990)

After 30 years of governance based on the mobilisation of consensus in health care policy, the general election of 1979 marked a dramatic turning point. Conservative

---

[82] HC Second Reading 2 May 1946, vol 422, cols 323–417, 398–99.
[83] Edwards, Linton and Potter, above (n 42) 4.
[84] National Health Service Act 1946, Part I.
[85] Edwards, Linton and Potter, above (n 42) 4.

Prime Minister Margaret Thatcher within the span of a decade would accomplish one of the most radical changes to the NHS to enforce a new culture based mostly on conflict management.[86] The medical profession would then see its role, within the health care system and in the realm of policy making, dramatically changed.

In the early 1980s, Prime Minister Thatcher and her government undertook a programme of important economic and social reform. The Conservatives sought to reduce public expenditure and the government's involvement in social policy, both thought to be at the root of the economic downturn.[87] As a result, a shift towards rationalisation and privatisation was initiated. First, to increase efficiency, ancillary services such as laundry, catering and cleaning in public facilities were contracted out to private providers.[88] Tenders remained open to the usual providers, but the private sector was also invited to participate. Whoever offered the lowest price would win the contract; most often the in-house services would lower its workers' wages to secure the deal.[89] These changes caused discontent in the sector and made the medical profession more wary of what they thought was an attempt to privatise health care services.[90]

Naturally, NHS spending also had to be reviewed to optimise public resources, as the health care system had become most emblematic of the 'institutionalised stagnation'.[91] Health care services were in deadlock because the NHS had to cope with contradicting demands. Advances in technology and the ageing population required more resources, whereas the period of economic austerity called for a restriction in health care spending,[92] both of which, to a different extent, impacted the medical profession.[93] Thatcher had initially planned to curb expenses and more strategically weaken the power of public sector unions to achieve her high-efficiency goals.[94]

Although past governments had been mostly preoccupied with the structure of the NHS, Thatcher, bearing in mind these considerations, ordered an inquiry[95] that focused mainly on the organisation's dynamics.[96] Sir Roy Griffiths, managing

---

[86] P Day and R Klein, 'The Mobilisation of Consent versus the Management of Conflict: Decoding the Griffiths Report' (1983) 287 *British Medical Journal* 1813, 1813.

[87] R Robinson and A Dixon, *Health Care Systems in Transition: The United Kingdom* (Copenhagen, European Observatory on Health Care Systems, 1999) vii, 7.

[88] C Cousins, 'The Restructuring of Welfare Work: The Introduction of General Management and the Contracting out of Ancillary Services in the NHS' (1988) 2 *Work, Employment & Society* 210, 219–25.

[89] Vetter, above (n 6) 65; see generally, S Harrison, DJ Hunter and C Pollit, *The Dynamics of British Health Policy* (London, Unwin Hyman, 1990).

[90] Vetter, above (n 6) 66.

[91] R Griffiths, *NHS Management Inquiry: Report to the Secretary of State for Social Services* (Department of Health and Social Security, 1983) 9e.

[92] Klein, *The New Politics of the NHS*, above (n 21) 105.

[93] ibid, 106–07.

[94] Pollock, *NHS plc*, above (n 66) 38.

[95] Griffiths, above (n 91).

[96] P Nairne, 'Managing the DHSS Elephant: Reflections on a Giant Department' (1983) 54 *Political Quarterly* 243.

director of Sainsbury's supermarkets was designated to lead the review. His private sector experience made him the best candidate to investigate the NHS' inefficiency.[97] In his report, he recommended a move towards a more managerial approach and away from the old style consensus that had traditionally character-ised the management of health care services.[98] According to the Griffiths Report, it was necessary to appoint general managers to provide leadership at every level, be it in health care units or district and regional health care authorities. Health authorities were 'being swamped with directives without being given direction'.[99] It was difficult to understand the chain of command and to pinpoint who was in charge at each level.[100] However, it was crucial to 'stimulate initiative, urgency, and vitality'[101] in order to optimise the resources allocated to health care. Thus, line management was to replace the decision-making process of professional groups.[102]

Griffiths was first to imagine a more dynamic and 'business-like' NHS that had a clear sense of direction.[103] He was critical of the status quo[104] that character-ised the institution and he believed that it made it 'extremely difficult to achieve change'.[105] Unsurprisingly, Griffiths' innovative market approach was not well received by the health care workforce and his proposal was perceived as an unsta-ble and suspicious project.[106] The medical profession was convinced that general managers at any level were bound to become powerless and, like in the past, would defer any decisions back to them. Even though the report had diminished the Conservatives' popularity and produced no significant changes, it was nonetheless precursor to the dramatic change that would overtake the NHS seven years later.[107] The Conservative government was nonetheless successful in instilling some struc-tural changes with the enactment of the Health Services Act (1980) removing a bureaucratic layer in the organisation and giving power to the Secretary of State to establish district health authorities.

During the general election campaign of 1987 many debates focused on further reforms of the NHS. The Labour Party targeted Thatcherite social policies and the Social Democratic Party/Liberal Alliance's manifesto heavily emphasised the NHS' 'state of fundamental crisis and malaise'.[108] Despite the attacks, the Conserv-atives were brought back into power, but with a severely diminished majority.[109]

---

[97] Webster, *The National Health Service: A Political History*, above (n 17) 167.
[98] Day and Klein, above (n 86) 1813.
[99] Griffiths, above (n 91) 6.
[100] Vetter, above (n 6) 66.
[101] Griffiths, above (n 91) 9.
[102] Vetter, above (n 6) 66.
[103] C Ham, *Management and Competition in the NHS* (Abingdon, Radcliffe Medical Press, 1997) 2; Griffiths, above (n 91) 1.
[104] Griffiths, ibid, 15.
[105] ibid, 8.
[106] Webster, *The National Health Service: A Political History*, above (n 17) 174.
[107] Robinson and Dixon, above (n 87) 8.
[108] Webster, *The National Health Service: A Political History*, above (n 17) 124.
[109] ibid, 125.

The general election having been a difficult experience, so the Party needed to restore its reputation. Every Tuesday and Thursday during Prime Minister's Question Time at the House of Commons Margaret Thatcher 'had thrown at her case after case of ward closures, interminably postponed operations and allegedly avoidable infant deaths, all of them attributed to Government parsimony'.[110]

Funding levels combined with mismanagement had put the NHS in serious difficulty.[111] Government funding had not sufficiently increased to fill the widening gap. Hospital services were affected the most, as the 'efficiency trap' penalised productivity improvements, and expenses were on the rise while incomes were merely stable. Hospital managers were left with no other choice than to partially close beds, cancel non-emergency admissions and freeze staff hiring to reduce expenditures.[112] Doctors and patients were greatly dissatisfied. The BMA was requesting additional resources to overcome the shortfall. The Royal Colleges of Surgeons, Physicians, Obstetricians and Gynaecologists had also decided to issue a joint statement denouncing the critical state of the NHS.[113] Thus, on 31 January 1989, Thatcher announced the launch of a new inquiry that would lead to the publication of the White Paper *Working for Patients*.[114] The new policy formulation would ultimately lead to another major health care reform with the enactment of the NHS and Community Care Act (1990).[115]

## A. Working for Patients

During its first two terms in office the Thatcher government was not entirely successful in fostering policy that would create value-for-money in health care. Despite the increase in human resources and the progress made with treatment of patients, the government was unable to diffuse the negative perception of its policies. The population believed that Conservative parsimony was to blame for the inefficient NHS.[116] For-profit stakeholders together with the parties of the opposition entered into a 'dialogue of the deaf'[117] with Whitehall, which made it even more difficult to find concrete solutions.

The Chancellor of the Exchequer, Nigel Lawson, therefore suggested another review of health care services to guarantee, this time, that spending would yield real value and improve patient care.[118] Convinced, Thatcher accepted immediately and began to organise the review. On 25 January 1988, during the BBC

---

[110] N Lawson, *The View from No 11* (London, Corgi Books, 1993) 612.

[111] Webster, *The National Health Service: A Political History*, above (n 17) 133.

[112] Ham, above (n 103) 3.

[113] ibid.

[114] Department of Health, *Working for Patients* (Cm 555, 1989).

[115] Edwards, Linton and Potter, above (n 42) 146.

[116] Webster, *The National Health Service: A Political History*, above (n 17) 182–83.

[117] Klein, *The New Politics of the NHS*, above (n 21) 142–43.

[118] ibid, 141.

television programme *Panorama*, she unexpectedly announced that a small group of her ministers would initiate a high-level inquiry into the NHS.[119] Thatcher had purposely set up the Cabinet committee to challenge the medical profession and to signal the new and lesser role she wanted to give it in health care policy. The announcement triggered an immediate reaction from the BMA. Not invited to participate in the exercise, the medical profession was slighted. Doctors interpreted the government's lack of consultation as a deliberate snub to the profession.[120]

The inquiry had to explore the possibility of a radical reform. The committee discussed a new financing system based on private insurance to reduce public involvement in health care and hopefully increase patient choice. The universal health care model was challenged as it was argued that it would be most optimal for patients to behave like consumers with the power to purchase health care services in a competitive market place. Other possibilities were also discussed, among which were a European model of social insurance and a health voucher system. The committee however concluded that general taxation remained the most adequate model to finance the NHS.[121]

Even though problems of rampant health care costs in the United States were not directly relevant to the British system's underfunding issues, the committee took interest in the American health care model.[122] American Defence Economist and Professor of Public and Private Management at Stanford University, Alain Enthoven, was called to provide some expertise, having previously worked on the HMO model and market solutions in health care. Enthoven, in his monograph *An American Looks at Incentives to Efficiency in Health Services Management in the UK*,[123] provided some insight on the issues affecting the NHS. He reaffirmed that money was not following the patient. Even though as an organisation the NHS was efficient, it lacked control over clinical services.[124] He advocated more incentives to stimulate productivity in health care and set out the provocative idea of an internal market for the provision of health care services. Competitive tendering from public or private health care providers to obtain NHS contracts could bring down consultant charges and introduce some form of auto-regulation for health care prices, quality of care and cost-effectiveness. The internal market could also tackle access issues. Health authorities would 'trade' with one another the health care services purchased from the private sector, thereby guaranteeing that all services were available irrespective of the area in which the authority was located.[125]

---

[119] ibid, 140–41.
[120] Edwards, Linton and Potter, above (n 42) 151.
[121] Klein, *The New Politics of the NHS*, above (n 21) 146–47; Vetter, above (n 6) 66.
[122] Klein, ibid, 148–49.
[123] See generally, AC Enthoven, *Reflections on the Management of the National Health Service: An American Looks at Incentives to Efficiency in Health Services Management in the UK* (London, Nuffield Provincial Hospitals Trust, 1985).
[124] Vetter, above (n 6) 66.
[125] ibid, 67.

The review completed, on 31 January 1989, the White Paper *Working for Patients* was published to sum up its conclusions and provide a concrete policy proposal.[126] Although radical change had been promised, the founding principles of the NHS, for the most part, remained intact,[127] and although the concept was extensively discussed, the words 'internal market' never appeared in the pages of the White Paper. The document was promoting a culture of consciousness, the expansion of patient choice, and called for an innovative split between the purchasers and the providers of health care services.[128] Efficiency was mentioned only discreetly,[129] and the government's new plan to increase competition by creating entities to run hospitals and services was unveiled. These entities would take the form of self-governing NHS trusts. District authorities would also undergo a transformation and assume a new purchasing role.[130]

The medical community's reaction was immediate and severe. Medical professionals argued that no major restructuring of the health care system was needed and that all that was required was a small increase in funding.[131] The strong opposition created by the review also fostered an unspoken alliance between the BMA and the Labour Party, both convinced that the new radical approach would lead to 'market medicine as practised across the Atlantic'.[132] The attempt to introduce financial incentives into the NHS was a betrayal of its foundational principles.[133] According to the BMA, this dangerous cost-cutting exercise was likely to hurt the doctor–patient relationship.[134] In many ways the beginning of these tough negotiations greatly resembled the 1946 showdown; however this time, Whitehall expected that 'the leaders of the profession [would] summon their troops to battle but [would] not make them fight'.[135]

The propositions that more specifically impacted primary care services aggravated GPs. Primary care doctors knew that a reform had been in the making for over a decade and that the government's goal was to create efficiency and choice in health care. The Conservatives' general perception was that providers that lacked accountability dominated health care services.[136] *Working for Patients* therefore proposed dramatic changes with new GP contracts and the creation of a purchaser–provider divide. The government hoped that GPs would become patients' representatives to help them voice their preferences and that they would

---

[126] Webster, *The National Health Service: A Political History*, above (n 17) 190.

[127] Department of Health, *Working for Patients*, above (n 114).

[128] H Davies and H Powell, 'How to Ration Health Care-and be Re-elected: The UK Experience' (1991) 3 *Stanford Law & Policy Review* 138, 142.

[129] Webster, *The National Health Service: A Political History*, above (n 17) 190.

[130] Ham, above (n 103) 9.

[131] Klein, *The New Politics of the NHS*, above (n 21) 147–48.

[132] ibid, 152–53.

[133] ibid 146.

[134] Edwards, Linton and Potter, above (n 42) 151.

[135] Klein, *The New Politics of the NHS*, above (n 21) 158.

[136] Crinson, above (n 19) 65.

become 'fundholders' in charge of purchasing services for their patients. The idea was for patients to voice their satisfaction or dissatisfaction directly to their GP and to allow them to enrol in another practice if they so desired.[137]

GP practices would also be forced to stay within a budget and, where possible, to generate surplus. This would lead practitioners to deny their patients the most expensive treatments or limit enrolment to the healthiest applicants.[138] However, doctors were unlikely to be responsive to market incentives. They refused to base their treatments upon financial considerations rather than their patients' needs.[139] Although GPs had always thought of themselves as NHS 'shopkeepers', they still could not agree to a reform that would transgress the system's fundamental principles. GPs felt that the government was purposely antagonising them.[140]

In February 1989, nonetheless, *Working for Patients* was presented and debated in the House of Lords. Much of the debate revolved around the internal market project. Some Members supporting the radical change contended that subsidiarity was the most efficient method to allocate health care resources. For instance, Conservative Member Lord Trafford, welcomed the proposition to decentralise the decision-making process in health care, stating:

> We are supposed to be equalising care throughout the country, so these are some of the things that desperately need to be addressed ... In my view the White Paper addresses some of these central problems. It devolves downwards so that we do not have a massive centralised bureaucracy. One of the most remarkable things on reading it is how much power the centre is prepared to surrender.[141]

Others criticised the libertarian rhetoric that had taken over the health care policy discourse[142] and made appeals to protect the egalitarian values that had characterised the NHS throughout its history.[143] Most eloquent was Labour Member Lord Ennals, explaining that:

> What most people see in the National Health Service – an embodiment of social justice – is anathema to her philosophy ... The public have tolerated a succession of Conservative reorganisations over the past 10 years and more. Frankly, those reorganisations have not achieved much in terms of an improvement of the National Health Service but I emphasise that none of them has challenged the basic principles on which the National Health Service was founded. However, throughout this period of Conservative reorganisation there has been the lurking fear that one day an over-confident Conservative Government would decide to introduce its free market, profit-orientated dogma into our National Health Service. That is why there has been a suspicion that the National Health Service is not safe in the hands of the Prime Minister. I must say that today it is

---

[137] Klein, *The New Politics of the NHS*, above (n 21) 159–60.
[138] ibid, 158.
[139] ibid.
[140] ibid, 160–61.
[141] HL Deb 22 February 1989, vol 504, cols 658–749, 686.
[142] ibid, 681, 685, 692, 720, 721.
[143] ibid, 668, 669, 690, 692, 694, 697.

no longer a suspicion, it is a certainty ... I believe that this would be the beginning of the end for a service based on patients' welfare ... In my view the proposals put producers before patients and profits before people.[144]

The fear that the market paradigm would take over was also palpable and was relayed through anti-libertarian discourses. The antagonistic debate between supporters of a new market approach in health care and Members who wanted to uphold NHS core values illustrated a shift in health care policy. The egalitarian principles had been enshrined in the NHS for over 40 years and this represented a drastic change.

After the debates in Westminster, the BMA vehemently disagreeing with the proposal, launched a campaign against the White Paper. It started with an editorial published in the *British Medical Journal*.[145] The medical council argued that the proposals in *Working for Patients* could 'cause serious danger to patient care'.[146] It was adamant that the reform would fragment health care services and destroy the comprehensive nature of the NHS without concretely increasing patients' choice in health care.[147] Patients would not gain more choice, nor would doctors feel more incentivised.[148] The BMA was also openly critical of the government's decision to ignore the medical profession's input in the reform, stating that it 'very much regret[ed] that no steps were taken to discuss the proposals with representatives of the profession before they were published'.[149] Most of all, the White Paper seemed to ignore the issue of inadequate funding that was crippling the NHS.[150]

The review and resulting White Paper nevertheless signalled a defeat for the medical profession. It marked the end of the BMA-policy veto and highlighted the weakness of doctors in the local administration of health care. Despite the government's dependence on the medical profession to implement its reform, doctors were given a 'back-seat' role in health care policy.[151]

## B. Ideas of Utilitarian Justice

The government ultimately decided to go forward with the proposals and turned *Working for Patients* into legislation. The National Health Service and Community Care Bill was to guarantee health care for the greatest number and the greater good of the community. For the Conservatives it involved the introduction of

[144] ibid, 668.
[145] L Beecham, 'BMA Launches Campaign Against White Paper' (1989) 298 *BMJ* 676, 676.
[146] ibid.
[147] ibid.
[148] Edwards, Linton and Potter, above (n 42) 147.
[149] Beecham, above (n 145) 676.
[150] ibid.
[151] Klein, *The New Politics of the NHS*, above (n 21) 155.

market dynamics. The split between purchasers and providers in health care would produce a level of uncertainty that could trigger enough competitiveness to tackle inefficiency.[152]

On the purchaser side, health authorities would commission the best services available, regardless of whether they were provided by entities from the public or private sector. They would have the duty to offer services that satisfied their population's health care needs. GP fundholding practices would also directly purchase secondary health care services for their patients. On the provider side, the hospitals in the form of NHS trusts would supply the services commissioned by the health authorities and GP fundholding practices.[153] Medical professionals would be involved in the ranking of the treatments' cost-effectiveness to guide health authorities in their investments. The utilitarian ranking exercise would help authorities provide the most beneficial services to the greatest numbers.[154] The reform thus would combine libertarian and utilitarian means to achieve the NHS' egalitarian goals.

During the Second Reading of the National Health Service and Community Care Bill before the House of Lords the influence of these ideas of justice were most apparent in the debates. Problems of efficiency affecting health care services were brought forward and support was given to the government's initiative. Lord McColl of Dulwich's intervention was representative of the Conservative argument in favour of competition in health care. He contented that increased competition was necessary despite the grievances voiced by the medical community, he then stated that

> the solution lies in the introduction of competition. We believe that it will help to solve that problem. It is fair to say that the Royal Colleges are fearful that competition will result in some hospitals going to the wall. Competition is much more subtle than that. It will provide the missing incentive for people to make sure that they give the kind of service that customers will appreciate. It will keep them just that little bit more on their toes. The great variations in quality and quantity will tend to disappear as the patients or customers become more and more the centre of the National Health Service activities. I believe that the right attitude should be: the customer is always right.[155]

Achieving the greatest good for the greatest number by maximising utility in health care was the goal of the proposition. Conservative Members were on board with utilitarian principles and argued in favour of the optimisation of resources to better address health care needs in Britain. Lord Henley said that the reform would 'provide a service that makes the most cost-effective use of resources'[156]

---

[152] Ham, above (n 103) 9.
[153] Davies and Powell, above (n 128) 142.
[154] Edwards, Linton and Potter, above (n 42) 149–50.
[155] HL Second Reading 3 April 1990, vol 517 cols 1255–1387, 1306.
[156] ibid, 1382.

and that this should be regarded as 'a virtue, [and] not a vice'.[157] The government had a 'duty to make sure that money [was] used to bring the maximum benefit'.[158] Other instances also relayed the ambition to set priorities in health care in order to reap maximum benefit from the resources invested.[159] Baroness Lockwood, for example, supported the ranking of needs, even though she believed it was important to differentiate the pound amount associated with treatment from the population's health care necessity. She explained that '[n]obody [was] suggest[ing] that the National Health Service should have a bottomless purse ... [P]riorities and choices [must be set] but they should be properly evaluated and not just costed'.[160]

Some instances also addressed the proposals made for community and primary care.[161] Baroness Cox and other Labour Members involved in the debate hoped that the more vulnerable groups in the community would not be forgotten in a system focused on effectiveness and priority setting. In an emotional plea, Baroness Cox stated:

> I have a nightmare – which I fear could become reality – of many very vulnerable people finding that community care is a Utopian myth. They find instead that the community does not or cannot care and that the services that should be caring for them are not available to help them in their time of need ... That is why I plead for systematic, vigorous evaluation and inspection not only of the National Health Service, but also of community care.[162]

Some aspects of the reform could nonetheless help address the needs of the community more locally. According to the Lord Bishop of Manchester, health authorities could more easily act as a 'link with the people and their communities'.[163]

The ideas of liberal equality at the core of the NHS were also the focus of many of the discussions. During these debates, universality, comprehensiveness and equality in health care were contrasted with the market approach and utilitarian rhetoric. Members mentioned that they '[did] not want the change to be so drastic that the continuity [would be] broken',[164] evidencing path dependency in health care policy instilled since 1946 with these values.[165] On nine occasions Members shared their attachment to these principles,[166] one of which was Baroness Cox's intervention stating:

> I believe the National Health Service is one of the most humanitarian institutions the world has ever known. It has provided a popular and generally equitable health

---

[157] ibid.
[158] ibid.
[159] ibid, 1289, 1304, 1382.
[160] ibid, 1302.
[161] ibid, 1278, 1319, 1322, 1336, 1354.
[162] ibid, 1322.
[163] ibid, 1278.
[164] ibid, 1304.
[165] ibid, 1263–64, 1316, 1369, 1376, 1381.
[166] ibid, 1276, 1292, 1322, 1323, 1332, 1354.

service, ... Therefore, I will wholeheartedly support any policies which help to put the principles which the National Health Service enshrines into practice more effectively; but I, and my professional colleagues, cannot and will not support proposals which appear to us to risk damaging this precious institution and thereby possibly harming those whom it serves.[167]

Lord Rea, for his part, challenged the purpose of the review, the results published in *Working for Patients* and the introduction of a new health care Bill. According to him:

[T]he White Paper that introduced the Bill pays lip service to the National Health Service, it seems to have missed two fundamental advantages of the NHS as it now stands. The first, which has been mentioned by many speakers, is its truly comprehensive nature. Not only is it available to anyone, however poor, but high standards are available throughout the country ... I can only ask why, if the present system is popular with the public and professions alike and is comprehensive and economical, is it necessary to make such fundamental changes.[168]

Ultimately, the legislative process came to a close and the National Health Service and Community Care Act received royal assent on 29 June 1990. The health care reform attracted significant attention, perhaps more so because of its form than its content. Indeed, it was the commercial language that generated the most anxiety. The British public did not want to see the NHS turned into a business venture.[169] Doctors were still anxious about the impact the Act could have on the profession. The non-clinical considerations they now had to balance while deciding on a course of treatment were a threat to their professional autonomy. Managers were therefore urged to 'clean up' the language and reaffirm the government's commitment to the founding principles.[170] In a blunder, Health Minister Kenneth Clarke had said: 'medicine is more important than baked beans but most baked bean companies are run better than most hospitals'.[171] Thus, even though the NHS was not to become a business, it was intended to be managed like one. The Act proposed to use utilitarian principles to allocate resources equally by having health authorities rank and prioritise health care services.[172]

The internal market was therefore implemented, but the egalitarian foundations of the NHS were preserved, services remaining free at the point of use.[173] As noted by NHS historian Charles Webster, "internal" was clearly inconsistent with

---

[167] ibid, 1322.
[168] ibid.
[169] Edwards, Linton and Potter, above (n 42) 154.
[170] ibid, 155.
[171] ibid, 154
[172] Davies and Powell, above (n 128) 142.
[173] G Bevan and R Robinson, 'The Interplay Between Economic and Political Logics: Path Dependency in Health Care in England' (2005) 30 *Journal of Health Politics, Policy and Law* 53, 55.

the aspiration to maximise the involvement of outside agencies and the private sector'.[174] In fact, when the reform was rolled out the BMA's opposition started to flounder. Even though equity of access might have been challenged in principle, the reform was not profoundly affecting their professional autonomy.[175] Patients had also not become consumers; they were subject to the expertise and choices of health authorities, GP fundholding practices and treating doctors.[176] Thus, the policy shift that the review and White Paper had announced was greatly moderated during the implementation phase.[177]

## IV. The Health and Social Care Act (2012)

During the course of two decades from 1990 to 2010 the NHS underwent a progressive transformation conveying a change in ideology. Universalism had lost its positive connotation and had started to be associated with the 'equity of the mediocre'. Ideas of consumerism and choice that had entered the political discourse during the New Labour era continued to influence health care policy.[178]

In 2010, denied of an outright victory during the general election, the Conservative Party had to negotiate the first post-war coalition government with the Liberal Democrats.[179] Adding to this period of political change were economic difficulties looming in the country and the NHS. The organisation was facing its longest period in history of low funding growth and experts projected that the next decade would be the most challenging for health care services.[180] The NHS had to be more efficient to meet the needs of the ageing population and to absorb the cost of new drugs and treatments. Many lifestyle factors such as obesity, alcohol-related illness, cancer, coronary diseases along with technological advances had contributed to significant spending in health care.[181] Since 1997, variations in access, utilisation and quality of care had also widened health inequalities and mortality rates were worryingly high.[182]

---

[174] Crinson, above (n 19) 66–67.

[175] ibid, 66.

[176] Webster, *The National Health Service: A Political History*, above (n 17) 202.

[177] CH Tuohy, 'Dynamics of a Changing Health Sphere: The United States, Britain, and Canada' (1999) 18(3) *Health Affairs* 114, 115.

[178] J Newman and E Vilder, 'Discriminating Customers, Responsible Patients, Empowered Users: Consumerism and the Modernisation of Health Care' (2006) 35 *Journal of Social Policy* 193, 199.

[179] T Quinn, 'From New Labour to New Politics: The British General Election of 2010' (2011) 34(2) *West European Politics* 403, 403.

[180] D Buck and A Dixon, 'Improving the Allocation of Health Resources in England' (The King's Fund, 2013) 1, 2.

[181] A Dixon and C Ham, 'Liberating the NHS: The Right Prescription in a Cold Climate' (The King's Fund, 2010) 2.

[182] R Thorlby and J Maybin (eds), 'A High-Performing NHS? A Review of Progress 1997–2010' (The King's Fund, 2010) 2.

Nonetheless, the Coalition government did not initially plan a health care reform. Yet, less than three months after a modest programme for the NHS was announced, the Department of Health, along with Secretary of State for Health, Andrew Lansley, published a ground-shaking White Paper that proposed substantial changes to the provision of health care services.[183] *Equity and Excellence: Liberating the NHS* revealed the government's intention to promote greater diversity in health care services and for the for-profit sector to play a greater role in the NHS; this, of course, without forsaking the organisation's core principles.[184] The government also wanted to 'stop the top-down reorganisation of the NHS that [had] got[ten] in the way of patient care'.[185] The goal was to set up an ambitious but speedy reform that would put patients first and significantly improve health care outcomes.[186]

Controversy and animosity came immediately after the publication of the White Paper. The government initiated a period of consultation; opinions and opposition were coming from all sides. Politicians, the public and the medical profession were outraged by what they saw as an attack on NHS foundational values.[187] The Labour Party, the Royal College of General Practitioners, the Royal College of Nursing and the BMA joined forces and formulated a response. The government's reply itself came in December 2010 with the White Paper *Liberating the NHS: The Legislative Framework and Next Steps*[188] outlining some minor modifications to the proposed policy. As the BMA and patient groups put together online petitions, street demonstrations and voiced open objections, the government moved forward and introduced the draft legislation into Parliament. In June 2011, the legislative process had to come to a halt. The Coalition had to pause, reflect and listen to the main stakeholders and so it did. After the government had opened the Future Forum to collect feedback once more, an altered and edited version of the Bill was reintroduced.[189] Each clause was discussed and negotiated until a patched-up version incorporating more than 1,000 amendments emerged to receive royal assent on 27 March 2012.[190]

Overall, the Health and Social Care Act (2012) has been the biggest transformation of the NHS to date.[191] The consumerist policies it has promoted have changed the character of a patient's entitlement. Focusing on the individual's

---

[183] R Klein, 'The Twenty-Year War Over England's National Health Service: A Report from the Battlefield' (2013) 38 *Journal of Health Politics, Policy and Law* 849, 853.

[184] DJ Hunter, 'A Response to Rudolf Klein: A Battle May Have Been Won but Perhaps Not the War' (2013) 38 *Journal of Health Politics, Policy and Law* 871, 871; Klein, ibid, 851.

[185] Klein, ibid, 852; Baggott, above (n 71) 41.

[186] Dixon and Ham, above (n 181) 1.

[187] Klein, 'The Twenty-Year War Over England's National Health Service', above (n 183) 849.

[188] Department of Health, *Liberating the NHS: Legislative Framework and Next Steps* (2010).

[189] E Speed and J Gabe, 'The Health and Social Care Act for England 2012: The Extension of 'New Professionalism'' (2013) 33 *Critical Social Policy* 564, 565.

[190] Klein, 'The Twenty-Year War Over England's National Health Service', above (n 183) 850.

[191] Webster, *The National Health Service: A Political History*, above (n 17) 23.

ability to choose public or private providers to satisfy their health care needs, it has given patients some freedom and a claim right against the state. Although the fundamental egalitarian concept of justice remains virtually untouched, for the first time the founding principles have come into question with the new and more direct role given to the private and independent sectors. Essentially, the 2012 reform has transformed commissioning and promoted a market approach for the provision of health care services.[192]

## A.  Two White Papers, One Reform

*Equity and Excellence: Liberating the NHS* was published at breakneck speed. After only six weeks, the document emerged to set a policy agenda that included a broad plan for reform with no concrete details on the implementation.[193] For the Coalition, avoidable deaths across the health care system justified yet another and more drastic reorganisation of the NHS.[194] In a nutshell, the far-reaching White Paper offered to take a market approach to the provision and commissioning of health care services in order to increase patient choice.[195] Within the first pages of the White Paper, however, the government introduced itself as the guardian of the NHS and its values of liberal equality and universality of care:

> It is our privilege to be custodians of the NHS, its values and principles. We believe that the NHS is an integral part of a Big Society, reflecting the social solidarity of shared access to collective healthcare, and a shared responsibility to use resources effectively to deliver better health. We are committed to an NHS that is available to all, free at the point of use, and based on need, not the ability to pay. We will increase health spending in real terms in each year of this Parliament. The NHS is about fairness for everyone in our society. It is about this country doing the right thing for those who need help.[196]

This stated commitment to the principles at the core of the NHS was a necessary note of caution to introduce more substantial changes because a libertarian, and in some instances neoliberal reform, was to completely redesign health care services. Three 'buzz' words[197] were 'efficiency', 'competition' and 'accountability'. The Coalition wanted to 'free up provision of healthcare, so that in most sectors of care, any willing provider [could] provide services'. It was thought that more competition would stimulate innovation and improve productivity.[198]

---

[192] ibid.

[193] K Walshe, 'Reorganisation of the NHS in England' (2010) *BMJ* 341, 341.

[194] R Jones, 'The White Paper: A Framework for Survival?' (2010) 60 *British Journal of General Practice* 635, 635.

[195] S Asthana, 'Liberating the NHS? A Commentary on the Lansley White Paper, "Equity and Excellence"' (2011) 72 *Social Science & Medicine* 815, 815.

[196] Department of Health and Social Care, *Equity and Excellence: Liberating the NHS* (Cm 7881, 2010) 7.

[197] Each of these words was mentioned at least 20 times in the document.

[198] Department of Health and Social Care, above (n 196) 37.

All the commissioning and provision of health care services would therefore be within the reach of the for-profit sector. The NHS had to transform to be more patient-centred and had to increase the quality of its services. This meant allowing patients to 'top-up' their public entitlements with the services offered by private providers.[199] Change was also to come at the governmental level. The new Department of Public Health would work alongside the Department of Health and the NHS Commissioning Board to minimise top-down political interference. The Commissioning Board would also work on behalf of the Secretary of State to oversee the work of GP commissioners. This way, the Board would be able to provide leadership on the commissioning of quality health care, the promotion of patient and public involvement, and the commissioning of services that could not be dispensed by GP consortia.[200]

On the whole, the policy signalled a shift from solidarity to subsidiarity with a greater devolution of power to local authorities and health care providers.[201] The government hoped that '[g]reater autonomy [would] be matched by increased accountability to patients and democratic legitimacy'.[202] The Coalition aimed at reducing the state's involvement in health care. Instead of micromanaging health services, the Department of Health was to fulfil its duties from a distance. The medical profession would be granted more managerial responsibilities and decision-making power in the allocation of health care resources.[203] In the new NHS, 'front-line' professionals, rather than the government, would structure, choose and provide the services that were most adequate for their patients.[204] The government was also accepting of devolving part of its commissioning power to GPs and their practices for them to work in consortia and purchase care for local populations.[205]

The reform was meant to 'free' NHS providers and grant them with more autonomy to commission care strategically and more adequately to meet local populations' health care needs.[206] The White Paper suggested pursuing the work undertaken by previous reforms that aimed at regrouping Strategic Health Authorities (responsible for the enacting directives and implementing fiscal policy at a regional level) and Primary Care Trusts (responsible for the commissioning of primary, community and secondary health services) into Foundation Trusts. However, under the new reform, Foundation Trusts would be freed 'from constraints they [were] under, in line with their original conception, so they [could] innovate to improve care for patients'.[207] That implied subjecting them to

---

[199] K Walshe and C Ham, 'Can the Government's Proposals for NHS Reform be made to Work?' (2011) 342 *BMJ* 804, 804.
[200] Dixon and Ham, above (n 181) 5.
[201] ibid, 3.
[202] Department of Health and Social Care, above (n 196) 27.
[203] Walshe and Ham, above (n 199) 805.
[204] Asthana, above (n 195) 816.
[205] Department of Health and Social Care, above (n 196) 4.
[206] ibid, 35.
[207] ibid.

the same regulation as any other providers from the voluntary or private sector, to enable patients to choose treatment from the provider they believed was best suited to their needs.[208] Cost-effectiveness was an obvious underlying theme of the document.[209] Many propositions were made to optimise the allocation of resources, be it outsourcing the management, the administration of commissioning duties or the provision of services to the private sector.[210]

An increase in competition among providers was also a call for more regulation. Monitor,[211] the main economic regulator, would continue to fulfil its duties as regulator of Foundation Trusts and would be given additional responsibility to encourage and promote competition, set prices, guarantee the continuity of essential services, prevent anti-competitive behaviour and even apply necessary sanctions.[212]

The propositions made in *Equity and Excellence: Liberating the NHS* immediately created some controversy. On the one hand, the public found the lack of justification for the reform hard to digest[213] and on the other, supporters of a market-based reform welcomed the proposal.[214] Disgruntled stakeholders nonetheless quickly outnumbered the supporters. Civil servants in local authorities and NHS managers strongly opposed the idea of competition in the sector and were outraged by the possibility of having private health care providers interfering with the NHS.[215] Equally, if not more strongly, the government felt the discontent of the medical profession. The BMA and Royal Colleges had regrouped to form a joint opposition to protest against the potential negative effects the reform could have on the doctor–patient relationship.[216]

Thus, once the period of consultation drew to a close the government felt the need to share the insights and suggestions that were provided mostly by the stakeholders challenging the reform.[217] *Liberating the NHS: Legislative Framework and Next Steps* was the Coalition's response White Paper. The report criticised the scale and speed of the reform, as it seemed to be detracting from the real and more

---

[208] Asthana, above (n 195) 815.

[209] ibid, 815–16.

[210] ibid, 816.

[211] *About Monitor | Monitor*, available at: www.gov.uk/government/organisations/monitor/about 'Monitor is the sector regulator for health services in England. It is meant to protect and promote the interests of patients by ensuring that the whole sector works for their benefits'.

[212] Webster, *The National Health Service: A Political History*, above (n 17) 23.

[213] N Timmins, *Never Again? The Story of the Health and Social Care Act 2012* (Institute for Government and the King's Fund, 2012), available at: www.kingsfund.org.uk/publications/never-again.

[214] Simon Stevens, president of global health at United Health Group, and a trustee of the King's Fund stated: 'More patient power; a greater role for GPs in planning and funding decisions; a stronger focus on clinical outcomes; NHS hospitals with operating freedoms similar to universities; an end to day to day politicisation thanks to arm's length regulation and an expert national commissioning board what's not to like about the new NHS White Paper?': BMJ, 'More Brickbats than Bouquets?' (2010) *BMJ* 341, c3977.

[215] Walshe and Ham, above (n 199) 804–05.

[216] Timmins, above (n 213).

[217] Department of Health and Social Care, above (n 196) 1.4.

pressing financing issues affecting the NHS.[218] The government's strategy to lead a more general and broader reform of public services, with health care as part of this project, could have explained the haste.[219] Nonetheless, in some aspects the proposal had to be modified because the 'original thinking was flawed'[220] and ultimately consensus had to be reached before the Health and Social Care Bill (enclosed in the White Paper) was introduced into Parliament.[221]

The Coalition would therefore allow piloting of some of the policy and had to plan a longer period of transition and implementation. This included providing clearer guidelines for the creation of GP consortia and greater transparency relating to their commissioning powers.[222] The document also addressed the unions' and the public's apprehensions with regard to the privatisation of health care services. Fear was that the reform was threatening 'the core principles of the NHS and [would] undermine its future'.[223] In a similar manner as in the initial proposal, the government introduced the White Paper by declaring that their vision was 'founded on [its] enduring commitment to the values and principles of the NHS as a comprehensive service, available to all, free at the point of use and based on clinical needs, not the ability to pay'.[224]

Nevertheless, as the tension grew the White Paper was transformed into legislation and introduced into Parliament. The scale and speed of the reorganisation and the potential 'privatisation' of the NHS became the focal points of all parliamentary debates on health care.[225] In April 2011, the government had to reluctantly launch the NHS Future Forum, a quasi-Royal Commission put together to listen and reflect on the proposed reform.[226] Again opposition from the primary doctors and NHS interest groups was reported, but many of the recommendations were also adopted by the Department of Health. Nevertheless, negotiations remained fierce as the legislative process resumed.[227]

## B. Ideas of Libertarian Justice and Neoliberalism

Parliament had to reconvene for a second time to discuss the latest version of the draft legislation in January 2012. The Second Reading of the Health and Social Care Bill in the House of Lords relayed the heated debates that had been taking

---

[218] 'Too Far, Too Fast: The King's Fund Verdict on Coalition Health Reforms' (The King's Fund, 7 October 2010), available at: www.kingsfund.org.uk/press/press-releases/too-far-too-fast-kings-fund-verdict-coalition-health-reforms.
[219] Department of Health and Social Care, above (n 196) 1.6.
[220] ibid, 1.4
[221] ibid, 1.5.
[222] ibid, 1.13.
[223] ibid, 1.16.
[224] ibid, 1.1.
[225] Timmins, above (n 213).
[226] Klein, 'The Twenty-Year War Over England's National Health Service', above (n 183) 855.
[227] ibid.

place outside Westminster. Two groups were confronting their ideas and using distinct rhetoric of justice to back their arguments. The 'reformers', in support of the Bill, favoured a libertarian and consumerist approach in health care. In their eyes, more competition in the realm of health care services would empower patients, and although advocating consumerist means to foster more efficiency,[228] they seemed unwilling to forfeit the NHS' original values. Advocates of the status quo, however, focused on preserving equality in treatment and access to care. Vastly critical of the market approach, they worried about the impact of the reform on the most vulnerable groups.[229]

More particularly, among the consumerist, libertarian and neoliberal concepts mentioned throughout the debate, Conservative Member Earl Howe evoked the importance of a subsidiary approach to the organisation of health care services, stating that '[The Act] allows power to be devolved from the centre so that innovation is unleashed from the bottom up, supported by clear lines of accountability. It is, in fact, the inverse of a topdown reorganisation'.[230] Indeed, one of the purposes of the reform was to enact this consumerist approach by adopting a more decentralised provision and administration of health care services. Also notable was Earl Howe's intervention pushing for competitiveness[231] for better health care:

> Where competition can operate to improve the service on offer to patients, or to address a need that the NHS fails to meet, we should let the system facilitate it. However, competition only has a place when it is clearly and unequivocally in the interests of patients.[232]

Adopting a similar position Baron Naseby, also a member of the Conservative Party, explained that:

> [C]ompetition is good for any industry. It makes it possible for new innovations, for better value for money and for solutions to be found. Competition gives people pride and responsibility. Even within the NHS there are numerous examples ... The state does not have to undertake everything. It has to be a demanding purchaser, an experienced demanding purchaser, and vigorously assess outcomes.[233]

Conversely, more than half a dozen instances referenced ideas of liberal equality in health care,[234] and others explicitly argued against a market approach for the commissioning and provision of services.[235] Among these interventions, was

---

[228] HL Second Reading 12 October 2011, cols 1469–1720, 1474, 1492, 1683, 1706.
[229] ibid, 1479, 1481, 1482, 1497, 1499, 1500, 1502, 1506, 1507, 1508, 1509, 1511, 1675, 1680, 1689, 1702, 1703, 1708.
[230] ibid, 1472.
[231] ibid, 1474.
[232] ibid.
[233] ibid, 1505.
[234] ibid, 1479, 1481, 1482, 1497, 1499, 1500, 1502, 1506, 1507, 1508, 1509, 1511, 1675, 1680, 1689, 1702, 1703, 1708.
[235] ibid, 1479, 1511, 1702.

Baroness Thornton's statement criticising the consumerist tactics of the Coalition government:

> [The reform] will change the NHS from a health system into a competitive market. It will turn patients into consumers and patient choice into shopping. Most crucially, it will turn our healthcare into a traded commodity … We do not support making our NHS into a regulated market, as advocated by some.[236]

Baroness Billingham, for her part, qualified the reform as senseless explaining that 'there [was] an underlying sinister motive to advance the market philosophy into the NHS, which [would] ultimately destroy it. The cherished principles of the NHS as a universal service [would] indeed be lost forever'.[237] Obviously, the defenders of the NHS' core principles saw the market as an ill-suited tool to allocate health care resources simply because 'health is different'.[238] As Lord Beecham explained:

> The health service is of great utility to the people of this country. It is not a utility like gas, water or electricity – still less an insurance fund. It falls to this House to preserve the principles of the National Health Service and facilitate its continuous improvement in the service of the people.[239]

The path dependency the egalitarian tenets instilled in health care policy evidently permeated the discussions. Baroness Bakewell[240] stated that:

> In 1946 the National Health Service was just such a bold and significant leap forward. As we consider how it might be improved, we need to bear in mind what we are changing: one of the finest, most highly regarded and valued institutions of British life, with a global reputation. The enduring essence of the NHS must not be yielded up to the transient imperatives of an external free market.[241]

Essentially, the tension between the consumerist neoliberal ideology and the preservation of the universal health care model structured the debate. The Health and Social Care Act was inspired by some libertarian principles inherited from the Thatcher era and would have advanced a consumerist conception of health care services delivery, but it would also have to honour the NHS legacy of liberal equality. The goal was to offer a decentralised system to cater for all patients' health care needs with a greater amount of choice.

After its enactment, heavy criticism targeted the unprecedented intensity with which market principles had to be employed in the realm of health care provision. The fear was that the entitlement to equality in treatment would be eroded

---

[236] ibid, 1479.
[237] ibid, 1510.
[238] ibid, 1497.
[239] ibid, 1680.
[240] Among many these occurrences explicitly the importance of NHS fundamental value: HL Second Reading 12 October 2011, cols 1469–1720, 1499, 1502, 1510, 1680.
[241] ibid, 1506.

and would lead to the 'death' of the NHS.[242] Echoing the reforms made in the education sector, the Coalition government wished to remove itself from the allocation process and to have the market distribute public goods like any other commodities.[243] For this, the health care sector had to be open to 'any qualified provider'.[244] Bids for community care, sexual health services, and even prison health care services would come from large corporate companies such as Virgin Healthcare, Serco or United Health.[245] However, this would also mean that certain areas of care would be at risk of having a fragmented service due to lack of coordination among the many actors present in the market. Overseas corporations strictly accountable to their shareholders and out of the British regulators' reach would be free to provide lower-quality services in the UK.[246] Although Monitor would guarantee that all providers compete on an equal footing, it had not been assigned the mission to safeguard the collaboration or integration of health care providers.[247]

The Act foreshadowed the advent of a two-tier or even 'hybrid' health care system. Having been granted general powers, local authorities were expected to step into the shoes of the health secretary and assume public health functions, despite their extremely limited resources.[248] The Secretary of State's duty to promote a comprehensive service was maintained, but the duty to provide comprehensive health services was abolished[249] and substituted with a lesser duty to 'act with a view to securing'[250] comprehensive services. Also striking was the milder duty of the Secretary of State to 'reduce inequalities between the people of England with respect to the benefits that they can obtain from the health service',[251] replacing the important and broader duty to promote equal access.[252]

Neither the NHS Commissioning Board supervising the GP commissioning consortia, now renamed Clinical Commissioning Groups (CCGs), nor the CCGs themselves were invested with the duty to ensure equal access to health care services based on need. CCGs were only mandated to meet 'reasonable requirements'[253] by providing the 'services or facilities [they] consider appropriate'.[254] Furthermore,

---

[242] AM Pollock et al, 'How the Health and Social Care Bill 2011 Would End Entitlement to Comprehensive Health Care in England' (2012) 379 *The Lancet* 387, 387.

[243] Hunter, 'A Response to Rudolf Klein', above (n 184) 873.

[244] N Black, '"Liberating the NHS" – Another Attempt to Implement Market Forces in English Health Care' (2010) 363 *New England Journal of Medicine* 1103, 1104.

[245] Speed and Gabe, above (n 189) 568; Hunter, 'A Response to Rudolf Klein', above (n 184) 873.

[246] Hunter, ibid.

[247] ibid, 852–53.

[248] Health and Social Care Act 2012.

[249] ibid, part I, s 1.

[250] ibid.

[251] ibid, part I, s 4, 1(c).

[252] AM Pollock and D Price, 'How the Secretary of State for Health Proposes to Abolish the NHS in England' (2011) 342 *BMJ* 747.

[253] Health and Social Care Act 2012, part I, s 13, 2(a).

[254] ibid, part I, s 14, 3(a)(1).

CCGs would only owe these duties to the enrolled population within their commissioning groups. Risk spreading was also critically endangered because CCG enrolees had to be drawn from a list of general members instead of from a pool of residents in a specific geographical area. Practice boundaries were thereby abolished, and patients had to be accepted irrespective of their place of residence.[255]

Thus, it was difficult to comprehend how public interest could be preserved and strengthened when the delivery of health care services was taken out of the hands of the government.[256] Promises might be fulfilled, but the risk of costs rising and quality decreasing, creating more health inequalities, was looming.[257] The conflict between welfare and market ideologies inherited from the Thatcher era had the Coalition government resorting to competition to solve health care issues.[258] The government would have a buyer's rather than a provider's role,[259] but unlike the reforms undertaken in the sector of public utilities, the desire to privatise the NHS was never explicitly formulated.[260] The NHS would continue to be funded by central taxation, available to all and free at every point of use.[261]

# V. Conclusion

Reforms of social policy after the Second World War were brought about by feelings of empathy and solidarity and the need to provide an adequate welfare structure for the British population. Aneurin Bevan's negotiations with medical consultants and GPs indirectly vested the medical profession with the 'mission' to protect the unified health care system. Although medicine was not divorced from the money at the onset, the agreement between the government and the medical profession led the practice of medicine to be separate from doctors' income.[262] The system's core values also ignited path dependency in health care policy. Ideas of equality and collectivism provided a solid foundation for a comprehensive and universal health care system that would allow the medical profession to exercise its expertise autonomously. Thereby, with the NHS Act (1946), the status of medical professionals in the United Kingdom became intertwined with the future and the success of the NHS.

---

[255] See generally, Pollock and Price, above (n 252); M Powell and R Miller, 'Privatizing the English National Health Service: An Irregular Verb?' (2013) 38 *Journal of Health Politics, Policy and Law* 1051, 1054.

[256] Pollock and Price, ibid.

[257] Hunter, 'A Response to Rudolf Klein', above (n 184) 874.

[258] MJ Sandel, *Justice: What's the Right Thing to Do?* (New York, Macmillan, 2010) 60–64.

[259] Speed and Gabe, above (n 189) 571.

[260] Timmins, above (n 213).

[261] Klein, 'The Twenty-Year War Over England's National Health Service', above (n 183) 849.

[262] Klein, *The New Politics of the NHS*, above (n 21) 155.

As demands and costs of health care grew in the 1970s, the medical profession remained determined to protect its position and the values of liberal equality that characterised the NHS. Margaret Thatcher's government, however, had the ambition to introduce competition and efficiency in social policy as it came into power in the 1980s until the end of the decade. The cost-cutting exercise led to the introduction of the internal market in health care and the redefinition of the medical profession's role in health care policy. Although the medical profession had, once again, organised its resistance it had lost most of its leverage. Path dependency, nevertheless, curtailed the libertarian ambitions of the Conservatives. Certainly, money had to follow the patient, but most importantly the system's core values had to be preserved. The NHS and Community Care Act (1990) introduced libertarian and utilitarian methods to provide health care services and maintain universality of care.[263]

The latest health care reform, in continuance of the Thatcherite and New Labour policies, had the ambition to inscribe a consumerist culture into the NHS. The shift operated by the Health and Social Care Act (2012) led health care policy to deviate from its liberal egalitarian foundations to embrace a neoliberal approach for the provision of health care services. The controversy and debates leading to the enactment of this law were representative of the shock that policies of decentralisation and privatisation for the provision of health care services had brought in and outside the system.[264]

By and large, the rhetoric of equality, efficiency and patient choice that were, over the last 70 years, brought in turn within the walls of Parliament during the negations of each of these watershed moments of health care policy signal the importance of ideas of justice in NHS law and policy making. The health care laws that were enacted in order to implement these health care reforms bear justice attributes as a result of the role played by the medical profession outside the legislative institutions and path dependency created by the principles at the heart of the NHS.

---

[263] Bevan and Robinson, above (n 173) 53.
[264] Speed and Gabe, above (n 189) 565; P Bailey, 'Primary Care Duped: The Government's Bill Will Wreck the NHS' (2012) 344 *BMJ* 1, 1.

# 7

# Conclusion

'I do know that the right words, spoken from the heart with conviction, with a vision of better place and a faith in the unseen, are a call to action. So when you hear my words, or speak your own to your neighbours, hear them and speak them as a call to action.'[1]

Deval Patrick

As life expectancy improves and advances in medical technology are made in Western welfare states, resources available for health care no longer measure up to populations' needs. Governments are struggling to honour basic health care entitlements and are unable to eradicate barriers to access health care services. In spite of suitable theoretical frameworks for the just distribution of scarce resources offered by political philosophy, legislative efforts undertaken to reform health care systems are unable to tackle distributive issues. The purpose of this book was therefore to assess whether the misalignment between the theory and the practice of health care law-making was responsible for failing health-care systems. The book also proposed to establish whether stakeholders involved in the elaboration of major health care reforms had chosen to inform their decisions with ideas and theories of justice. The enquiry essentially calls attention to a dimension of justice in health care law using a philosophical analysis of the legislative process. The book also provides a systematic framework to describe, analyse and compare policy paths that goes beyond the mere description of the history of health care law.[2]

The context and historical events that gave rise to health care reforms in the United States and the United Kingdom is present throughout, but particular attention is given to laws enacted between 1945 and 2012. For both the case studies, the events leading up to the enactment of laws reforming these systems helped put into perspective the discourses of for-profit actors engaging in the legislative

---

[1] Deval Patrick, Massachusetts Governor candidate, 'Rally for Change' (Speech at the Rally for Change on Boston Common, 15 October 2006).

[2] See the comments made about a lack of comparative analysis in the field in, R Klein, 'Carolyn Hughes Tuohy, *Accidental Logics: The Dynamics of Change in the Health Care Arena in the United States, Britain and Canada*' Book Review (2000) 20 *Journal of Public Policy* 105, 105; I Crinson, *Health Policy: A Critical Perspective* (London, Sage Publications, 2009) 1.

process. Discourse analysis was pivotal to the enquiry as the linguistic occurrences reflect the actors' and societies' perception of health care issues at a particular point in time and provide evidence of whether ideas of justice were considered during reformative periods. The language used in policy documents, such as White Papers, helped explain the underlying tensions around, or consensus on, particular issues leading to the enactment of new law. The analysis of the final version of each Act, on the other hand, relays the compromises reached by stakeholders through the democratic process.[3] On this matter, even though occurrences relaying theories of justice may have been instrumentalised and mentioned purely rhetorically, the enquiry concludes that the language of justice used during the negotiation of health care laws is an appeal for greater justice in the allocation of health care resources. Congressional testimonies or statements made during the Second Reading of a Bill go beyond linguistics; they anticipated action and change through the discussions of justice in health care. The words of for-profit actors during these negotiations essentially constitute a call to action.

Thus, the enquiry mostly focused on the discourses of for-profit actors or the discourses of their representatives during strategic stages of the legislative process. In the case of the American health care system, largely dominated by the private sector, the enquiry explored the role of the medical profession, employers and the insurance industry in health care policy. With regard to the NHS, a comprehensive and publicly funded health care system, the enquiry focused on the influence of the medical profession and the independent sector (that comprises private and commercial actors involved in schemes to finance and provide health care services) on the actions taken inside Parliament.

The analysis led in chapter three demonstrated that the for-profit sector in the United States had participated in the advent of a fragmented system and fostered path dependency in health care policy, which has allowed only incremental changes throughout its history.[4] Medical professionals, employers and insurers having vested interest in the system pushed their agenda during periods of reform.[5] Doctors had sought to protect their autonomy and economic interests by institutionalising their power with the American Medical Association. Later, as the Association and the profession lost political traction, it continued to lobby against a universal health care system and allied with insurers to promote a private system of coverage. More recently, with the Clinton proposal and the Affordable Care Act (ACA 2010), doctors have given their support to proposals that offer the possibility of achieving a type of universal coverage but preserve commercial insurance dominance.

---

[3] J Newman and E Vilder, 'Discriminating Customers, Responsible Patients, Empowered Users: Consumerism and the Modernisation of Health Care' (2006) 35 *Journal of Social Policy* 193, 195.

[4] K Patel and ME Rushefsky, *Healthcare Politics and Policy in America*, 4th edn (Armonk, NY, ME Sharpe, 2014) 358.

[5] N Daniels, *Just Health Care* (Cambridge University Press, 1985) 115.

With regard to insurance, not-for-profit health care coverage developed during the course of the 1950s with the 'Blue' insurers. Shortly after, commercial under-writers had started to develop plans, but in the 1960s they left the financing of the health care needs of the elderly and the poor to the federal government. American insurers had thereby strategically posited themselves as middlepersons between the providers and the government, and reserved themselves the most lucrative portion of the health care market. Throughout the twentieth century, the insur-ers' alliance with providers and the support they have given to the fee-for-service system triggered rampant health care costs, an issue that the ACA 2010 aimed to manage, along with the restrictions the industry has imposed on applicants with pre-existing conditions. Also important is the contribution of employer-based insurance to the edification of a largely privately run health care system. After the war, American employers were able to form large risk pools offering health care benefits to their employees to preserve their control over the workforce and keep unions at bay. During the 1970s and 1990s employers also engaged in the insurance industry's reforms, be it with ERISA or HIPAA but as a heteroge-neous group and, because of their lack of unity, they have lost their dominance in health care policy. Nevertheless, employer-based insurance is still the most prominent form of coverage among working adults in the United States.

The analysis focused on the United Kingdom in chapter five. Here, the for-profit sector's role had to be analysed in parallel with the public sector's achievements because of the public nature of the NHS. For-profit stakeholders, GPs and medi-cal consultants were persuaded to collaborate with the government to establish a centralised health care system. Successive governments have had to manage their relationship with the medical profession and, for the first 40 years following the creation of the NHS, were successful in fostering a collaborative partnership. Doctors had preserved their clinical independence and their input was valued in the realm of health care policy.[6] Medicine had become a powerful and dominant profession. Nonetheless, because of financial strains, during the 1970s the system had to be reorganised. Thereafter, the medical profession was drastically excluded from the policy-making process by the Thatcher government. In the 1990s, a set of new for-profit actors belonging to the independent sector, namely commercial and private entities, were invited to take part in the financing and provision of health care services. The consumerist approach promoted by the New Labour govern-ment put the patient at the heart of the system. Thus, NHS providers and private entities were put at the service of this project.

On the role of for-profit actors in health care policy, the enquiry concludes that medical professionals play different roles across welfare states; thus, incentives may vary, and so does their ability to promote these interests. Assumptions that

---

[6] PL Bradshaw and G Bradshaw, *Health Policy for Health Care Professionals* (London, Sage Publications, 2004) 15.

for-profit actors participating in private health care systems have a stronger role in health care policies and are better able to impose their interests must be nuanced. For-profit actors' roles in a publicly financed system, although limited because of the boundaries set by the government, may also significantly influence health care reforms. The private sector in the American health care system has certainly made policy path dependent, and created an incremental system. Nonetheless, the medical profession in the United Kingdom has played an equally important role in the development of NHS policies and has been able to safeguard the fundamental values of universality and equality of care that constitute the core of the system.

In order to address the book's central research question, a reflection on the role of justice in health care law also had to be included. Chapter two offers an analysis of theories of political philosophy, organising principles for health care systems and theories of health care rights, to create the framework of analysis used in chapter four and chapter six. The egalitarian, utilitarian, communitarian, libertarian and neoliberal approaches to the allocation of health care resources are unpacked to understand how each of these theories envisions the intervention (or lack thereof) of social institutions to guarantee the just allocation of health care resources. Each model takes a stance for or against universality of care having a direct impact on the partner of allocation it prescribes. The principles outlined for each theory, along with principles organising health care systems, form the reading grid used to critically analyse the American Congressional hearings in chapter four and the British Second Reading of proposed health care Bills in chapter six. The principles of solidarity and subsidiarity that transcend all theories of justice were also fundamental to the enquiry as they propose two different, but potentially complementary, methods to organise health care systems. Solidarity requires that members of a society adopt a benevolent attitude towards weaker social groups, whereas subsidiary mandates that the lowest and least central level of authority should deal with the allocation of resources. Finally, the last portion of this theoretical chapter bridges these concepts explaining how these theories and principles can help formulate health care rights. This also helped determine whether the laws later analysed had emulated these theoretical models.

Indeed, the enquiry into health care reforms in the United States and the United Kingdom reveals that theories for the just allocation of health care resources have made their way into the law. Laws that aimed to reform the distribution of resources to finance and provide services in the United States have been informed by ideas of liberal equality in the 1960s mirroring the more general movements of social solidarity among the population. Discourses during the Congressional hearings, leading to the enactment of the Kerr–Mills Act (1960) and the amendments to the Social Security Act (1965) creating the federal programmes of Medicare and Medicaid, relay a desire to provide more vulnerable members of society with health care coverage. The reaction of the for-profit sector to these proposals, namely the medical profession is, however, indicative of a libertarian approach to health care policy. These debates attest to the constant oscillation of health care policy between the need to promote equality of health care resources or the equality in access to care, and the market and libertarian approach to the distribution of health care. In fact, the enactment of the Health Maintenance Organization and Resources Development Act (HMO 1973) made a return to the market ideology as the government struggled with rising health care costs and uncontrolled federal spending on Medicare and Medicaid. Negotiations of this law conveyed ideas of libertarianism and many elements of the doctrine of communitarian justice that appeal to greater subsidiarity in health care and a local decision-making process in order to produce a more cost-efficient system. Finally, the ACA (2010) and the uphill battle led by the Obama Administration provide an interesting example of discussions that have risen above political interests as they engaged with the welfare egalitarianism and libertarian rhetoric.

On the other hand, ideas of justice in British health care policy are present at the inception of the centralised system in 1946 and have led to path dependency in health care policy up until the latest health care reform in 2012. The foundational National Health Service Act (1946), initially negotiated without the input of the medical profession, conveyed ideas of liberal equality that constitute the core of the NHS. The revolutionising Act built on the review and recommendations made in the Beveridge report. The conclusions of the inquiry foreshadowed a system based on equality in health care and the universal provision of health care services. Social utility was also a prime concern of the founders of the NHS, but values such as respect for human dignity were first put forward to advance the egalitarian justice principles in the negotiation process. The inefficiencies crippling the public sector during the 1980s led the Conservative government to order a series of policy papers and reports that culminated with the enactment of the National Health Service Community Care Act (1990). Debates during the Second Reading of the precursor White Paper *Working for Patients* (1989) relay the libertarian ambition of the government with the creation of an internal market for medicine. The divide between health care purchasers and providers put forward in the proposal signals a turn towards a market approach embracing competition in health care. Nevertheless, the discussions during the negotiation of the National Health Service and Community Care Act (1990) revolved around a utilitarian rhetoric. The purpose of the reform was to make health care services more efficient using utilitarian principles, but the foundational egalitarian goals of the NHS could not be compromised. Over the course of the 1990s and the beginning of the new millennium, the libertarian rhetoric used by the proponents of a market approach had transformed into a consumerist approach for the allocation of health care resources. The NHS had to be more patient-focused to better address health care needs. The equal entitlement would remain even though private providers had been formally invited to collaborate with the NHS. Thus, the reform proposal formulated by the Coalition government in its first White Paper *Equity and Excellence: Liberating the NHS* conveyed a libertarian approach and prominent consumerist rhetoric. During the Second Reading of the Health and Social Care Bill in the House of Lords those in favour of the reform put forward discourses that argued in favour of a libertarian and neoliberal approach to the allocation of health care resources. Conversely, rhetoric of liberal equality present in the discourses of MPs in opposition to the reform dominate the debate. The final version of the Act reflects a compromise. The NHS principles of equality in health care were preserved but a neoliberal approach to the delivery of health care services had been adopted. Essentially, the enactment of each of these laws represents watershed moments in health care policy. Even though the creation of the international market in 1990 and the introduction of private entities for the provision of health care services in 2012 represent major shifts for the NHS, the policy remains deeply path dependent. Despite these systemic overhauls, the NHS' core continues to be unwavering.

Finally, the conclusions of this enquiry may also have some implications for policy and health care law scholarship. A bird's-eye view of the comparison between the health care systems of the United States and United Kingdom highlights a new trend in health care policy. Traditionally, health care systems have been classified along a continuum, with private systems at one end of the spectrum and state-funded systems at the other.[7] The taxonomy now seems to be outdated. Health care systems are responding differently to social and economic contexts and are now adopting hybrid approaches.[8]

For instance, some academics have argued that the ACA (2010) constitutes an important departure from previous reforms as it brings the American health care system closer to an international standard.[9] Indeed, the analysis of discourses in the negotiation of the latest health care reforms reveals a desire to bring health care coverage closer to a universal model of health care financing. The individual mandate and the end of insurance discrimination based on pre-existing conditions could be interpreted as attempts to align health care financing and delivery in the United States with the standard set by European Western welfare states.

Conversely, the NHS is undergoing a transition in the opposite direction. The regulatory role of the state focusing on the structure and organisation of health care services has, in some aspects, been delegated to the private sector.[10] The latest health care reform in England reinforces and takes further the idea of a health care market established by the Thatcher and New Labour reforms in the 1980s and 1990s.[11] This new phase aims to optimise the performance of the NHS beyond the provision of health care services. Performance indicators have set new benchmarks, costs now need to be accounted for to make the allocation of health care

---

[7] JG Cullis and PA West, 'French Health Care: Viewpoint A-System X?' (1985) 5 *Health Policy* 143, 148.

[8] CH Tuohy, 'Reform and the Politics of Hybridization in Mature Health Care States' (2012) 37 *Journal of Health Politics, Policy and Law* 611, 612.

[9] See generally, J White, 'The 2010 US Health Care Reform: Approaching and Avoiding How Other Countries Finance Health Care' (2013) 8 *Health Economics, Policy and Law* 1.

[10] AM Pollock and D Price, 'How the Secretary of State for Health Proposes to Abolish the NHS in England' (2011) 342 *BMJ* 747.

[11] See generally, A Talbot-Smith and AM Pollock, *The New NHS: A Guide* (New York, Routledge, 2006).

resources most optimal.[12] Prior to the Health and Social Care Act (2012), health care services were publicly provided and financed, success was solely assessed on the basis of quality of care and responsiveness. The reform now opens the provision of services to the private sector in order to achieve new objectives and meet the expectations of 'patients-consumers'.[13]

While the book focuses on two specific health care systems, the theoretical framework based on models for the just distribution of health care resources could be used to analyse health care allocation laws in any other welfare state. This book certainly contributes to solving these issues, as it reveals the importance of a philosophical understanding of the legislative process. It constitutes a stepping stone to engage the for-profit sector in a different way. Nevertheless, the principles of justice relayed in the drafting of health care financing and provision laws neither guarantee the just application of these norms, nor do they imply the just allocation of health care resources. Regardless, awareness that path dependency affects health care policy-making and the enactment of allocation laws provides an important contribution to the research in the field of health care law. Lawmakers may be able to use this research to circumvent or use these constraints to create optimal health care financing and provision legislation. Hopefully, revealing a link between different perspectives on health care allocation issues and offering a comparative and philosophical analysis of health care laws will help elaborate more just policies and norms needed for the allocation of health care resources.

[12] Tuohy, above (n 8) 612.
[13] J Clarke et al, *Creating Citizen-Consumers: Changing Publics, Changing Public Services* (London, Sage Publications, 2007) 27.

# APPENDIX

| Theoretical Archetypes | Discourse Occurrences |
|---|---|
| Egalitarianism | Equity, equality, fairness, inequality, welfare, vulnerable group, right to health/health care, category, opportunity |
| Utilitarianism | Utility, happiness, maximisation, priority, ranking (of applicants' needs) |
| Communitarian | Community, society, common good, local needs, social needs |
| Libertarianism and neoliberalism | Autonomy, charity, market, competitiveness, property, proximity, privatisation, decentralisation, consumers, cost-effectiveness |
| Organising principles | Solidarity/Subsidiarity |

# BIBLIOGRAPHY

'About the National Health Service (NHS) in England' *NHS Choices* (13 April 2016).

Adonis, A, *5 Days in May: The Coalition and Beyond* (London, Biteback Publishing, 2013).

Ahmed, PK and Cadenhead, L, 'Charting the Developments in the NHS' (1998) 24 *Health Manpower Management* 222.

Ainsworth, A, 'The Birth of the NHS' (2008) 36(1) *Practice Nurse* 38.

Allsop, J, *Health Policy and the NHS Towards 2000* (London, Longman, 1995).

Almgren, GR, *Health Care Politics, Policy and Services: A Social Justice Analysis* (New York, Springer Publishing Company, 2012).

Altman, SH and Weiner, SL, 'Regulation as a Second Best Choice' in US Federal Trade Commission and W Greenberg (eds), *Competition in the Health Care Sector: Past, Present, and Future* (Washington DC, Government Printing Office, 1978).

American Civil Liberties Union, *Legislative Briefing Kit: Lifestyle Discrimination in the Workplace* (Washington DC, American Civil Liberties Union, 1998).

Anderson, OW and Alksne, H, *An Examination of the Concept of Medical Indigence* (Health Information Foundation, 1957).

Annas, GJ, *American Health Law* (Boston, MA, Little Brown, 1990).

Appleby, J, 'Employers Tie Financial Rewards, Penalties to Health Tests, Lifestyle Choices' *Kaiser Health News* (2 April 2012).

—— 'Making Sense of PFI' (Nuffield Trust, 2017).

Arneson, R, 'Egalitarianism' [2002] *Stanford Encyclopedia of Philosophy*.

Arora, S, Charlesworth, A, Kelly, E and Stoyel, G, 'Public Payment and Private Provision' (Nuffield Trust/Institute for Fiscal Studies, 2013).

Arrow, KJ, 'Uncertainty and the Welfare Economics of Medical Care' (1963) 53 *American Economic Review* 851.

Arts, W and Gelissen, J, 'Welfare States, Solidarity and Justice Principles: Does the Type Really Matter?' (2001) 44 *Acta Sociologica* 283.

Asthana, S, 'Liberating the NHS? A Commentary on the Lansley White Paper, "Equity and Excellence"' (2011) 72 *Social Science & Medicine* 815.

Baggott, R, *Understanding Health Policy* (Bristol, Policy Press, 2015).

Bailey, P, 'Primary Care Duped: The Government's Bill Will Wreck the NHS' (2012) 344 *BMJ* 1.

Baily, MA, 'Managed Care Organizations and the Rationing Problem' (2003) 33(1) *Hastings Center Report* 34.

Banaszak-Holl, JC, Levitsky, SR and Zald, MN, *Social Movements and the Transformation of American Health Care* (Oxford, Oxford University Press, 2010).

Beauchamp, TL and Childress, JF, *Principles of Biomedical Ethics* (Oxford, Oxford University Press, 2001).

Beauchamp, TL and Faden, RR, 'The Right to Health and the Right to Health Care' (1979) 4 *Journal of Medicine and Philosophy* 118.

Beecham, L, 'BMA Launches Campaign Against White Paper' (1989) 298 *BMJ* 676.

Béland, D, Rocco, P and Waddan, A, 'Obamacare and the Politics of Universal Health Insurance Coverage in the United States' (2016) 50 *Social Policy & Administration* 428.

Bennahum, D, 'The Crisis Called Managed Care' in D Bennahum (ed), *Managed Care: Financial, Legal, and Ethical Issues* (Cleveland, OH, Pilgrim Press, 1999).

Bennett, JT and Di Lorenzo, TJ, *Destroying Democracy: How Government Funds Partisan Politics* (Washington DC, Cato Institute, 1985).

Bentham, J, *An Introduction to the Principles of Morals and Legislation* (Oxford, Clarendon Press, 1879).

Berliner, HS, 'Medicaid After the Supreme Court Decision' (2013) 8(1) *Health Economics, Policy and Law* 133.

Bernstein, I, *Guns or Butter: The Presidency of Lyndon Johnson* Oxford, Oxford University Press, 1996).

Bernstein, MC and Bernstein, JB, *Social Security: The System That Works* (New York, Basic Books, 1988).

Besley, T, Hall, J and Preston, I, 'Social Security and Health Care Consumption: A Comparison of Alternative Systems Private and Public Health Insurance in the UK' (1998) 42 *European Economic Review* 491.

Bevan, A, *In Place of Fear* (New York, Simon and Shuster, 1952).

Bevan, G and Robinson, R, 'The Interplay Between Economic and Political Logics: Path Dependency in Health Care in England' (2005) 30 *Journal of Health Politics, Policy and Law* 53.

Beveridge, WH, *Social Insurance and Allied Services* (London, HM Stationery Office, London 1942).

Black, D, 'Change in the NHS' (1992) 13 *Public Health Policy* 156.

Black, N, '"Liberating the NHS" – Another Attempt to Implement Market Forces in English Health Care' (2010) 363 *New England Journal of Medicine* 1103.

Blair, T, MP (Speech at the Trimdon Labour Club, Trimdon, 30 April 1997).

Blavin, A et al, 'Employer-Sponsored Insurance Stays Strong, with No Signs of Decay under the ACA: Findings through March 2016' (2016) *Urban Institute: Health Policy Centre*.

Blendon, RJ et al, 'Satisfaction with Health Systems in Ten Nations' (1990) 9(2) *Health Affairs* 185.

Blumenthal, D, 'Employer-Sponsored Health Insurance in the United States: Origins and Implications' (2006) 355 *New England Journal of Medicine* 82.

BMJ, 'More Brickbats than Bouquets?' (2010) *BMJ* 341.

Bobbitt, P, *The Shield of Achilles: War, Peace, and the Course of History* (New York, Random House, 2007).

Bode, I, 'The Welfare State in Germany' in C Aspalter (ed), *Welfare Capitalism Around the World* (Hong Kong, Casa Verde, 2003).

Bodenheimer, T, 'Should we Abolish the Private Health Insurance Industry?' (1990) 20 *International Journal of Health Services* 199.

Bovbjerg, RR, Griffin, CC and Carroll, CE, 'US Health Care Coverage and Costs: Historical Development and Choices for the 1990s' (1993) 21 *Journal of Law, Medicine & Ethics* 141.

Boyle, S, 'United Kingdom (England): Health System Review' (WHO Regional Office of Europe, 2011).

Bradshaw, PL and Bradshaw, G, *Health Policy for Health Care Professionals* (London, Sage Publications, 2004).

Brady, D et al, 'Path Dependency and the Politics of Socialized Health Care' (2016) 41 *Journal of Health Politics, Policy and Law* 355.

Breslow, L and Hochstim, JR, 'Sociocultural Aspects of Cervical Cytology in Alameda County, Calif' (1964) 79 *Public Health Reports* 107.

Brook, RH and Stevenson, RL, 'Effectiveness of Patient Care in an Emergency Room' (1970) 283 *New England Journal of Medicine* 904.

Brown, LD, *Politics and Health Care Organization: HMOs as Federal Policy* (Washington DC, Brookings Institution Press, 1983).

—— 'Pedestrian Paths: Why Path-Dependence Theory Leaves Health Policy Analysis Lost in Space' (2010) 35 *Journal of Health Politics, Policy and Law* 643.

Brown RE, 'Medicare and Medicaid: Band-Aid for the Old and Poor' in VW Sidel and R Sidel (eds), *Reforming Medicine: Lessons of the Last Quarter Century* (New York, Pantheon, 1983).

Buchanan AE, 'The Right to a Decent Minimum of Health Care' (1984) 13 *Philosophy & Public Affairs* 55.

—— 'Managed Care: Rationing Without Justice, But Not Unjustly' (1998) 23 *Journal of Health Politics, Policy and Law* 617.

Buck, D and Dixon, A, 'Improving the Allocation of Health Resources in England' (The King's Fund, 2013).

Buettgens, M, Garrett, B and Holahan, J, 'Why the Individual Mandate Matters' (The Urban Institute, 2010).

Burrow, JG, *AMA: Voice of American Medicine* (Baltimore, MD, The Johns Hopkins Press, 1963).

Cabinet Office, *Modernising Government* (London, Stationery Office, 1999).

Callahan, D and Wasunna, AA, *Medicine and the Market: Equity v Choice* (Baltimore, MD, Johns Hopkins University Press, 2006).

Carpenter, DP, Esterling, KM and Lazer DMJ, 'The Strength of Weak Ties in Lobbying Networks: Evidence from Health-Care Politics in the United States' (1998) 10 *Journal of Theoretical Politics* 417.

Carroll, A, 'What Makes the US Health Care System So Expensive' *The Incidental Economist* (20 September 2010).

Cawson, A, *Corporatism and Welfare: Social Policy and State Intervention in Britain* (London, Heinemann Educational Publishers, 1982).

Chapin, CF, 'The American Medical Association, Health Insurance Association of America, and Creation of the Corporate Health Care System' (2010) 24 *Studies in American Political Development* 143.

Chernichovsky, D, 'Health System Reforms in Industrialized Democracies: An Emerging Paradigm' [1995] *The Milbank Memorial Fund Quarterly* 339.

Clarke, J et al, *Creating Citizen-Consumers: Changing Publics, Changing Public Services* (London, Sage Publications, 2007).

Commission on the Future of Health and Social Care in England, *The UK Private Health Market* (The King's Fund, 2014).

Commonwealth of Pennsylvania, Department of Public Welfare, Informational Leaflet No 8, 'If You Need Medical Assistance for the Aged' (1962).

Conservative Party, *Invitation to Join the Government of Britain: The Conservative Manifesto 2010* (London, Conservative Research Department, 2010).

Cookson, R et al, 'Effects of the Blair/Brown NHS Reforms on Socioeconomic Equity in Health Care' (2012) 17 *Journal of Health Services Research and Policy* 55, 55.

Cortese, DA and Smoldt, RK, 'Healing America's Ailing Health Care System' (2006) 81 *Mayo Clinic Proceedings* 492.

Cousins, C, 'The Restructuring of Welfare Work: The Introduction of General Management and the Contracting out of Ancillary Services in the NHS' (1988) 2 *Work, Employment & Society* 210.

Cowan, R and Cornwell, S, 'House Votes to Being Repealing Obamacare' *Reuters* (Washington DC, 13 January 2017).

Crimmins, JE, 'History of the Utilitarian Social Thought' in J Wright (ed), *International Encyclopedia of the Social & Behavioral Sciences*, 2nd edn (Oxford, Elsevier, 2015).

Crinson, I, *Health Policy: A Critical Perspective* (London, Sage Publications, 2009).

Cullis, JG and West, PA, 'French Health Care: Viewpoint A-System X?' (1985) 5 *Health Policy* 143.

Cunningham, PW, 'Rebellion by States Could be Hazardous to Health Care Overhaul' *The Washington Times* (25 August 2011).

Daniels, N, 'Health-Care Needs and Distributive Justice' (1981) 10 *Philosophy & Public Affairs* 146.

—— *Just Health Care* (Cambridge, Cambridge University Press, 1985).

—— *Just Health: Meeting Health Needs Fairly* (Cambridge, Cambridge University Press, 2007).

—— 'Justice and Access to Health Care' [2008] *Stanford Encyclopedia of Philosophy*.

—— 'Broken Promises: Do Business-Friendly Strategies Frustrate Just Healthcare?' in DG Arnold (ed), *Ethics and the Business of Biomedicine* (Cambridge, Cambridge University Press, 2009).

Daniels, N and Sabin, JE, *Setting Limits Fairly: Learning to Share Resources for Health* (Oxford University Press, 2008).

David, SI, *With Dignity: The Search for Medicare and Medicaid* (Westport, CT, Greenwood, 1985).

Davidson, S, *Still Broken: Understanding the US Health Care System* (Stanford, CA, Stanford University Press, 2010).

Davies, H and Powell, H, 'How to Ration Health Care-and be Re-elected: The UK Experience' (1991) 3 *Stanford Law & Policy Review* 138.

Davis, K and Reynolds, R, *The Impact of Medicare and Medicaid on Access to Medical Care* (Washington DC, Brookings Institution, 1976).

Day, P and Klein, R, 'The Mobilisation of Consent versus the Management of Conflict: Decoding the Griffiths Report' (1983) 287 *British Medical Journal* 1813.

Delamothe, T, 'NHS at 60: Founding Principles' (2008) 336 *British Medical Journal* 1216.

Den Bakker, EK and De Wit, GE, 'Social Security in a European Perspective' (1983) 8 *Geneva Papers on Risk and Insurance* 248.

Department of Health, *Working for Patients* (Cm 555, 1989).

—— Press Release, 'A National Plan for a National Health Service: Five Teams to Focus on NHS Challenges' (23 March 2000).

—— *For the Benefit of Patients: A Concordat with the Private and Voluntary Health Care Provider Sector* (2000).

—— *The NHS Plan: A Plan for Investment, A Plan for Reform* (Cm 4818-I, 2000).

—— *Shifting the Balance of Power within the NHS* (2001).

—— *The Expert Patient: A New Approach to Chronic Disease Management for the 21st Century* (2001).

—— Delivering the NHS Plan – Next Steps on Investment, Next Steps on Reform (Cm 5503, 2002).

—— *A Code of Conduct for Private Practice* (2004).

—— *Guidance on NHS Patients Who Wish to Pay for Additional Private Care* (2009).

—— *Liberating the NHS: Legislative Framework and Next Steps* (2010).

Department of Health and Social Care, *High Quality Care for All: NHS Next Stage Review Final Report* (Cmd 7432, 2008).

—— *Equity and Excellence: Liberating the NHS* (Cm 7881, 2010).

Department of Health and Social Security, *National Health Service Reorganisation: England* (Cmnd 5055, 1972).

—— *Primary Health Care: An Agenda for Discussion* (Cmnd 9771, 1986).

Dickinson, H et al, 'The Limits of Market-Based Reforms' (2013) 13(1) *BMC Health Services Research* 1.

Dixon, A and Ham, C, 'Liberating the NHS: The Right Prescription in a Cold Climate' (The King's Fund, 2010).

Dorsey, JL, 'The Health Maintenance Organization Act of 1973 (PL 93-222) and Prepaid Group Practice Plans' (1975) 13 *Medical Care* 1.

Downing, R, *Suffering and Healing in America: An American Doctor's View from Outside* (Seattle, WA, Radcliffe Publishing, 2006).

Driver, S and Martell, L, *Blair's Britain* (Cambridge, Polity Press, 2002).

Dunshire, A, 'Then and Now Public Administration, 1953–1999' (1999) 47 *Political Studies* 360.

Dworkin, R, 'What is Equality? Part 2: Equality of Resources' (1981) 10 *Philosophy and Public Affairs* 283.

—— *Sovereign Virtue: The Theory and Practice of Equality* (Cambridge, MA, Harvard University Press, 2002).

Eckstein, H, 'Pressure Group Politics' (1960) 35 *Academic Medicine* 1069.

Edwards, B, Linton, J and Potter, C, *The National Health Service: A Manager's Tale 1946–1992* (London, Nuffield Provincial Hospitals Trust, 1993).

Eilers, RD, *Regulation of Blue Cross and Blue Shield Plans* (Homewood, IL, SS Huebner Foundation for Insurance Education, 1963).

'Eldercare Branded Empty Propaganda' *AFL–CIO News* (20 February 1965) RG 233, Records of the House of Representatives, 89th Congress, Committee on Ways and Means, Legislative Files, Box 21, File: HR 6675-3 of 94.

Elhauge, E, 'Allocating Health Care Morally' (1994) 82 *California Law Review* 1449.

—— *The Fragmentation of US Health Care: Causes and Solutions* (Oxford, Oxford University Press, 2010).

Emanuel, EJ, 'Where Civic Republicanism and Deliberative Democracy Meet' (1996) 26(6) *Hastings Center Report* 12.

Emmerson, C, Frayne, C and Goodman, A, 'Should Private Medical Insurance Be Subsidised?' (The King's Fund, 2001).

Engelhard Jr, HT, *The Foundations of Bioethics*, 2nd edn (New York, Oxford University Press, 1996).

Enthoven, AC, *Reflections on the Management of the National Health Service: An American Looks at Incentives to Efficiency in Health Services Management in the UK* (London, Nuffield Provincial Hospitals Trust, 1985).

Enthoven, AC and Singer, SJ, 'Markets and Collective Action in Regulating Managed Care' (1997) 16(6) *Health Affairs* 26.

European Commission, 'Government Investment in the Framework of Economic Strategy' (1998).

European Commission Directorate General, 'Making the Most of the Opening of Public Procurement' (1997).

—— 'Public Procurement in the European Union: Exploring the Way Forward (1997).

European Investment Bank, 'The EIB and Public Private–Partnerships' (1998) 2 *EIB Information* 97.

Evans, HM, 'Do Patients Have Duties?' (2007) 33) *Journal of Medical Ethics* 689.

Executive Hearings Before the H Comm on Ways and Means, 89th Cong (1965).

Falkson, JL, *HMOs and the Politics of Health Service Reform* (Chicago, IL, American Hospital Associations, 1980).

—— 'Market Reform, Health System, and HMOs' (1981) 9 *Policy Studies Journal* 213.

Federal Trade Commission and Department of Justice, *Improving Health Care: A Dose of Competition* (2004).

Fernandez, B and Mach, AL, *Health Insurance Exchanges Under the Patient Protection and Affordable Care Act* (Washington DC, Congressional Research Service, 2013).

Field, RI, *Mother of Invention: How the Government Created 'Free-Market' Health Care* (Oxford, Oxford University Press, 2013).

Fine, S, 'The Kerr–Mills Act: Medical Care for the Indigent in Michigan, 1960–1965' (1998) 53 *Journal of the History of Medicine and Allied Sciences* 285.

Finlayson, JG, *Habermas: A Very Short Introduction*, Vol 125 (Oxford, Oxford University Press, 2005).

Fleischacker, S, *A Short History of Distributive Justice* (Cambridge, MA, Harvard University Press, 2009).

Fleming, S, 'Wellness Programs Lighten Health Costs' (2005) 120(3) *American City & County* 8.

Føllesdal, A, 'Survey Article: Subsidiarity' (1998) 6 *Journal of Political Philosophy* 190.

Foot, M, *Aneurin Bevan: A Biography Vol 2, 1945-60* (London, Paladin, 1975).

Fotaki, M et al, *Patient Choice and the Organisation and Delivery of Health Services: Scoping Review* (Manchester, NCCSDO, 2005).

Foubister, T et al, *Private Medical Insurance in the United Kingdom* (Copenhagen, European Observatory on Health Systems and Policies, 2006).

Fourie, C, 'What Do Theories of Social Justice Have to Say About Health Care Rationing? Well-being, Sufficiency and Explicit Age-rationing' in A den Exter and M Buijsen (eds) *Rationing Health Care: Hard Choices and Unavoidable Trade-Offs* (Antwerp, Maklu, 2012).

Fried, C, 'The June Surprises: Balls, Strikes, and the Fog of War' (2013) 38 *Journal of Health Politics, Policy and Law* 225.

Fries, JF et al, 'Reducing Health Care Costs by Reducing the Need and Demand for Medical Services' (1993) 329 *New England Journal of Medicine* 321.

Froud, J et al, 'Persuasion Without Numbers? Public Policy and the Justification of Capital Charging in NHS Trust Hospitals' (1998) 11 *Accounting, Auditing and Accountability Journal* 99.

Gabel, JR and Monheit, AC, 'Will Competition Plans Change Insurer–Provider Relationships?' (1983) 61 *Milbank Memorial Fund Quarterly/Health and Society* 614.

Gaffney, D et al, 'The Private Finance Initiative: NHS Capital Expenditure and the Private Finance Initiative – Expansion or Contraction?' (1999) 319 *BMJ* 48.

—— 'The Private Finance Initiative: PFI in the NHS – Is there an Economic Case?' (1999) 319 *BMJ* 116.

—— 'The Private Finance Initiative: The Politics of the Private Finance Initiative and the New NHS' (1999) 319 *BMJ* 249.

Geertz, C, *The Interpretation of Cultures: Selected Essays* (New York, Basic Books, 1977).

Germain, S, 'Taking "Health" as a Socio-Economic Right Seriously: Is the South African Constitutional Dialogue a Remedy for the American Healthcare System?' (2013) 21 *African Journal of International and Comparative Law* 145.

Giaimo, S, *Markets and Medicine: The Politics of Health Care Reform in Britain, Germany, and the United States* (Ann Harbor, MI, University of Michigan Press, 2002).

Ginsburg, PB, 'Public Insurance Programs: Medicare and Medicaid' in HE Frech (ed), *Health Care in America: The Political Economy of Hospitals and Health Insurance* (San Francisco, CA, Pacific Research Institute for Public Policy, 1988).

Girod C, Hart S and Weltz S, '2017 Milliman Medical Index' *Milliman* (2017).

Glaser, WA, *Health Insurance in Practice: International Variations in Financing, Benefit, and Problems* (San Francisco, CA, Jossey-Bass Publishers, 1991).

Glennerster, H, 'The Coalition and Society (III): Health and Long-Term Care' in A Seldon and M Finn (eds), *The Coalition Effect, 2010–2015* (Cambridge, Cambridge University Press, 2015).

Goldhill, D, *Catastrophic Care: How American Health Care Killed My Father – and How We Can Fix It* (New York, Alfred A Knopf, 2013).

Golemboski, D, 'The Flip Side of Subsidiarity: Sometimes It Takes More Than a Village' (2012) 139 *Commonweal* 9.

Goodman, JC, *The Regulation of Medical Care: Is the Price Too High?* (San Francisco, CA, Cato Institute, 1980).

—— *Priceless: Curing the Health Care Crisis* (Oakland, CA, Independent Institute, 2012).

Gordon, C, *Dead on Arrival: The Politics of Health Care in Twentieth-Century America* (Princeton, NJ, Princeton University Press, 2004).

Greener, I et al, 'How Did Consumerism Get into the NHS? An Empirical Examination of Choice and Responsiveness in NHS Policy Documents' (2006) 29 *Cultures of Consumption Paper Series* 1.

Griffin, J, *Well-Being: Its Meaning, Measurement, and Moral Importance* (Oxford, Clarendon Press, 1986).

Griffiths, R, *NHS Management Inquiry: Report to the Secretary of State for Social Services* (Department of Health and Social Security, 1983).

Gutmann, A, 'For and Against Equal Access to Health Care' in R Bayer, AL Caplan and N Daniels (eds), *In Search of Equity* (Boston, MA, Springer, 1983).

Habermas, J, *Between Facts and Norms: Contributions to a Discourse Theory of Law and Democracy* (Chichester, John Wiley & Sons, 2015).

Hacker, JS, *The Road to Nowhere: The Genesis of President Clinton's Plan for Health Security* (Princeton, NJ, Princeton University Press, 1997).

—— 'The Historical Logic of National Health Insurance: Structure and Sequence in the Development of British, Canadian, and US Medical Policy' (1998) 12 *Studies in American Political Development* 57.

—— *The Divided Welfare State: The Battle over Public and Private Social Benefits in the United States* (Cambridge, Cambridge University Press, 2002).

Hacker, JS and Pierson, P, 'Business Power and Social Policy: Employers and the Formation of the American Welfare State' (2002) 30 *Politics & Society* 277.

Haidt, J, *The Righteous Mind: Why Good People are Divided by Politics and Religion* (New York, Vintage Books, 2012).

Hall, JP and Moore, JM, 'The Affordable Care Act's Pre-Existing Condition Insurance Plan: Enrollment, Costs, and Lessons for Reform' (2012) *The Commonwealth Fund* 5.

Hall, M and Brewbaker, WS (eds), *Health Care Corporate Law: Managed Care* (Gaithersburg, MD, Aspen, 1996).

Hall, MA, Bobinski, MA and Orentlicher, D, *The Law of Health Care Finance and Regulation*, 3rd edn (New York, Wolters Kluwer Law & Business, 2014).

Halls, WD (trans) and Durkheim, E, *The Division of Labour in Society* (London, Macmillan, 1984).

Ham, C, *Health Policy in Britain*, 2nd edn (Basingstoke, Macmillan, 1992).

—— *Management and Competition in the NHS* (Abingdon, Radcliffe Medical Press, 1997).

Hamburger, T and Geiger, K, 'Healthcare Insurers Get Upper Hand' *Los Angeles Times* (24 August 2009).

Hanson, R, 'Why Health is not Special: Errors in Evolved Bioethics Intuitions' (2002) 19(2) *Social Philosophy and Policy* 153.

Hare, RM, 'Ethical Theory and Utilitarianism' in A Sen and B Williams (eds), *Utilitarianism and Beyond* (Cambridge, Cambridge University Press, 1982).

Harris, J, *William Beveridge: A Biography* (Oxford, Clarendon Press, 1997).

Harris, R, *A Sacred Trust* (New York, New American Library, 1966).

Harrison, S and McDonald, R, *The Politics of Healthcare in Britain* (London, Sage Publications, 2008).

Harrison, S, Hunter, DJ and Pollit, C, *The Dynamics of British Health Policy* (London, Unwin Hyman, 1990).

Hayes, MT, *The Limits of Policy Change: Incrementalism, Worldview, and the Rule of Law* (Washington DC, Georgetown University Press, 2001).

Haysom, N, 'Constitutionalism, Majoritarian Democracy and Socio-Economic Rights' (1992) 8 *South African Journal on Human Rights* 451.

Health Committee, *Independent Sector Treatment Centres*, 4th Report (2005–06, HC 934-I).

'Health Insurance Coverage of the Total Population' (Henry J Kaiser Family Foundation, 2016).

'Healthcare Disparities and Barriers to Healthcare' (Stanford eCampus Rural Health, 2010).

Hedinger, FR, *The Social Role of Blue Cross as a Device for Financing the Costs of Hospital Care: An Evaluation* (Graduate Program in Hospital and Health Administration, 1966).

Hellowell, M, 'Unhealthy Option?' *Public Finance* (30 October 2008).

Hellowell, M and Pollock, AM, 'The Private Financing of NHS Hospitals: Politics, Policy and Practice' (2009) 29(1) *Economic Affairs* 13.

Hessler, K and Buchanan, AE, 'Specifying the Content of the Human Right to Health Care' in R Rhodes, MP Battin and A Silvers (eds), *Medicine and Social Justice: Essays on the Distribution of Health Care* (Oxford, Oxford University Press, 2002).

HM Treasury, *PFI: Meeting the Investment Challenge* (London, HM Stationery Office, 2003).

Hockett, R, 'Justice in Time' (2008) 77 *George Washington Law Review* 1135.

Hoedemaekers, R and Dekkers W, 'Justice and Solidarity in Priority Setting in Health Care' (2003) 11 *Health Care Analysis* 325.

Hoffman, B, 'Health Care Reform and Social Movements in the United States' (2003) 1 *American Journal of Public Health* 75.

Holley, RT and Carlson, RJ, 'The Legal Context for the Development of Health Maintenance Organizations' (1971) 24 *Stanford Law Review* 644.

House of Commons, *NHS (England) Summarised Accounts 1996–97* (London, HM Stationery Office, 1998).

Houtepen, R and Meulen, R ter, 'The Expectation(s) of Solidarity: Matters of Justice, Responsibility and Identity in the Reconstruction of the Health Care System' (2000) 8 *Health Care Analysis* 355.

Hunter, DJ, *Desperately Seeking Solutions: Rationing Health Care* (London, Longman, 1997).

—— 'A Response to Rudolf Klein: A Battle May Have Been Won but Perhaps Not the War' (2013) 38 *Journal of Health Politics, Policy and Law* 871.

—— *The Health Debate* (Bristol, Policy Press, 2016).

Iacobucci, G, 'A Third of NHS Contracts Awarded Since Health Act Have Gone to Private Sector' (2014) 349 *BMJ* 1.

Ibbetson, D, 'Comparative Legal History: A Methodology' in A Musson and C Stebbings (eds), *Making Legal History: Approaches and Methodologies* (Cambridge, Cambridge University Press, 2012).

Iglehart, JK, 'The Carter Administration's Health Budget: Charting New Priorities with Limited Dollars' (1978) 56 *Milbank Memorial Fund Quarterly* 51.

Illich, I, *Limits to Medicine: Medical Nemesis – The Expropriation of Health* (London, Penguin Books, 1977).

Immergut, EM, *Health Politics: Interests and Institutions in Western Europe*, 6th edn (Cambridge, Cambridge University Press Archive, 1992).

Jackson, E, *Medical Law: Text, Cases, and Materials*, 3rd edn (Oxford, Oxford University Press, 2013).

—— *Medical Law: Text, Cases, and Materials*, 4th edn (Oxford, Oxford University Press, 2016).

Joachim, HH and Rees, DA (eds), *Aristotle: The Nicomachean Ethics* (Oxford, Clarendon Press, 1953).

Jones, R, 'The White Paper: A Framework for Survival?' (2010) 60 *British Journal of General Practice* 635.

Jones, S, 'The Failure of the NHS-Distributive Justice and Health Care in Britain' (1997) *UCL Jurisprudence Review* 163.

Jones, WA, 'Medicaid 101: History, Challenges, and Opportunities' (2006) 16 *Ethnicity & Disease* 56.

Jørgensen, MW and Phillips, LJ, *Discourse Analysis as Theory and Method* (London, Sage Publications, 2002).

Jost, TS, *Disentitlement?: The Threats Facing our Public Health-Care Programs and a Rights-Based Response* (New York, Oxford University Press, 2003).

—— 'Health Insurance Exchanges and the Affordable Care Act: Eight Difficult Issues' (The Commonwealth Fund, 2010).

'Kaiser Health Tracking Poll: The Public's Views on the Affordable Care Act' (Henry J Kaiser Family Foundation, 2017).

Kennedy, I, *The Unmasking of Medicine* (London, Allen & Unwin, 1981) 123.

Kennedy, I and Grubb, A, *Medical Law* (Oxford, Oxford University Press, 2000).

Keynes, JM, *The General Theory of Employment, Interest and Money* (New Delhi, Atlantic Publishers and Distributors, 1936).

King, D and Mossialos, E, 'The Determinants of Private Medical Insurance Prevalence in England, 1997–2000' 40(1) *Health Services Research* 195.

Kirsch, R, 'The Politics of Obamacare: Health Care, Money, and Ideology' (2013) 81 *Fordham Law Review* 1737.

Klarman, HE, 'Approaches to Moderating the Increases in Medical Care Costs' (1969) 7 *Medical Care* 175.

Klein, R, 'Carolyn Hughes Tuohy, *Accidental Logics: The Dynamics of Change in the Health Care Arena in the United States, Britain and Canada*' Book Review (2000) 20 Journal Public Policy 105.

—— *The New Politics of the NHS: From Creation to Reinvention*, 7th edn (London, Radcliffe Publishing, 2013).

—— 'The Twenty-Year War Over England's National Health Service: A Report from the Battlefield' (2013) 38 *Journal of Health Politics, Policy and Law* 849.

Knight, C, *Luck Egalitarianism: Equality, Responsibility, and Justice* (Edinburgh, Edinburgh University Press, 2009).

Krugman, P and Wells, R, 'The Health Care Crisis and What to do About It' (2006) 53(5) *The New York Review of Books* 1.

Kullgren, JT et al, 'Nonfinancial Barriers and Access to Care for US Adults' (2011) 47(1) *Health Services Research* 462.

Kuttner, R, 'Columbia/HCA and the Resurgence of the For-Profit Hospital Business' (1996) 335 *New England Journal of Medicine* 362.

Kymlicka, W, *Contemporary Political Philosophy: An Introduction* (Oxford, Oxford University Press, 2002).

LaFrance, KG, 'Preferred Provider Organization (PPO)' in MJ Stahl (ed), *Encyclopedia of Health Care Management* (Thousand Oaks, Sage Publications, 2004).

Lamm, RD, 'Rationing of Health Care: Inevitable and Desirable' (1992) 140 *University of Pennsylvania Law Review* 1511.

Landers, RM, 'The Dénouement of the Supreme Court's ACA Drama' (2012) 367 *New England Journal of Medicine* 198.

Landwehr, C, 'Procedural Justice and Democratic Institutional Design in Health-Care Priority-Setting' (2013) 12 *Contemporary Political Theory* 296.

Laugesen, MJ and Rice, TH, 'Is the Doctor In? The Evolving Role of Organized Medicine in Health Policy' (2003) 28 *Journal of Health Politics, Policy and Law* 289.

Lawson, N, *The View from No 11* (London, Corgi Books, 1993) 612.

Le Grand, J, Mays, N and Mulligan, J, *Learning from the NHS Internal Market* (London, King's Fund Publishing, 1998).

Lee, PR and Estes, CL, 'New Federalism and Health Policy' (1983) 468 *Annals of the American Academy of Political and Social Science* 88.

Levi, M, 'A Model, a Method, and a Map: Rational Choice in Comparative and Historical Analysis' (1997) in M Irving Lichback and AS Zuckerman (eds), *Comparative Politics: Rationality, Culture and Structure* (Cambridge, Cambridge University Press, 1997).

Liberal Democrats, *Change That Works for You: Liberal Democrat Manifesto 2010* (London, Liberal Democrat Publications, 2010).

Light, DW, 'The Restructuring of the American Health Care System' (1997) *Health Politics and Policy* 46.

Lindblom, CE, 'The Science of "Muddling Through"' (1959) 19 *Public Administration Review* 79.

Litman, TJ and Robins, LS, *Health Politics and Policy*, 2nd edn (New York, Delmar 1991).

Lorenzoni, L, Belloni, A and Sassi, F, 'Health-Care Expenditure and Health Policy in the USA Versus Other High-Spending OECD Countries' (2014) 384(9937) *The Lancet* 83.

Ludmerer, KM, *Time to Heal: American Medical Education from the Turn of the Century to the Era of Managed Care* (Oxford, Oxford University Press, 1999).

Maarse, H, 'The Privatization of Health Care in Europe: An Eight-Country Analysis' (2006) 31 *Journal of Health Politics, Policy and Law* 981.

Maarse, H and Paulus, A, 'Has Solidarity Survived? A Comparative Analysis of the Effect of Social Health Insurance Reform in Four European Countries' (2003) 28 *Journal of Health Politics, Policy and Law* 585.

MacLauchlan, G and Maynard, A, *The Public–Private Mix for Health* (Oxford, Nuffield Provincial Hospitals Trust, 1982).

Marmor, TR, *The Politics of Medicare* (New York, Aldine de Gruyter, 2000).

Martin, J, 'SEIU Takes Pragmatic Stance' *Politico* (24 September 2009).

Mays, N, Dixon, A and Jones, L, *Understanding New Labour's Market Reforms of the English NHS* (London, King's Fund, 2011).

McClure, W, 'Structural and Incentives Problems in Economic Regulation of Medical Care' (1981) 59 *Milbank Memorial Quarterly/Health and Society* 107.

McGregor, S, 'Neoliberalism and Health Care' (2001) 25 *International Journal of Consumer Studies* 82.

Mechanic, D, *The Truth About Health Care: Why Reform is not Working in America* (London, Rutgers University Press, 2006).

Milburn, A, Chief Secretary to the Treasury (Speech at the Private Finance Initiative Transport Conference, February 1999).

—— Secretary of State for Health (Speech at the Annual Social Services Conference, Cardiff, 16 October 2002).

Minister of Health, *Memorandum on the Future of the Hospital Services* (Ministry of Health, 13 December 1945).

Ministry of Health, *A National Health Service* (Cmd 6502, 1944).

Mitchell, L, 'Sick in the Head: Why America Won't Get the Health-Care System It Needs' [2009] *Harper's* 11.

Monahan, A and Schwarcz, D, 'Will Employers Undermine Health Care Reform by Dumping Sick Employees?' (2011) 97 *Virginia Law Review* 125.

Mooney, G, '"Communitarian Claims" as an Ethical Basis for Allocating Health Care Resources' (1998) 47 *Social Science & Medicine* 1171.

Moore, JD and Smith, DG, 'Legislating Medicaid: Considering Medicaid and its Origins' (2005) 27(2) *Health Care Financing Review* 45.

Moran, AE, 'Wellness Programs After the Affordable Care Act' (2013) 39 *Employee Relations Law Journal* 75.

Moran, DW, 'Whence and Whither Health Insurance? A Revisionist History' (2005) 24(6) *Health Affairs* 1415.

Morone, JA, 'Citizens or Shoppers? Solidarity Under Siege' (2000) 25 *Journal of Health Politics, Policy and Law* 959.

Morone, JA and Jacobs, LR, *Healthy, Wealthy and Fair: Health Care and the Good Society* (New York, Oxford University Press, 2005).

Mullard, M and Swaray, R, 'New Labour Legacy: Comparing the Labour Governments of Blair and Brown to Labour Governments since 1945' (2010) 81 *The Political Quarterly* 511, 511.

Nairne, P, 'Managing the DHSS Elephant: Reflections on a Giant Department' (1983) 54 *Political Quarterly* 243.

National Association of Manufacturers, *ManuFacts: Health Care Reform* (Washington DC, National Association of Manufacturers, 2011).

National Audit Office, *The Performance and Management of Hospital PFI Contracts* (London, HM Stationery Office, 2010).

—— *Memorandum on the Provision of the Out-of-Hours GP Services in Cornwall* (HC 2012–13, 1016).

National Business Group on Health, *Principles for National Health Care Reform: The View of the National Business Group on Health* (Washington DC, NBGH, 2008).

Navarro, P, *The Policy Game: How Special Interests and Ideologues Are Stealing America* (New York, Wiley, 1984).

Newdick, C, 'Promoting Access and Equity in Health: Assessing the National Health Service in England' in CM Flood and A Gross (eds), *The Right to Health at the Public/Private Divide: A Global Comparative Study* (Cambridge, Cambridge University Press, 2014).

Newman, J and Vilder, E, 'Discriminating Customers, Responsible Patients, Empowered Users: Consumerism and the Modernisation of Health Care' (2006) 35 *Journal of Social Policy* 193.

Nixon, RM, 'Message to Congress' in *Weekly Compilation of Presidential Documents* (Washington DC, Office of Federal Register, 1971).

'NHE Fact Sheet' (Centers for Medicare & Medicaid Services, 2017).

Nozick R, *Anarchy, State, and Utopia* (New York, Basic Books, 1974).

Nussbaum, MC, 'Aristotle, Politics, and Human Capabilities: A Response to Antony, Arneson, Charlesworth, and Mulgan' (2000) 111 *Ethics* 102.

Office for National Statistics, 'Expenditure on Healthcare in the UK: 2013' (2015).

Padgug, RA and Oppenheimer, GM, 'AIDS, Health Insurance, and the Crisis of Community' (1991) 5 *Notre Dame Journal of Law, Ethics & Public Policy* 35.

Patel, K and Rushefsky, ME, *Healthcare Politics and Policy in America*, 4th edn (Armonk, NY, ME Sharpe, 2014).

Patrick, D, Massachusetts Governor candidate, 'Rally for Change' (Speech at the Rally for Change on Boston Common, 15 October 2006).

Peckham, S and Sanderson, M, 'Patient Choice: A Contemporary Policy Story' in M Exworthy (ed), *Shaping Health Policy: Case Study Methods and Analysis* (Bristol, The Policy Press, 2012).

Penner, J et al, *McCoubrey & White's Textbook on Jurisprudence* (Oxford, Oxford University Press, 2012).

Peters, RA, 'The Social Security Amendments of 1960: Completing the Foundations of Medicare and Medicaid' (2004) 26 *Journal of Health and Human Services Administration* 438.

Peterson, MA, 'From Trust to Political Power: Interests Groups, Public Choice, and Health Care' (2001) 26 *Journal of Health Politics, Policy and Law* 1145.

'PFI: Meeting the Investment Challenge' (HM Treasury, 2003).

Pierson, P, 'Not Just What, But When: Timing and Sequence in Political Processes' (2000) 14 *Studies in American Political Development* 72.

Pollock, AM, 'Primary Care – From Fundholding to Health Maintenance Organisations?' (1998) *NHS Doctor and Commissioning* 1.

—— *NHS plc: The Privatisation of Our Health Care* (London, Verso, 2004).

—— 'NHS No More?' (2016) 89(12) *Community Practitioner* 28.

Pollock, AM et al, 'What Happens When the Private Sector Plans Hospital Services for the NHS: Three Case Studies Under the Private Finance Initiative' (1997) 314 *BMJ* 1266.

—— 'How the Health and Social Care Bill 2011 Would End Entitlement to Comprehensive Health Care in England' (2012) 379 *The Lancet* 387.

Pollock, AM, Gaffney, D and Dunnigan, M, 'Public Health and the Private Finance Initiative' (1998) 20(1) *Journal of Public Health Medicine* 1.

Pollock, AM and Price, D, 'How the Secretary of State for Health Proposes to Abolish the NHS in England' (2011) 342 *BMJ* 747.

—— 'Has the NAO Audited Risk Transfer in Operational Private Finance Initiative Schemes?' (2008) 28 *Public Money & Management* 173.

Pollock, AM, Price, D and Brhlikova, P, 'Classification Problems and the Dividing Line Between Government and the Market: An Examination of NHS Foundation Trust Classification in the UK' (2011) 82 *Annals of Public and Cooperative Economics* 455.

Pollock, AM, Price, D and Liebe, M, 'Private Finance Initiatives During NHS Austerity' (2011) 342 *BMJ* 324.

Pollock, AM, Shaoul, J and Vickers, N, 'Private Finance and "Value for Money" in NHS Hospitals: A Policy in Search of a Rationale?' (2002) 324 *BMJ* 1205.

Pope John Paul II, *On Social Concerns* (Boston, MA, St Paul Edition, 1987).

—— *Centesimus Annus* (1991).

Powell, M and Miller, R, 'Privatizing the English National Health Service: An Irregular Verb?' (2013) 38 *Journal of Health Politics, Policy and Law* 1051.

Preston, G, 'Preferred Provider Organization (PPO)' in MJ Stahl (ed), *Encyclopedia of Health Care Management* (Thousand Oaks, Sage Publications, 2004).

Pringle, AS, *The National Insurance Act, 1911* (Edinburgh, William Green & Sons, 1912).

Propper, C, 'The Demand for Private Health Care in the UK' (2000) 19 *Journal of Health Economics* 855.

Quadagno, J, 'Why the United States has no National Health Insurance: Stakeholder Mobilization Against the Welfare State, 1945–1996' (2004) (Extra Issue) *Journal of Health and Social Behavior* 25.

—— *One Nation, Uninsured: Why the US has no National Health Insurance* (Oxford, Oxford University Press, 2005).

—— 'The Role of Specific Political Factors: Interest-Group Influence on the Patient Protection and Affordability Act of 2010: Winners and Losers in the Health Care Reform Debate' (2011) 36 *Journal of Health Politics, Policy and Law* 449.

—— 'Right-Wing Conspiracy? Socialist Plot? The Origins of the Patient Protection and Affordable Care Act' (2014) 39 *Journal of Health Politics, Policy and Law* 35.

Quinn, T, 'From New Labour to New Politics: The British General Election of 2010' (2011) 34(2) *West European Politics* 403.

Rand, A, *The Virtue of Selfishness* (New York, Signet, 1964).

Rawlins, M, 'In Pursuit of Quality: The National Institute for Clinical Excellence' (1999) 353 *The Lancet* 1079.

Rawls, J, *Justice as Fairness: A Restatement* (Cambridge, MA, Harvard University Press, 2001).

—— *A Theory of Justice* (Cambridge, MA, Harvard University Press, 2005).

Reagan, MD, *The Accidental System: Health Care Policy in America* (Boulder, CO, Westview Press, 1999).

Reid, TR, *The Healing of America: A Global Quest for Better, Cheaper, and Fairer Health Care* (New York, Penguin Press, 2009).

Reinhardt, UE, 'The Rise and Fall of the Physician Practice Management Industry' (2000) 19(1) *Health Affairs* 42.

Rescher, N, *Distributive Justice: A Constructive Critique of the Utilitarian Theory of Distribution* (New York, Bobbs-Merrill, 1966).

Rich, RF, Cheung, E and Lurvey, R, 'The Patient Protection and Affordable Care Act of 2010: Implementation Challenges in the Context of Federalism' (2013) 16 *Journal of Health Care Law & Policy* 77.

Rivet, G, *From Cradle to Grave: The History of the NHS 1988 Onwards Second Part* (London, Blurb, 2017).

Robbins, RH, *Global Problems and the Culture of Capitalism* (Boston, MA, Pearson Allyn and Bacon, 2005).

Robinson, JC, 'The Future of Managed Care Organization' (1999) 18(2) *Health Affairs* 7.

Robinson, R and Dixon, A, *Health Care Systems in Transition: The United Kingdom* (Copenhagen, European Observatory on Health Care Systems, 1999).

Roemer, JE, *Theories of Distributive Justice* (Cambridge, MA, Harvard University Press, 1998).

Rösch, M, 'What Does Neoliberalism Mean?' (1998) *Eberhard Karls Universität Tübingen*.

Rosenbaum, WA, *Environmental Politics and Policy* (Washington DC, CQ Press, 1985).

Rosenberg, CE, *The Care of Strangers: The Rise of America's Hospital System* (Baltimore, MD, John Hopkins University Press, 1995).

Ruger, JP, *Health and Social Justice* (Oxford, Oxford University Press, 2010).

Russell, J et al, 'Recognizing Rhetoric in Health Care Policy Analysis' (2008) 13 *Journal of Health Services Research & Policy* 40.

Saltman, RB and Figueras J, *European Health Care Reform* (Copenhagen, World Health Organization, 1997).

Sandel, MJ, 'The Procedural Republic and the Unencumbered Self' (1984) 12 *Political Theory* 81.

—— *Liberalism and the Limits of Justice*, 2nd edn (Cambridge, Cambridge University Press, 1998).

—— *Justice: What's the Right Thing to Do?* (New York, Macmillan, 2010).

Sass, H-M, 'The New Triad: Responsibility, Solidarity and Subsidiarity' (1995) 20 *Journal of Medicine and Philosophy* 587.

Schatz, B, 'The AIDS Insurance Crisis: Underwriting or Overreaching?' (1987) 100 *Harvard Law Review* 1782.

Schieber SJ, 'The Future of Retiree Health Benefits in Higher Education in the United States' (2005) in RL Clark and J Ma (eds) *Recruitment, Retention and Retirement in Higher Education: Building and Managing the Faculty of the Future*.

Schneider, SK, 'Intergovernmental Influences on Medicaid Program Expenditures' (1988) 48 *Public Administration Review* 756.

Schoenfeld, E and Meštrović, SG, 'Durkheim's Concept of Justice and its Relationship to Social Solidarity' (1989) 50 *Sociological Analysis* 111.

Schweitzer, SO, 'The Economic of the Early Diagnosis of Disease' (Econometric Society, 1972).

Selznick, P, 'Foundations of Communitarian Liberalism' in A Etzioni (ed), *The Essential Communitarian Reader* (Rowman & Littlefield, 1998).

Sen, A, 'Why Health Equity?' (2002) 11 *Health Economics* 659.

Shaoul, J, 'Charging for Capital in the NHS Trusts: To Improve Efficiency?' (1998) 9(1) *Management Accounting Research* 95.

Shaoul J, Stafford, A and Stapleton, P, 'The Cost of Using Private Finance to Build, Finance and Operate Hospitals' (2008) 28 *Public Money and Management* 101.

—— 'NHS Capital Investment and PFI: From Central Responsibility to Local Affordability' (2011) 27 *Financial Accountability & Management* 1.

Shi, L and Singh, DA, *Delivering Health Care in America*, 2nd edn (Gaithersburg, MD, Aspen, 2001).

Sia, C et al, 'History of the Medical Home Concept' (2004) 113 (Supplement 4) *Pediatrics* 1473.

Sigerist, HE, 'From Bismarck to Beveridge: Developments and Trends in Social Security Legislation' (1943) 13 *Bulletin of the History of Medicine* 365.

Sirpal, S, 'The Affordable Care Act and Incentivized Health Wellness Programs: A Tale of Federalism and Shifting Administrative Burden' (2014) 37 *Journal of Health and Human Services Administration* 327.

Smith, JG, *Political Brokers: People, Organizations, Money and Power* (New York, Liveright, 1972).

Smith Mueller, M, 'Health Maintenance Organization Act of 1973' *Bulletin* (March 1974).

Smith R, 'The NHS: Possibilities for the Endgame' (1999) 318 *BMJ* 209.

Smyrl, ME, 'Beyond Interests and Institutions: US Health Policy Reform and the Surprising Silence of Big Business' (2014) 39 *Journal of Health Politics, Policy and Law* 5.

Sommers, BD, 'Health Care Reform's Unfinished Work: Remaining Barriers to Coverage and Access' (2015) 373 *New England Journal of Medicine* 2395.

Sommers, BD et al, 'The Impact of State Policies on ACA applications and Enrollment Among Low-Income Adults in Arkansas, Kentucky, and Texas' (2015) 34(6) *Health Affairs* 1010.

Sood, N, Ghosh, A and Escarce, JJ, 'Employer-Sponsored Insurance, Health Care Cost Growth, and the Economic Performance of US Industries' (2009) 44(5) *Health Services Research* 1449.

Speed, E and Gabe, J, 'The Health and Social Care Act for England 2012: The Extension of 'New Professionalism'' (2013) 33 *Critical Social Policy* 564.

Spidle, J, 'The Historical Roots of Managed Care' in D Bennahum (ed), *Managed Care: Financial, Legal, and Ethical Issues* (Cleveland, OH, Pilgrim Press, 1999).

Squires, DA, 'Explaining High Health Care Spending in the United States: An International Comparison of Supply, Utilization, Prices, and Quality' (2012) 10 *Issue Brief* 1.

Starr, P, *The Social Transformation of American Medicine* (New York, Basic Books, 1982).

—— *Remedy and Reaction: The Peculiar American Struggle Over Health Care Reform* (New Haven, CT, Yale University Press, 2013).

'State Health Insurance Marketplace Types' (Henry J Kaiser Family Foundation, 2018).

Status of Treaties Chapter IV: Human Rights (*United Nations Treaty Collection*, 2017).

Stein, MS, *Distributive Justice and Disability: Utilitarianism Against Egalitarianism* (New Haven, CT, Yale University Press, 2008).

Stewart, B, 'List of 27 States Suing Over Obamacare' *The Daily Signal* (17 January 2011).

Stinchcombe, AL, *Constructing Social Theories* (Chicago, IL, University of Chicago Press, 1987).

Stone, DA, 'At Risk in the Welfare State' (1989) 56 *Social Research* 591.

—— 'The Doctor Businessman: The Changing Politics of a Cultural Icon' (1997) 22 *Journal of Health Politics, Policy and Law* 533.

Law, SA, *Blue Cross: What Went Wrong?* (New Haven, CT, Yale University Press, 1974).

Talbot-Smith, A and Pollock, AM, *The New NHS: A Guide* (New York, Routledge, 2006).

Tanne, JH, 'Obama asks AMA to support his healthcare reform package' (2009) 338 *BMJ* 1522.

Taylor, AJ and Ward, DR, 'Consumer Attributes and the UK Market for Private Medical Insurance' (2006) 24 *International Journal of Bank Marketing* 444.

Taylor, C, 'Cross Purposes: The Liberal-Communitarian Debate' in ML Rosemblum (ed), *Liberalism and the Moral Life* (Cambridge, MA, Harvard University Press, 1989).

Terl, AA, 'Emerging Issues of AIDS and Insurance' (1987) 12 *Nova Law Review* 1291.

Terris, M, 'The Neoliberal Triad of Anti-Health Reforms: Government Budget Cutting, Deregulation, and Privatization' (1999) 20 *Journal of Public Health Policy* 149.

Teslik, LH and Johnson, T, 'Healthcare Costs and US Competitiveness' (2007) *Backgrounder*.

*The Family Doctor Charter* (London, HM Stationery Office, 1966).

'The Structure of the New NHS' (British Medical Association, May 2017).

Thomasson, MA, 'From Sickness to Health: The Twentieth-Century Development of US Health Insurance' (2002) 39(3) *Explorations in Economic History* 233.

Thorlby, R and Maybin, J (eds), 'A High-Performing NHS? A Review of Progress 1997–2010' (The King's Fund, 2010).

Timmins, N, *Never Again? The Story of the Health and Social Care Act 2012* (Institute for Government and the King's Fund, 2012).

Titmuss, R, *History of the Second World War: Problems of Social Policy* (London, HM Stationery Office, 1950).

'Too Far, Too Fast: The King's Fund Verdict on Coalition Health Reforms' (The King's Fund, 7 October 2010).

Tuohy, CH, 'Dynamics of a Changing Health Sphere: The United States, Britain, and Canada' (1999) 18(3) *Health Affairs* 114.

—— 'Reform and the Politics of Hybridization in Mature Health Care States' (2012) 37 *Journal of Health Politics, Policy and Law* 611.

US Census Bureau, *Income, Poverty, and Health Insurance Coverage in the United States: 2010* (Washington DC, US Census Bureau, 2011).

US Chamber of Commerce, *Employer Mandate* (2015).

US Health Resources Administration, *Health in America: 1776-1976* (Rockville, US Department of Health, Education, and Welfare, 1976).

Uyehara, E and Thomas, M, 'Health Maintenance Organization and the HMO Act of 1973' (1975) Rand Corporation Paper Series 1.

van der Vossen, B and Vallentyne, P, 'Libertarianism' [2002] *Stanford Encyclopedia of Philosophy*.

Vetter, N, *The Public Health and the NHS: Your Questions Answered* (Oxon, Radcliffe Medical Press, 1998).

Wall, A and Owen, B, *Health Policy*, 2nd edn (London, Routledge, 2002).

Wallace, SP and Carroll, EL, 'Health Policy for the Elderly' (1989) 26(6) *Society* 66.

Walshe, K, 'Improvement through Inspection? The Development of the New Commission for Health Improvement in England and Wales' (1999) 8 *Quality in Health Care* 191.

—— 'Reorganisation of the NHS in England' (2010) *BMJ* 341.

Walshe, K and Ham, C, 'Can the Government's Proposals for NHS Reform be made to Work?' (2011) 342 *BMJ* 804.

Walzer, M, *Spheres of Justice: A Defense of Pluralism and Equality* (New York, Basic Books, 2008).

Webster, C, *The Health Services Since the War: Problems of Health Care* (London, HM Stationery Office, 1988).

—— *The Health Services Since the War: Problems of Health Care*, 2nd edn (London, HM Stationery Office, 1990).

—— *The National Health Service: A Political History* (Oxford, Oxford University Press, 2002).

Weinstock, D, 'Health Care in Political Philosophy: What Kind of a Good is it?' (Centre de recherche en éthique de l'Université de Montréal, 2010).

Wetenschappelijke Raad voor het Regeringsbeleid, *Volksgezondheidszorg* (Public Health Care) (The Hague, SDU, 1997).

White, J, 'The 2010 US Health Care Reform: Approaching and Avoiding How Other Countries Finance Health Care' (2013) 8 *Health Economics, Policy and Law* 1.

Williamson, C, 'The Quiet Time? Pay-beds and Private Practice in the National Health Service: 1948-1970' (2015) 28 *Social History of Medicine* 576.

Wilsford, D, *Doctors and the State: The Politics of Health Care in France and the United States* (Durham, NC, Duke University Press, 1991).

—— 'The Logic of Policy Change: Structure and Agency in Political Life' (2010) 35 *Journal of Health Politics, Policy and Law* 663.

Wilsford, D and Brown, LD, 'Path Dependency: A Dialogue' (2010) 35 *Journal of Health Politics, Policy and Law* 681.

Wittgenstein, L, *Philosophical Investigations* (Oxford, Blackwell, 1952).

Zuckerman, S and Holahan, J, 'Despite Criticism, the Affordable Care Act Does Much to Contain Health Care Costs' (2012) (October) *The Urban Institute Policy Center* 1.

# INDEX